What they are saying about

Release Your Brakes!

By James W. Newman

"This is a fabulous book! I recommend it to anyone looking for an extra edge in their life and work."

–KEN BLANCHARD, coauthor of
The One Minute Manager® and *Gung Ho!*®

"Release Your Brakes! is one of the seminal works that influences my thinking and my life. It's a timeless classic as effective today as it ever has been. James Newman's witty, easy-flowing style, combined with his staggering belief in human potential, proudly affirms your own human potential and gives practical advice on releasing it."

–DR. STEPHEN R. COVEY, author of
The 7 Habits of Highly Effective People

"Release Your Brakes! clearly offers personal growth methods that easily translate into the corporate environment. I loved it!"

–SHARI LIPPERT,
Human Assets and Learning Manager
AT&T

"I promise you this is one success book you'll read again and again. Underline those sentences which are most meaningful to you. Put stars and exclamation points next to paragraphs that you know you can apply to your own way of life. There is no better way to learn, study and remember–you should see my copy!"

–OG MANDINO in *Success Unlimited*

"I encourage everyone–regardless of their goals in life–to attend a (***PACE***™) session..."

–ZIG ZIGLER author of
Raising Positive Kids in a Negative World

"I have personally been using the techniques learned in ***PACE***™.., and I am delighted with the results. Anyone, regardless of age, will benefit greatly from the ***PACE***™ experience."

–SANFORD N. MCDONNELL, Chairman
McDonnell Douglas Corporation

"Jim Newman has been a mentor to me. He has changed thousands of lives and is one of America's most respected seminar leaders."

–DENIS WAITLEY author of
The Psychology of Winning

"Release Your Brakes! is the premier manual for achieving optimal performance. I use it personally and in my seminars. The book's powerful, user-friendly information is priceless."

–DIANA K. WEISS, PH.D.
Cardiac Psychologist
Optimal Performance and Health Educator

to get where you want to go faster . . . .

RELEASE YOUR BRAKES!

JAMES W. NEWMAN

THE *PACE*™ OWNER-OPERATOR MANUAL
FOR THE HUMAN SYSTEM

Published by

The **PACE**™ *Organization*

Enhancing Personal And Company Effectiveness Since 1961

Del Mar, California

ISBN 0-9638918-0-4

This second edition contains the entire text of the original. It has been updated with a new foreword, preface, and afterword.

Editor
Charles Sale

Cover Design
Robert Howard

Interior Design
Valery Alean

Production
Richard Fowler
Exalt! Communications LLC

Dedicated to Nan–constantly changing, growing, adventuring–and always exciting, loving and encouraging. The best person that's ever happened to me!

About the Author

James W. Newman was a pioneer in the study of high-performance behavior. By the time of his death in the summer of 1997, his reputation was worldwide and his theories clearly proven. *The **PACE**™ Organization*, which he founded in 1961, continues to provide consulting services; conduct seminars and workshops; and publish books, pamphlets, and other training media. Jim Newman's legacy is in the work being done today by the organization he founded.

Mr. Newman's ideas and innovations have blended into the fabric of American culture. The term, "comfort zone," was, for example, a Jim Newman invention. Mr. Newman's teaching empowered millions of people to do more and to be more than they ever thought they could. Companies, professional associations and governmental agencies today make use of management and communication tools created by Jim or inspired by his ideas. Indeed, much of the personal development and interpersonal communications training being offered today is grounded in the principles Jim discovered.

Jim Newman was a master at motivating people and enhancing their ability to achieve. He was one of the few speakers in the world to have been honored with the CPAE (Council of Peers Award for Excellence) awarded by the prestigious National Speakers Association. He was also a member of Speakers Roundtable and of Mensa.

In 1988 Mr. Newman served as Chairman of the Los Angeles County Task Force to Promote Self-Esteem and Responsibility. He also served on the President's National Private Resources Advisory Committee to the Office of Economic Opportunity.

Jim's early years were spent in Webster Groves, Missouri. His undergraduate education was at Washington University, Iowa State College and Westminster College, and he served three years of active duty as a naval officer in World War II. He spent his later years in Studio City, California.

In his leisure hours, Jim enjoyed photography, tennis, computers and magic. He was a performing member of Hollywood's famous Magic Castle. When Jim died, he left two grown children, Colby and Jim, Jr., and his wife, Nan.

Table of Contents

Chapter 1   **Take charge of your life**   1

Change, in your self and in your life, is inevitable. You are
guiding that process of change, and you have been doing so all
of your life, by intent or by default. Now is the time to decide
what you want to accomplish, what kind of person you want
to become and make it happen, deliberately, intentionally.

Chapter 2   **A system of release**   9

A new approach to increased effectiveness and success. Instead
of "pressing"–trying harder to do better–*release* the wealth
of unused potential which is available to you.

Chapter 3   **Potential and performance**   13

The key to more effective, productive use of your potential is to
be found in the emotional patterns which you have adopted–how
you *feel* about yourself, your job, your family, and the rest of
the world which surrounds you.

Chapter 4   **The whole person system**   23

The human mechanism is a complex system of complex
systems. Every change in any part of the Whole Person causes
reactions or adjustments throughout the entire system.

Do you want to *know* more? Do you want to *do* more? Read this section.
The work that Jim Newman began in 1961 is being carried on today by
*The **PACE**™ Organization. The **PACE**™ Organization* provides consulting
services; conducts seminars and workshops; and publishes books, pamphlets,
and other training media. The curriculum is extensive–filling the needs of
individuals, couples, small groups, and organizations. Read here about
what you can expect in a ***PACE***™ seminar. Contact us at the address and
telephone numbers found in this section, or through *The **PACE**™ Organization*
web site at *http://www.paceorg.com*. We will be happy to provide you with
further information or to enroll you in one of our courses.

Lindsey L. Davidson
President and CEO
*The **PACE**™ Organization*
Del Mar, California

January 31, 2001

Foreword

I first met Jim Newman when my wife, Lois, and I enrolled in a **PACE**™ Seminar a few years ago. At the time I was starring in two of the longest running series in broadcast history, serving on the boards of directors of seven national corporations, actively heading up a half dozen businesses of my own, and enjoying life with a family of five. In short, I was financially successful, professionally secure, and socially responsible. So what was I doing in middle age going "back to school"? And, most surprising to most of my associates, what was I doing at this point in my life trying to learn how to be more effective?

It's really simple.

I believe none of us should ever stop growing, learning, changing, and being curious about what's going to happen next. None of us is perfect, so we should be eager to learn more and try to be more effective persons in every part of our lives.

Nobody grows old by living a certain number of years. People can grow old at sixteen if they desert their ideals, let their thinking become clouded with pessimism, or permit worry, self-doubt, fear, and anxiety to prevent them from taking risks. Therefore, I believe that this book could be a "fountain of youth"–keeping one's thinking alive, elastic, and expanding, no matter what the calendar says. This book could easily be one of the most important events of your life. It is not a compilation of high-flown phrases, noble-sounding philosophy, and ego-soothing cliches. Hundreds of thousands of men and women have attended **PACE**™ Seminars over the years and personally validated the concepts and techniques about which Jim writes. Each chapter is a sort of roadmap for a more effective life, helping you to decide where you want to go and how to get there.

The chances are that you have attended some kind of a "how to" seminar. No doubt you have read at least one book dedicated to rekindling your enthusiasm for life. You may think you've heard it all before. But–take my word for it–THIS book can change your life. And, since change and growth are essential to a rewarding life, release YOUR brakes and start right now to accelerate your movement through the years ahead.

Art Linkletter
Author and CBS
radio and television host

1977

Foreword to the Second Edition

The book you are about to read can change your life. In the pages ahead, you will learn a series of profoundly important principles and practices that you can apply to unlock your inborn potential and accomplish more than you ever thought possible.

Jim Newman was one of those incredible teachers who come along only once or twice in a generation. He has the wonderful ability to bring together the most helpful discoveries in personal success and then synthesize them into a complete system that changes people's lives forever.

Many of the most respected and influential people in our society attribute much of their success to Jim Newman's **PACE**™ Seminar. In this easy to read book, Jim once more demonstrated his mastery of the complex by making these life-changing ideas accessible to you in the form of clean, clear principles for better living that you can implement immediately in every area of your life.

Jim Newman and I lived and shared together for many years as members of a small, exclusive group of committed speakers and trainers. During that time, I developed my own teaching system for success and achievement, and taught it to more that one million people in twenty languages worldwide.

Even though I had invested twenty-five years and thousands of hours in developing my own material on the development of human potential, I never met or spoke with Jim without learning something new and wonderful, something that added another dimension to my understanding of individual achievement.

I invited Jim to address my worldwide group of professional trainers and educators and watched, happily, while he entertained and illuminated them, sending them out with renewed inspiration and dedication to their work.

Jim Newman was a great man, a fine friend and a great teacher. He made a profound difference in the world. This amazing book, *Release Your Brakes!*, is his gift to mankind, a tribute to his belief in the unlimited goodness and value in each person.

As Jim always said, "The best is yet to be." The best days of your life lie ahead of you, and this book will guide you every step of the way.

Brian Tracy
Chairman
Brian Tracy International

January 31, 2001

Preface

The *PACE* philosophy and methods which you will encounter in this book have evolved through the years in response to one pivotal question: "What is it about successful people that makes it possible for them to excel?" That puzzle first started gnawing at me when I studied psychology and philosophy in college and the search for answers has been, and is still, an exciting quest.

Probably the greatest insights have come from participants in the many *PACE* Seminars and Conferences which I have been privileged to conduct. In a very real sense the teacher has learned at least as much as the students. There have been special people along the way who have provided models, frameworks, or pieces of the puzzle. Abraham Maslow stands out as one of the most adventurous, challenging minds of our time, and as a primary influence on my thinking. Other third force psychologists—Carl Rogers, Rollo May, Viktor Frankl, William Glasser and others—have helped to piece things together. The great pioneers in the science of General Semantics—Korzybski, Hayakawa and Johnson—have added to the *PACE* structure.

Others with whom I have had the privilege to work and exchange ideas have included John K. Boyle, George Haddad, Howard Westphall, and my brother, Bill Newman. Their ideas—and challenges—have made significant contributions to the *PACE* system. There have been too many others to list—college professors, clergymen, coaches and athletes, physicians, business executives who have been willing to share their ideas and experiences. In a way it all started with Bill and Dorothy Newman, a pair of high-performance parents who truly believed that leaving the world a better place than you found it was what life was all about.

The format of this book is different from others you have read. You will find wide margins so that you can make notes as you read. Then, when you read a section a second time, you will find your own ideas and experiences along with mine.

In the back of the book are some exercises to help you to implement some of the *PACE* methods and a Glossary to help clarify how I am using key words. There is a section at the very end of the book which will be helpful if you would like to obtain information about *PACE* Seminars, Youth Conferences, Cassette programs and various reminders which are available to help keep the principles and tools working for you on a day-to-day basis.

I hope you will use *Release Your Brakes!* as a manual. Write in it, underscore parts that seem especially meaningful, turn down page corners so that you can find key sections easily, and go back to read it again periodically to reinforce what you have learned. You will find that each time you read it the ideas will be clearer and you will have new experiences to illustrate what I have written.

Preface to the Second Edition

From 1961 until his death in the summer of 1997, James W. Newman devoted himself to transforming the lives and work of thousands of people. He was one of the key founders of the human potential movement, particularly the elements of it that advanced the disciplines of organizational development and personnel management. His writings, speeches and seminars had a profound influence on these disciplines during the 36 years of his work. That influence is continued today through the programs and publications of *The PACE™ Organization,* which he founded.

Jim devoted himself primarily to his seminars and speaking engagements, sparing himself time for only one book–this book. It is a classic. There is no other like it. It contains the essence of Jim's unique wisdom and insight, spoken during his life to thousands in live audiences, and captured here in clear, concise detail. It is written for results, not casual reading. As Brian Tracy says in his forward to this second edition, "It can change your life."

There have been ten printings of *Release Your Brakes!* since its original publication in 1977. When the tenth printing sold out, I considered publishing a "revised and expanded edition." Fortunately, these considerations led me to re-read Jim's book, and doing so brought me to an altogether different conclusion.

I decided that readers should have this classic in a second edition preserving Jim's words just as he wrote them. He was the founder of a great movement, and his book–this book–clearly and comprehensively delivers the technology he created. The book works–and always has. I decided not to tamper with it. It inspired me. It transformed my life and work, and that of thousands of others. It can do the same for you.

Brian Tracy wrote the foreword to this second edition, and I wrote the preface to it. Art Linkletter's original foreword and the author's preface appear just as they did in the first edition. This second edition contains the complete text of James Newman's famous book. It will tell you step-by-step how to use your untapped potential to get where you want to go faster and easier–while having a lot more fun along the way.

James Newman was blessed with a great gift: He could distill the essence of what he called "high-performance behavior," into practical, easy-to-follow steps. He devoted his life to sharing this gift with others. Those of us fortunate enough to have known him are infinitely richer for it. He is gone now, but this book remains as part of his gift to us. I am confident it will enrich you as it has thousands of others.

After Jim died, I purchased his company, *The PACE™ Organization,* and am carrying on the work he began. I have a degree in construction engineering from California State Polytechnic University, and spent my early years in the construction industry. I worked on large projects, where I sometimes ran into seemingly insurmountable obstacles. At first, I thought of these obstacles as unavoidable aspects of the many technical problems of construction. With time and experience, however, I saw that the vast majority of these problems were not technical at all. They were interpersonal. They were breakdowns in communication between people. I realized that what I was "saying" to my subcontractors was often not what they were "hearing."

Over the next 15 years, I took many courses in management, relationships, communications, women's studies, and psychology. While I learned much about myself and others, the growth in my ability to communicate was average at best. Then I met Jim Newman. It was in his three-day **PACE™** Seminar that the principles of effective human communication became clear, and I became an effective and empathic communicator. I applied these skills in the construction company I founded.

I learned to embrace rather than merely tolerate differences among people. With my team of managers, I strongly emphasize the principles of personal responsibility and practical communication in all aspects of company operations. The result was a quantum leap in personal and corporate effectiveness.

Jim had a remarkable ability to decipher the complexities of human behavior and describe them in readily understandable terms. You will appreciate this as you read his book. He also provided unique affirmations and other tools for permanently altering behavior and therefore, results. These tools are also described in the pages that follow.

Jim believed strongly in taking personal responsibility. He felt this was the universal attribute of high performers. In Chapter 15, entitled, "You are 'They'," you will read how the entire **PACE**™ philosophy and method is based upon this concept. Employees who truly take personal responsibility are promoted rapidly and contribute directly to the positive growth of their organizations. I have seen this again and again in my own company and the companies for which I conduct team-building seminars. Problems are solved quickly and there are fewer negative interpersonal reactions when individual team members take responsibility for their own contribution to a problem and its solution.

In Chapter 16, "Building Better Bridges," Jim discusses the technology of effective communication. After instructing thousands of people from all walks of life, Jim became convinced that nearly everyone is challenged by communications problems. In this chapter, he gives specific guidance for dissolving such problems. This was the guidance I had been seeking in my early years in contracting. It is guidance I have found nowhere else.

The work that Jim Newman began in 1961 is being carried on today by *The* **PACE**™ *Organization.* We offer many programs and publications, which are detailed in the back of this book and on our web site at *http://www.paceorg.com.* Please contact us through this web site or by phone at (858) 755-8604 or fax at (858) 755-8468. Correspondence can be sent to *The* **PACE**™ *Organization,* P.O. Box 2949, Del Mar, California 92014. We will be delighted to equip you with further information or to enroll you in one of our courses.

Lindsey L. Davidson
President and CEO
The **PACE**™ *Organization*
Del Mar, California

January 31, 2001

Take charge of your life

How do you feel about the fact that you are constantly changing? Of course, you *know* that you are different today than you were a year ago—even six months ago. You have only to look at a photograph or the home movies that were taken last Christmas. But those are the physical changes that show up in photographs—the differences in weight, hair, style of clothing. How about the rest of you—the behavioral part of your system? Can you see that you are thinking and acting differently now than a year ago, or five years ago? Differently than yesterday!

Change—physical, emotional change in your abilities and in your relationships with your world—is absolutely inevitable! It has been in the past, and even more important, it will be in the future. The experiences of each day have an effect on your personality, your outlook, and your reactions to the opportunities which you encounter.

Of course, you-a-year-from-now will be a lot like you-today in many ways. But there will be some very important differences, too. The changes may be dramatic in some areas, more subtle in others, but the one prediction that we can make about you is that a year from today you will be different.

Back to the all-important question—how do you **feel** about that? Get in touch with your emotions for a moment. As you look toward the future, are you excited about the prospect of change in yourself and your world? Or do you find yourself a little apprehensive, fearful because you are not quite sure which direction that inevitable process of change is going to take? If the prospect strikes you as a little scary, you're certainly not alone. The unknown can be very frightening—especially if you are pretty sure that you cannot do much about it.

I hope to convince you in the pages that follow that you **can** do something about your future. You can do a **lot** about it in fact. Oh yes, there will be many unexpected, unpredictable events in your life—events over which you have little or no control. But even in those areas, you have the ability to determine and manage your **reaction** to what's happening.

Your decisions, your actions—and your reactions—are creating your future. Within the framework of your own unique potential, you are guiding and directing your destiny, by intent or by default!

The goal of this book is to provide you with a very simple but comprehensive method for guiding and managing the inevitable process of change so that you can accomplish the things that you want to accomplish in life a lot more easily, become the kind of person you really want to be, with an increased sense of joy and personal fulfillment in the process.

A participant in one of our *PACE* (Personal and Company Effectiveness) Seminars summed it all up very simply. Paul and Gretchen had just bought a small foreign sports car, and on the week-end preceding the Seminar they had driven down the California coastline in their new car, reveling in the pleasure of the new addition to their environment. As they made their way down the coast and back, while one drove the other read aloud from the owner-operator manual. They studied the various dials, knobs, and control levers, knowing that the more they understood about the automobile the more likely they were to take proper care of it and use it properly for many years to come.

With this experience vividly in mind from the recent week-end, Paul told the Seminar group that the whole *PACE* experience seemed to them like an owner-operator manual for the human system.

As you move through the pages ahead, it may help if you think of this book as an owner-operator manual for your system, designed to help you understand yourself a lot better, to take better care of your whole system so that it will function effectively and take you where you want to go, quickly and enjoyably. With this owner-operator manual comes the *PACE* tool kit with which to "tune up" and enhance your own personal effectiveness, health, and happiness.

Let me put this another way. If you just let the inevitable process of change happen in its "own way," take your chances with it, the end result may turn out very well—or it could be disastrous. But it is not necessary to drift along like a feather in the breeze and hope that everything will turn out all right, that you will be "lucky." You are *not* "stuck with" the conditioning and habits of your past, nor do you need to allow others to determine your future. "They" are not in charge of your future! One of the most limiting attitudes a person can possibly have is, "Well, that's just the way I am."

You can **decide** where you want to go, what you want to become—and then deliberately **guide** the process of change in that direction. This book is going to show you exactly how to do that.

What are the results that you can expect from reading this book? That is a little difficult for me to tell you right now, because the book will mean something different to each person who reads it. I don't know (and right now you probably don't either) just which areas of your life you will *want* to change. You will be making some decisions about that as we go along. But I *can* tell you this: When you have finished reading *Release Your Brakes!* you will know a lot more about *how* to move your life in the direction that you want it to go. The ideas, techniques, and images we are going to work with together will have already brought about a change in your thinking and your behavior. You will be looking at yourself and your world in some profoundly different ways.

One of our *PACE* Seminar participants put it this way: "I feel like I've been driving through a muddy rainstorm all of my life—and someone just turned on the windshield wiper."

Come with me through an exercise that may help to prepare you for the experience you are about to have.

What do you see when you look at this picture?

The chances are about four to one that it looks like the profile of a rather attractive young lady, with her face turned away from you—a sort of Toulouse-Lautrec picture. But for about one person in five, it is a picture of an old witch with a large nose and no teeth. Which one do you see?

Regardless of which picture you see first, if you keep looking you will soon be able to see the other image. When that happens—when the other picture "snaps in"—you will have what I call an "Aha!" experience. It is a feeling of discovery—"Oh, *there* she is!"

If you still see only the young girl's picture, try this. Look at the black line that represents the choker or necklace around her neck. See if you can see that line as a mouth—the thin-lipped mouth of an old hag. Or, if the old hag is the image you have locked onto, try this. Cover her mouth and chin with your finger. Now see if you can see the left side of the picture to be a profile of a young girl. You can just see the tip of her nose and her eyelash across her cheekbone.

The "Aha!"—a sudden recognition of something you have been looking at but not seeing—can be a very exciting, rewarding breakthrough. You will have a lot of them as we move together through the pages that follow, and they will be a lot more significant than seeing a second picture in an artist's drawing. They will be "Aha's" about *you,* your behavior, and your relationships with your world.

Even though you have been living with yourself for a lot of years, you are going to experience some very fascinating discoveries about how and why you act as you do and how you can further sharpen your abilities, skills, and patterns of success.

The "Aha's" will come as you see how all of your experiences, ideas, and study fit together into a whole, meaningful pattern. As you develop a clearer insight into *why* some self-improvement methods have worked for you, and why some have not, there will be a "Well, of course!" feeling. The most exciting "Aha's" will come as you find yourself applying the *PACE* methods to your own life and realize that you are in charge of what's happening more than you have ever been in the past.

The systems and ideas which you will learn always work. No exceptions, no escape hatches, no cop-outs.

How your life will change—the degree of change and the parts of your life that change—will be the result of some decisions you will make as we proceed. Using the *PACE* system will not involve teeth-gritting will-power, but it will be necessary for you to make some decisions and to devote some time to a few very simple and productive exercises.

If you play golf, tennis, or bridge, or if you bowl or ski, you know that an understanding of the principles of the game or sport—and some practice—help you to do it better. As you have learned, and practiced, your golf game (or other sport skill), you probably haven't thought of it as "hard work." It may have involved some *effort,* but because the results were rewarding—and immediately evident—the energy expended was a lot of fun—recreation. How you **felt** about learning, practicing, and improving in that sport had a lot to do with the speed with which you progressed.

I would like to urge you to have the same view toward expanding your personal horizons. We will explore together some principles of personal growth and some step-by-step methods for you to practice, in much the same way that you would practice a golf swing, a tennis stroke, or driving an automobile. The results will be quickly evident—to you and to others—and will prove far more rewarding and exciting than any skill you have ever practiced before.

There is one more suggestion which I believe will help you to receive the maximum return on the time and effort you are investing in this book. Remember that this is a book about **you**! It starts from the assumption that *you* have a considerable amount of untapped potential. I want to introduce you to some simple, proven keys with which you can unlock that potential and release it. Please be very *selfish* as you read on.

I know that you probably learned when you were very young that selfishness is bad. We will take a longer look at that concept later on, but for now, set that idea aside and look for the principles and methods which apply to *you*. What can you find here which can help *you* to get where you want to go faster and to become the kind of person *you* are capable of being?

Unless you are a very unusual person, you will sometimes be tempted to see how directly the material we will be examining applies to others—your mate, your boss, your children, the home office. You may find yourself thinking how much better life would be if only "they" would practice some of the *PACE* methods.

Observing how all of this applies to someone else can waste a lot of time—and energy—which might more profitably be invested in your own personal growth. It can be very frustrating, too.

Yes, this would be a much better world if everyone else would just shape up (whatever that means). But first, see what *PACE* can do for *you*. See what kind of effect it has on increasing *your* effectiveness. The changes in you will be contagious. Then, if there are others you admire or love who you think would find these ideas to be valuable, give them a copy of *Release Your Brakes!*

Now, let's begin our journey. A guided tour through the wondrous labyrinth of the human system—*your* system. I believe that you will find it one of the most exciting, absorbing, and rewarding experiences you have ever had. I promise you that your life will never be quite the same.

A system of release

Have you ever driven your automobile with the brakes on? I suppose that most of us who have driven for any length of time have had that experience. I can remember times when I have arrived at my destination, reached down to pull on the parking brake, and found that it had been on all the time that I had been driving. What a ridiculous way to drive a car!

Not only was it inefficient—the miles per gallon must have been a lot less than they usually were—but it wasn't very good for the car either. If one did much driving with the brakes on, the brake linings wouldn't last very long.

Perhaps you have had this experience. You pulled away from the curb in your car, and as you drove along you began to wonder what was wrong. The car seemed sluggish, didn't have the pep and pick-up you had come to expect. You had just had the engine tuned. It should be functioning well, but even pushing harder on the accelerator didn't seem to help very much. And when you took your foot off the gas pedal the car slowed down quickly. Then, the "Aha!" You reached down, perhaps a little sheepishly, and released the hand-brake.

Remember how you felt as the brakes were released? As the horsepower which had been under the hood all along began to make its way to the wheels without the dragging, inhibiting friction of the braking mechanism, how did you feel? Sure, there was the "Aha!" feeling that you have when you solve a puzzle. But there was also a kind of *relief* feeling—a sense of "That's more like it."

9

Keep that image—and the **feeling** of release—in mind as we proceed.

Consider how ridiculous it would be for an Olympic runner to strap on a twenty-five pound weight belt before starting his race. Or how much slower a boat would go if it were towing a bucket or sea-anchor.

Of course, no one would deliberately wear extra weights to run a race, or tow a bucket behind a boat if he were in a hurry to get somewhere. Nor would you intentionally drive your car with the brakes on. You wouldn't get where you were going as fast—and a lot of energy would be wasted, too.

Yet, without realizing it—or intending to do so—you are moving through life with your brakes partly set! The horsepower is there, but vast areas of potential are blocked, bottled up, restricted from effective application. Puzzling? Indeed, and frustrating, too. But that's not the worst of it.

When you have the ability to do something and that ability is not functioning or flowing the way that you want it to flow, you may find yourself "trying harder"—pressing. Then when that extra grit and determination doesn't work you may think, "What's wrong with me, anyway?" In fact, the "try harder" approach may even further diminish the flow of your ability, at the expense of a lot of wasted energy.

Isn't that a lot like pushing harder on the accelerator when the hand-brake is set? It may work—temporarily. But it is not very good for the system, it wastes energy, and the end result is more likely to be negative than positive!

We know enough about the automobile that, given a choice between pressing harder on the gas pedal or releasing the parking brake, the decision is obvious. Unfortunately, the human system is not delivered with a set of directions to help you make the best use of its marvelous potential—or to help you to care for it so that it will give long and trouble-free service.

So, here is the manual. As with any such book, we will not attempt to explore all of the details of design and manufacture of the system—only the directions for using it in a productive, effective, satisfying way.

The system we will be applying is not a teeth-gritting, will-power, try-hard-to-shape-up method. You have tried that already: *I'm going to try hard to get organized!* or *I'm going to put my will-power to work and stop smoking!* Probably the harder you tried the more frustrated you became. Now we are going to look at a proven system for *releasing* that potential, allowing it to flow. You will be surprised at how quickly and how easily it works.

Potential and performance

The average person uses only a fraction of his potential.

As many times as you have heard that—or even said it—I wonder how much you have thought about what it means. What is "potential"? To be more specific, what is **your** potential? As we will be using the term, a person's potential is the present combination of three elements or components.

First, there is the basic design or blueprint of your system—the original equipment with which you began your life. This dimension includes your physical stature; the color of your skin, eyes and hair; whether you are in a male or female body; musical and artistic talents. Your intellectual capacity is a part of this first component, too—not the I.Q., but the original wiring of your thinking mechanism. This part of your potential is simply the genetic endowment, your heritage from prior generations. It is unique. Your original blueprint is different from everybody else's.

There isn't much that we can do about this first dimension except to understand it. Once the sperm has found the egg and a new life form is begun, the blueprint is set. We can make some minor changes, but the most productive effort would seem to be to get acquainted with what sorts of talents and capacities we may have as a built-in part of the original equipment package.

CHAPTER 3

13

The second part of your potential is the complex mass of knowledge, information, data, and skills which you have acquired since the genetic blueprint was set. What you have learned about yourself and the world around you, whether or not it is immediately available to recall, is also unique. No one else in the world has ever had—or ever will have—exactly the same accumulation of knowledge and information that you have. This second dimension includes the skills which you have developed—the coordination information about how to stroke a tennis ball, how to ride a bicycle, how to walk.

The first two dimensions are fairly mechanical. We can see an interesting comparison in these two areas with a computer. The "electronic brain" also has a basic design which equips it very well to handle certain kinds of tasks, and not very well to handle others. Moreover, the computer must be programmed with data in order to function. If the information is inaccurate, then we get some wrong answers. The same principle applies to human systems. If the knowledge or information which you have acquired in a particular area is false, then your behavior in that area is very likely to be unproductive or even destructive.

The third component in your human potential is not to be found in the computer. It is the inner motivation or drive to make productive use of the first two dimensions. Built into your system is the desire, the inclination, to apply your talent and knowledge. This is the inborn urge to grow, to achieve, to excel, to become the kind of person you are capable of being. Your inner motivation is not a learned skill; it is a part of your being which has been there from the start of your life. You have only to watch a small child to see this intrinsic, natural drive in action. A baby is curious, energetic, enthusiastic, reaching out to explore the world—highly motivated.

Sometimes this built-in motivation can be squelched or limited in the early years—and we will be looking at some of the experiences which can have that effect—but it is never destroyed.

In recent years, most of the theories, programs, and methods of motivation have focused on *external* forces. *How can we get Charlie motivated? What can we do to get our kids motivated?* While it is perfectly legitimate to use the word *motivation* in this context, it is important to draw the distinction between *outer* and *inner* motivation. On the one hand we have someone motivating someone else—a process which could just as well be called "manipulation." On the other hand, we have the natural, inner drive or urge to use the talents and knowledge that we possess.

While external motivation—whether based on fear or rewards—does work, releasing the inner motivation that is a vital part of all human systems works a lot better and can be depended upon to last longer.

One more look at the computer analogy. It is almost absurd to think of a computer being motivated. An electronic mechanism lacks the capacity to care about whether it is ever programmed, whether the data it receives is correct, or whether it is even taken out of the shipping crate. Not so with your system! A vibrant part of your potential is the natural, built-in driving urge to function well—to use the talents and knowledge which you have in your system.

There are the three elements which make up your personal package of potential. Your **talent,** the **information** you have acquired about yourself and your world, and the built-in **motivation** to use the first two dimensions to grow, to become, to achieve.

Defined in this way, we can clearly see that we all have a lot of potential that is not being used. If you play golf, you probably have the physical equipment (talent) you need to play a good game; you have had lots of lessons (information) and practice—you know how to hit the golf ball—and you certainly have the motivation, the desire to hit it well.

If you are a parent, you probably know more about how to fulfill that responsibility than you sometimes act like you know.

If you are a salesperson, it's a good bet that you have more potential than you are using. The physical equipment is there. You know a lot about your product or service, and you have a lot of information about how to prospect, how to make appointments, how to present your story, and how to ask for the order. And, you are highly motivated. You really want to be successful in your chosen profession. So, when the time comes to close the sale, why do you change the subject? Not because of any lack of potential, but because of a *fourth* dimension in your behavioral system.

The fourth dimension is **emotion.** How you **feel** about yourself and your world. Here is the key dimension which will facilitate or restrict the flow of your potential. The negative emotional patterns are the braking mechanisms in your system.

Of course, the computer lacks emotion. When the electronic mechanism is programmed the process is one of cold, rational logic. There may be errors in the data, and resulting errors in the output, but computers do not experience fear, anger, or frustration. Not so with you and me! We never just "learn" anything as a pure informational input. In every instance, along with the "knowledge" we have some feelings—an emotional inclination toward or away from that activity, event, person, etc. The emotional element may be almost imperceptible sometimes, but it is there. You have feelings about everything that you know anything about—including, of course, your self! We will be calling that combination of knowledge and feeling *attitude patterns,* or, more simply, *attitudes.*

Your behavior, unlike the output of a computer, is far more a result of how you *feel* than of what you *know!* That is not to say that the knowledge, informa-

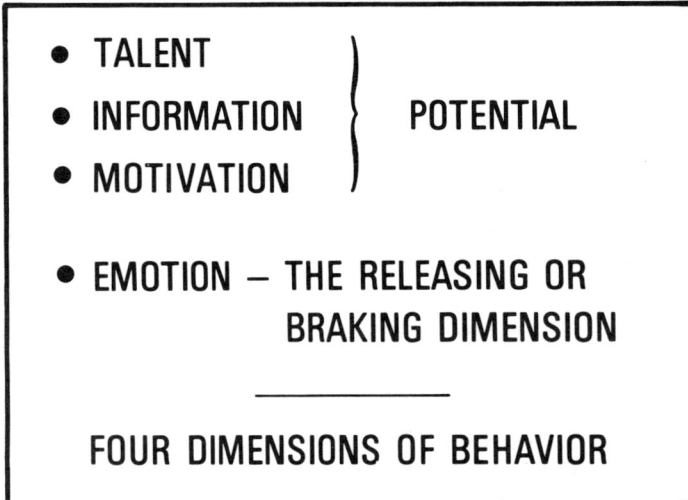

- TALENT
- INFORMATION   } POTENTIAL
- MOTIVATION

- EMOTION — THE RELEASING OR
             BRAKING DIMENSION

FOUR DIMENSIONS OF BEHAVIOR

tion, and skills which you have acquired are not important. Of course they are—very important. But your ability to *use* that knowledge, and the other aspects of your potential, is a function of this fourth dimension, your emotions.

Here is another definition. We will be using the word *effectiveness* to mean the degree to which a person uses his or her potential (the first three dimensions) in a natural, free-flowing, spontaneous, and consistent manner. Your ability to function well in a particular situation is partly the result of your potential, but it is also related to how you feel about all of the various aspects of that situation. How you feel about yourself, the other people who are involved in the activity, the feelings you have about the task itself, and many other factors that may be involved.

Dig into this concept and be sure that you have really grasped it clearly. It is a very important principle.

I have found that the importance of emotion in human behavior is often much more difficult for males to accept than for females. Both little boys and little girls receive a lot of negative messages about emotions, but it seems that, in our culture at least, boys are especially subject to the "Don't be emotional!" programming in the early years. They learn, more often than not, that boys are supposed to be logical, rational, and intellectual, but *not* emotional. "Don't get angry!" "Don't be afraid!" "Shut up and go to sleep; there's nothing in the closet!" "You stop that crying or I'll give you something to cry about!" It's easy to see how children—boys *and* girls—might learn that we are not supposed to have any emotions. And if we do slip up and have some feelings, for heaven's sake, don't let anyone know it!

If you have trained yourself, through the years, to feel uncomfortable about feeling, then the idea that your emotions are the most important part of your behavioral system may be difficult to look at, let alone accept. But stay with it. Not only are your emotional patterns the primary key to the use of your potential but, as we will see in a later chapter, the continued suppression of those natural feelings can lead to serious illness and even death!

Let's be more specific. How, exactly, can this fourth dimension, your emotional patterns, influence your behavior?

Imagine that there is a plate on a table in front of you right now. On the plate is a two-inch thick steak. It is charcoal-broiled, medium-rare, government-inspected, prime grade tenderloin. Is your saliva flowing? Oh, there is one more bit of information about the steak. It is a horsemeat steak.

What happened to your appetite? If you suddenly lost interest, can you see that your reaction—and what is going to happen with your knife and fork—has very little to do with what you *know* about the edibility of horsemeat, and a lot to do with how you *feel* about it?

The idea of eating horsemeat may not have turned off your appetite at all. What I am asking you to look at is that everyone who has some knowledge about horsemeat also has some feelings about it. The feelings, positive or negative, will guide, manage, control that person's behavior.

If you were traveling in the Orient and you were invited to dinner by some friends in Hong Kong, you might find yourself sitting down to a meal that is considered a great delicacy in that part of the world—boiled dog! How do you suppose you would respond to that? Would your behavior be logical, rational? Or would the *feelings* you have about dogs have an influence on your behavior?

Suppose your telephone were to ring right now, and when you answer it you find that the call is from the program chairman of a club or association to which you belong. He is calling to ask for your help. The speaker who was scheduled to address the meeting this evening has taken ill suddenly and will not be able to talk to the group after all. It is a real emergency. The program chairman would like for you to give a thirty-minute talk to the group this evening. You can select the topic. It can be about your hobby, vocation, a trip you have taken, or whatever you want to talk about.

What is your reaction? Do you leap at the opportunity, only regretting that you will be limited to thirty minutes? Or do you panic ("Who, *me*? You've got to be kidding!")? Your response may not be at either of those extreme ends of the scale, but we can be certain that how you react—and how you perform if you accept the invitation—will be only partly a function of your potential, and largely a function of how you feel about yourself as a public speaker.

You may have all of the necessary physical equipment, the intelligence, education, training, and even the *motivation* to give an excellent, dynamic, well-organized public speech. But whether or not you actually walk up to that microphone—and, if you do so, how well you use the potential that you possess—will be a result of the emotional dimension. Whether you express yourself clearly, forcefully, enthusiastically, and naturally, or find yourself at a loss for words, tense, and "trying hard" to get your ideas out, will be controlled by the feelings you have developed through the years of your life about yourself as a public speaker.

Positive emotions release your brakes—help your potential to flow spontaneously, freely, and easily. When you have feelings like joy, enthusiasm, pride, love, or confidence flowing through your system, your brakes are off. Whatever talents, knowledge and motivation you have available—your potential—will be working for you in a very natural manner.

The negative emotions are the braking mechanisms. Let's look at some of them. Think of specific times in your life when you did not handle a situation as well as you could have because of one of these patterns of emotion.

Probably the primary braking device in the human system is the emotion of **fear,** or the somewhat less intense but still limiting pattern called **anxiety.** If you have the potential to be a good public speaker, but you are not using that potential, can you see that fear is blocking your performance?

Sometimes it may be fear of actual physical pain which causes you to avoid certain kinds of activities—or to put them off as long as you can. Many people have taught themselves to fear a visit to the dentist's office because of the possibility of physical discomfort. So, they procrastinate. By the time they do get to the dentist the cavities or other problems have progressed to the point that there really is some discomfort!

More often, though, fear of less tangible pain ties up the system. Fear of failure, for example. Somewhere in childhood you may have learned that one of the worst things you can do is to *fail.* If so—and that is a very common lesson that many young people do learn—then you will do all sorts of things to try to avoid situations in which you might fail.

How about the fear of rejection? When you were very small, someone who meant a lot to you may have said, "Go to your room! I don't want you around me when you act like that. If you keep that up we'll just have to find someplace else for you to live!" That was pretty scary, and if it happened often enough there is a very good chance that you developed a fear pattern which can have a dramatically limiting effect on your behavior as an adult. Have you ever wanted to ask someone for a date, invite someone to come to dinner, or ask a prospect for an order and not done so? Can you get in touch with the fact that the braking mechanism which kept you from doing something you were capable of doing and really wanted to do was fear—fear that the person might say *No*—fear of rejection!

There's still another kind of fear which is remarkably widespread, extremely limiting and yet not likely to occur to you right away. The fear of *success!* Why on earth would anyone be afraid of success? That's what everyone is supposed to want, not fear! Think about that for a moment. What is there about success that can be a little frightening?

If I achieve success (however you may want to define that word) will I be able to maintain it? If I get up there will I be able to stay? If I become very successful can I handle the responsibility? I'll be making decisions which affect a lot of people. What if I make a mistake? What will other people think of me if I make a lot of money, live in a big house, belong to a country club? What if I can't handle that kind of lifestyle?

Seems strange, doesn't it, that one might—at an intellectual level—want to succeed, and at the same time have emotional patterns which restrict progress? But it happens with all of us to some degree. Just like driving the car with the brakes partly set!

Fear is not the only limiting emotional pattern. Have you ever been so angry that you could hardly function? When you have wanted to accomplish something but there was an obstacle blocking your progress, did the feeling of frustration have an adverse effect on your performance? The feeling of envy or jealousy can tie up your abilities. Hate, a disastrous combination of fear and anger, can short out all of the intellectual circuits.

Enough about the negative emotions. We are going to be working with the releasing mechanisms, tools for growth. Each of us has some attitude patterns which include negative feelings, but fortunately we are not "stuck with" our present accumulation of attitudes. In the course of this book you will learn how to use a technique called **Constructive Imagination,** a dependable, proven brake-releasing method.

With *Constructive Imagination* you can bridge the gap between potential and performance. Here is one example of how it worked for a professional salesperson.

> Several years ago I was conducting a series of conferences for a large national sales organization. At one of the meetings I met Dave, a handsome, enthusiastic young salesperson. His district manager told me that he was about to give up on Dave and let him go. He was really bewildered. "That kid has so much going for him. So much potential. He's a star pupil in our training sessions, knows our product inside out, and he really wants to succeed. He's married, and he and Doris just had a baby. He's got plenty of motivation. I just can't figure out what's wrong!"

It didn't take long to find the answer. Dave was a perfect example of a lot of horsepower with the brakes on.

Dave knew that one of the keys to success in selling—especially in his field—was a constant flow of prospects.

He understood that fact thoroughly and could explain the importance of prospecting to new trainees at great length. He knew how to prospect. Dave had attended several training sessions about how to use the telephone to find new prospects. And, yes, Dave was highly motivated. Still, he would sometimes sit at his desk and look at the telephone for twenty or thirty minutes without picking it up. Or, more often, he would find other "more important" things to do. Day after day would pass without any new prospects. It's pretty hard to keep your sales volume up when you don't have prospects.

Dave's difficulty was not related to what he knew or to his desire to use that knowledge. It was an emotional pattern which was blocking his performance—his feeling about calling a stranger on the telephone. Many years before Dave became a sales professional he had taught himself to be afraid of rejection and failure. Those fears were now destroying his performance—and his career.

I showed Dave how to apply the *PACE* technique called *Constructive Imagination* to the project of building a positive, enthusiastic feeling about using the telephone to find new prospects.

In a matter of days, the telephone had become one of Dave's best friends! His feeling of fear had been bridged with a new feeling of enthusiasm about meeting new people and developing rapport with them on the telephone. Now the natural talent, education and training—and Dave's built-in desire to excel—all got together and began to flow spontaneously and consistently. He released the brakes and within a month was the number three producer in his district. Today he is one of the top District Managers for his company.

The whole person system

In order to clearly understand the restricting effect of negative attitude patterns, how they have developed in your behavioral system, and what can be done to release the untapped potential that you have, it is important to develop a model of the very complex human system—**your** system.

We can use a simplified representation. It is not necessary to thoroughly understand all of the details of the manufacture of an automobile, or know about all of its working parts, in order to drive it—or take good care of it. One can sew beautiful garments without knowing exactly how the movement of a sewing machine bobbin is mechanically coordinated with the action of the needle. Many people solve remarkably complex mathematical problems with computers, despite a lack of knowledge about the exact working principles of the microscopic solid state electronic components which make it possible. Most top-notch secretaries are not the least bit concerned with the marvelous mechanisms which make it possible for them to type so rapidly.

To make effective use of any of these modern mechanical or electronic wonders does, however, require a certain amount of knowledge about its purpose and the overall scheme of its design and function. Even a steam iron or an electric carving knife comes with a folder that tells how to use and care for the device. Whether it is a simple household appliance or a jet airliner, you are a lot more likely to use it better—and it's a lot more likely to last longer—if you read the directions.

The model that we are going to be using, a very simplified representation of the complex human system, will almost certainly be somewhat different from the way that you have thought of it in the past. Whether you have made a long and searching study of human behavior or have only made some casual observations about what makes people "tick," I urge you to be open to a new and different approach. Not altogether new and different, but probably different enough to challenge your thinking.

Here, too, we can see a direct example of how the emotional patterns can limit performance or progress. If you find yourself feeling uncomfortable or irritated because our Whole Person model is different from the one you have used in the past, your learning process will be blocked or diminished. That doesn't mean that you need to buy or accept everything that you read in this book without any question or challenge. See if you can develop the feelings of interest, curiosity, perhaps even excitement about looking at familiar territory from a different point of view. An attitude of "open-minded skepticism" will permit you to explore new ideas with a sense of fascination along with a desire to experiment and test to see what really works in your own world.

The foundation of our **Whole Person System** concept is what the physicists call the *General System Theory.* This is simply the idea that whenever anything changes within a system, the whole system changes.

A great deal of attention has been given in recent years to the ecological system, for example. We know that when a particular species of plant or animal is destroyed, the entire system is affected. When a new animal is introduced—rabbits in Australia or the mongoose in Hawaii—the end result is often surprising, and the whole environmental system is affected by the change.

When there is a change in the solar system, a production system, an economic or political system, the change reverberates throughout the entire group of objects, events, or people that interact to make up that system.

So it is with the human system. When there is a change, the *whole person* responds. Moreover, there are so many variables that it is impossible to predict with complete accuracy where those changes may lead.

We can, however, increase the degree of accuracy by understanding the system better. In an attempt to facilitate that understanding, we will break the larger system into three, still complex subsystems.

The most tangible and obvious part of the Whole Person System is the physical vehicle in which you travel through life, your body. What a remarkable mechanism! The skin, muscles, bones, glands, and all of the other cell structures of the organism develop from a single cell. When the egg cell—or ovum—is "activated" by a sperm cell, a complete, detailed blueprint is established. All of the design specifications are created at that instant for the manufacture of an entire human organism.

Every blueprint is unique—no two will be exactly alike. Of course, after the design has been set, the system may not develop exactly according to the blueprint due to nutritional deficiencies in the mother during pregnancy, in the child after it is born, or because of other damage to part of the system.

Still, the body that you now have, whatever its age and condition, is a marvelous mechanism. An important

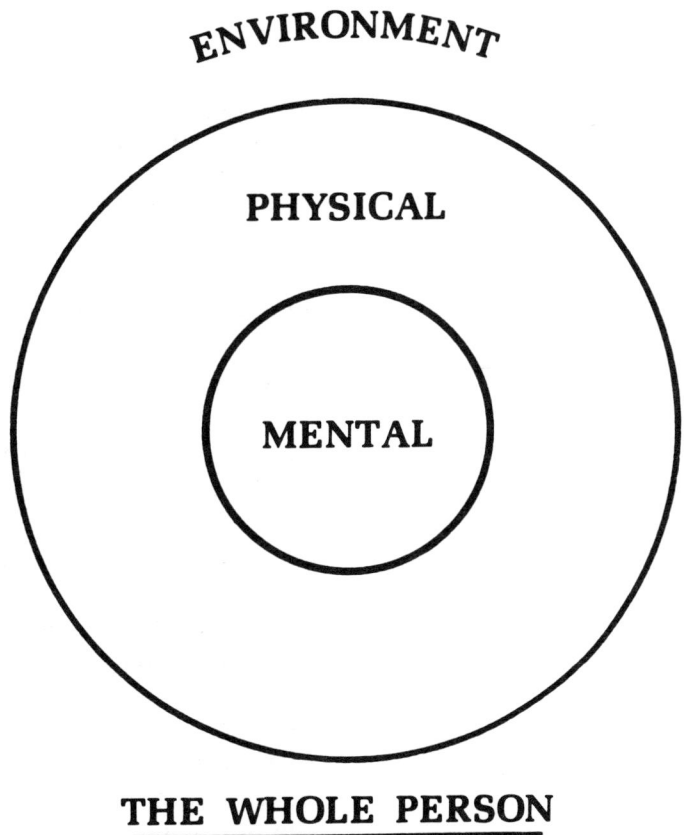

ENVIRONMENT

PHYSICAL

MENTAL

THE WHOLE PERSON

aspect of your potential is the physical equipment which you have at your disposal, and a vital part of your personal effectiveness—the degree to which you use your potential—is the way that you care for and condition that body of yours so that it will serve you well.

We will not deal here with the subject of nutrition and exercise, but there are some excellent sources of information listed in the bibliography which you will find in the back of this book. If you have not yet made a study of those areas, do so right away. Anyone who is sincerely interested in personal growth, success, or increased effectiveness will find that proper care of the physical system is an absolutely essential ingredient in the recipe.

Within the physical mechanism there are many kinds of processes or activities: digestive, circulatory, glandular, respiratory, and dozens more. The kind of activity within your system with which we will be primarily concerned is the complex set of processes which take place within that part of your physical mechanism called the "nervous system." That includes the brain and spinal cord, or central nervous system, along with the multitude of peripheral nerve cells which carry information or stimuli throughout the body.

We will not spend much time looking at the nervous system, though. Our interest is in what happens there, the mental processes, the flow of information within that system.

Here is the one part of the Whole Person over which we can exercise some direct guidance or control. You can **decide** what to think. By directing and managing your thoughts, you can bring about predictable changes in behavior and in the other parts of the Whole Person System. The mental processes are the control center of the entire system. As you increase your understanding of how this part of your system works, you can—to the degree that you choose to do so—develop new, more effective habits of thinking which will release your potential.

The third part of the Whole Person System is the universe outside of your skin surface. It may at first seem strange to include the environment as a part of the system, but of course you could not exist without it! The air you breathe, the atmospheric pressure, gravity, the temperature and the people in your world are all a part of your system. Whenever there is a change in any of those elements of your environment—or in many others—the other parts of your system change, too.

We need not be concerned with such questions as, "When does the oxygen stop being part of the environment and become part of the body?" Whether that happens as it enters the respiratory tract, the lungs, or the physical cells is not critical to our simplified view of the system. What is important is the fact that changes in the environment do stimulate changes in the physical mechanism and in the mental processes.

Consider this example. Suppose that the temperature in the room where you are right now were suddenly to go up to 120 degrees. That change in the environment would trigger some changes in your physical system, wouldn't it? You would begin to perspire, for example, as your body's cooling system went to work. You would begin to think in some different ways. Perhaps you would be thinking more slowly in the hotter environment. You would think, "Boy, it's sure getting hot in here!" and your mental processes might activate some physical muscles to move your body out of the room or to readjust the thermostat to a lower temperature.

As changes come about in your physical system, the entire system responds and adjusts, too. As you grow older, for example, the muscles in your eyes may weaken and the lenses may not be able to focus on objects which are very close to you. Your thought processes respond to this change, and may, in turn, bring about a change in the environment—hanging some lenses out in front of your eyes.

Even with these very simple examples there would, of course, be many other adjustments and responses beyond those that we have discussed. See if you can track each of them a little further and identify some other reverberations which might follow the ones we have noted.

Our primary concern is the changes which will develop in the physical mechanism and in the environment as we deliberately make some changes in the mental processes. The same sort of whole person adjustment happens in that direction, and by understanding how and why that happens, we can bring about the changes that we want to effect in the entire system with a high degree of predictability.

The conscious mental processes

Some mental activities are more available to your conscious awareness than others. These are processes which may be deliberately controlled or guided to some degree.

The key word here is *degree.* You do not have a compartment or place in your brain (or in your mental system) which can logically be called a "conscious mind." But you do have certain processes which seem to happen most of the time at a predominantly conscious level. It is not accurate to think of your thought processes as either conscious or subconscious; it is a matter of degree. And a particular type of mental activity will not always occur at the same level of consciousness.

Please avoid the trap of thinking in terms of the "Conscious Mind." Instead, let's look at those processes within your mental system which seem to happen, usually, at a largely conscious level.

We are going to examine four specific process areas which we will label **conscious.** Of course, this is an arbitrary, simplified view of a very complex part of your system, but it will suffice for our purpose of finding some methods with which we can increase effectiveness.

The first conscious process in our structure we will call PERCEPTION. This is the fraction of what is happening, inside and outside of your skin surface, which reaches a conscious level in your mental system—the fraction of which you become aware.

29

You have many sensory devices built into your physical mechanism: eyes, ears, odor detectors, taste buds, and tactile sensors which can pick up some of what is going on in your environment. Within your body there are many more which can provide information relating to balance, muscular position, hunger, thirst, temperature, and the like.

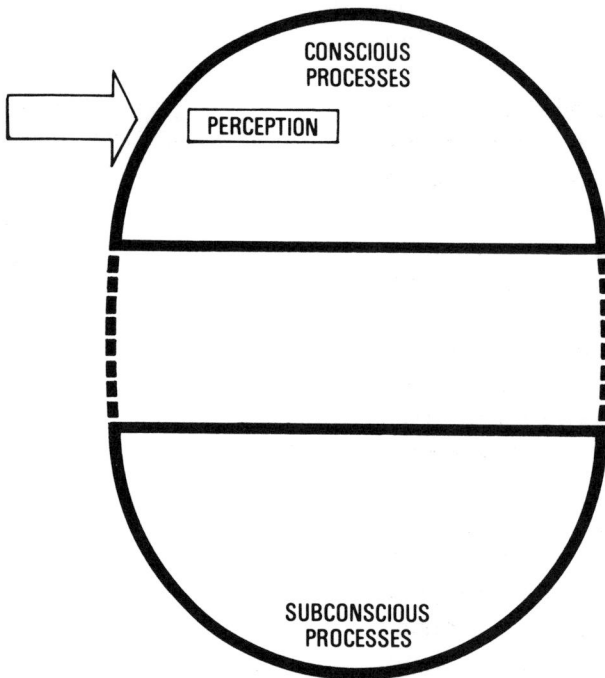

CONSCIOUS PROCESSES

PERCEPTION

SUBCONSCIOUS PROCESSES

Neurologists have estimated that about two million signals or stimuli come into the central nervous system every *second*. Of course, you do not perceive all of those two million per second inputs. A series of discriminating "filters" send most of the incoming signals to parts of the brain which process and use that information automatically, without your conscious attention.

When you walk, for example, a constant stream of thousands of signals comes into your mental system from various parts of your body. Messages from the balance mechanism in the inner ear, from your visual system, and from thousands of muscles throughout the body help you to stay erect and to coordinate your movements—automatically.

The filtering mechanism allows only that information which is "important" to you to pass through to a conscious, aware level. The degree to which you are aware is directly proportional to the degree of importance you assign to the input in your value system, based upon your prior experience and thought/feeling processes. Much as a radio receiver is designed to select only one narrow portion of the broadcast spectrum—only one of the hundreds of signals which reach it—your system selects the signals that you need to be aware of in order to survive and achieve your goals.

Look how this is working right now as you are reading. To the degree that your attention is focused, or concentrated, on reading these words, a multitude of visual inputs, sounds, odors, and information about what is happening outside and within your body are being "ignored." Much of what is being *sensed* is not being *perceived* at all. Other inputs are registering only in a fleeting, semiconscious way. As you shift your attention from one set of signals to another it is a little like turning the radio's station selector from one station to another.

What are some of the sounds which are going on in your environment right now that you have been filtering out? Notice, for a moment, the feeling of your clothing against your skin. Most of the time you are not conscious of that sensation—or, at best, you are barely aware of it. How about odors in the room you are in right now? You can perceive them if you want to do so—or if they signal danger. If you were to smell something burning, that stimulus would find its way to the conscious level right away. Or the fragrance of dinner being prepared in the kitchen may be perceived—whatever is important!

Now look inside your physical mechanism for a moment. You can probably sense some tensions in various muscles. Maybe there are some hunger or thirst signals reaching a conscious level. Lots of other happenings in your body right now are simply not available to your awareness. The circulation of your blood, glandular activity, digestion of your food, and many other processes are being monitored and controlled by your central nervous system, but you do not need to "think" about them. In many cases it is virtually impossible for you to perceive the processes as they are happening.

As an event, or stimulus, is perceived, you reach into your experience files—the vast bank of information and emotional patterns which you have accumulated through the years—to see whether anything like this has happened to you before. If nothing exactly like what is now happening has been recorded in the past, then you may find some experiences which are somewhat similar. This second process which happens most of the time at a predominantly conscious level we call ASSOCIATION.

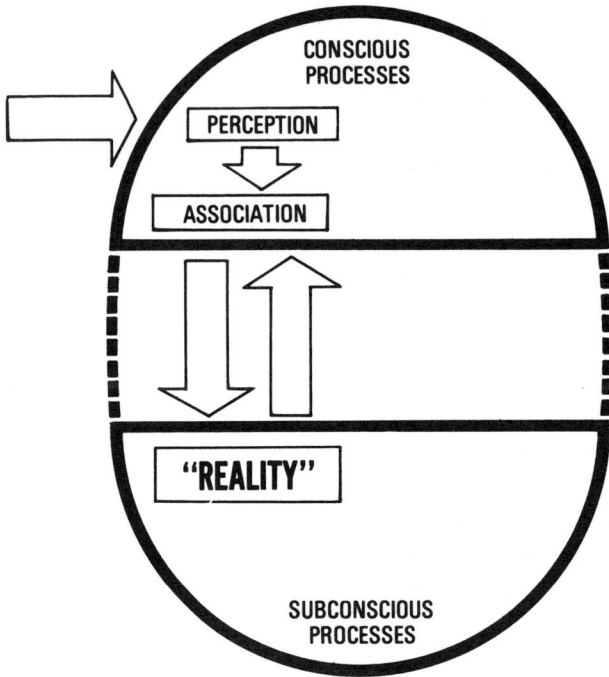

As you hear a sound, see a word on this page, feel a pain in your abdomen, or detect a new odor in your environment, you scan the storage files. What else has happened to you that is like this? Have you ever had a stomachache like this before—or ever heard about someone else having one? What does that smell like? Of course, what that means is, "What previous odors that I have experienced does that odor resemble?"

Only to the degree that you have some kind of experience already in the files with which to associate what is now happening does the present input have any "meaning" to you. If you have had a lot of previous thoughts and feelings about something, then the next time you come across it what you perceive will be very meaning**ful**. If the experience files are nearly empty in that department, then what you are perceiving will be relatively meaning**less**.

Look at this example of the association process in action.

$$\boxed{\text{ДО СВИДА́НИЯ}}$$

What happens in your thinking as you look at what is printed inside that rectangle? Does it have any meaning to you at all? What category or pigeon-hole did you put it in? Language? Meaningless marks?

If you associated it with the language department of your experience files, did you go beyond that stage to associate it with a particular part of the world?

It is a very familiar expression if you happen to have studied the Russian language. But even if you are not a student of that language, you may have associated it with that part of the world. You have seen pictures in newspapers and magazines of posters or signs in the Russian language. The Russian alphabet (or Cyrillic alphabet) is different enough that when you see something printed in those symbols you may find yourself associating them with that language. Go back a minute or two and review just what your associations were. Notice, particularly, the emotions. Did the association trigger any feelings? What were they?

If you had *heard* that expression instead of *reading* it, the association might have been different. It is pronounced *Da sveedahnya* and is Russian for "Goodbye."

A person who grew up with that language would immediately find the expression very meaningful—associating it with the many previous experiences which had been programmed into his mental filing system.

Everything that you perceive is associated with the already existing accumulation of information and emotion in your mental system.

The next process at a predominantly conscious level is the EVALUATION of what has been perceived and associated with the experience files. As you evaluate,

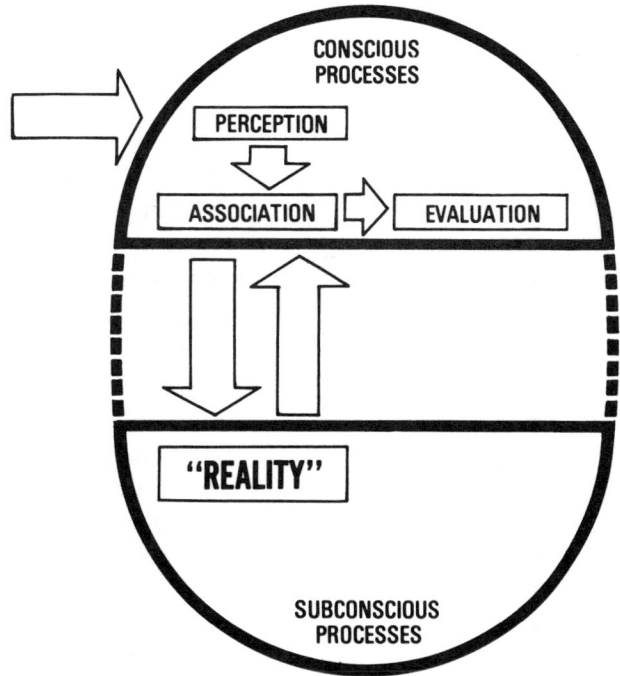

you are gauging probabilities—estimating the probable validity, significance, value, and predictive consequences of the event or message that you are perceiving.

Based upon your previous experiences with similar information or events, to what degree can you be sure that what you are hearing is "true"? To what degree is it likely to be of importance or value to you? What is this probably leading toward in the future—what are the probable consequences of what is now happening?

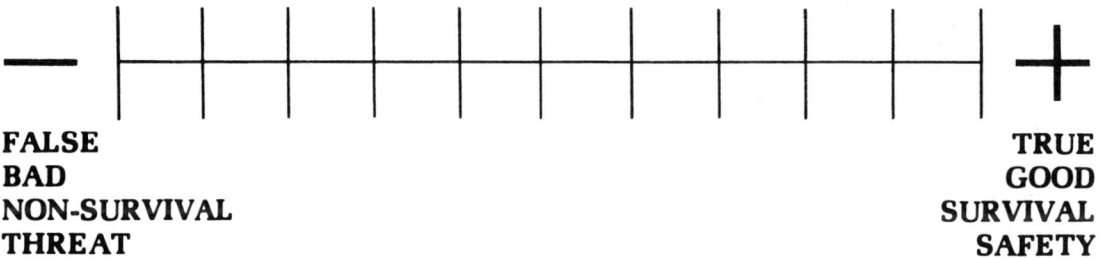

FALSE   **TRUE**
BAD   **GOOD**
NON-SURVIVAL   **SURVIVAL**
THREAT   **SAFETY**

Sometimes it may seem as though you are evaluating an input as "true" or "false," "good" or "bad." That kind of "either/or" evaluating can create some serious difficulties. We live in a world of probabilities. Your thinking, and resulting behavior, is much more likely to be effective and productive as you develop the habit of recognizing those probabilities.

Here is an example which you may have experienced. As you approach an intersection you stop at the boulevard *Stop* sign and look both ways to see what traffic may be approaching on the main, through street.

As you look to your left, you see a car coming toward the intersection, and you notice that an amber light below the right headlight is flashing. That's **perception.**

Then you check the experience files. What do you know—and how do you feel—about such situations? That's **association.**

On the basis of what you are perceiving (remember that you are not perceiving everything that is happening), and your association with your own unique accumulation of experiences, you now **evaluate** what is probably going to happen next.

If you "jump to the conclusion" that the approaching automobile is certain to turn right at the intersection, you might have a serious accident. Of course, the other driver's signal may be broken; the car may have just

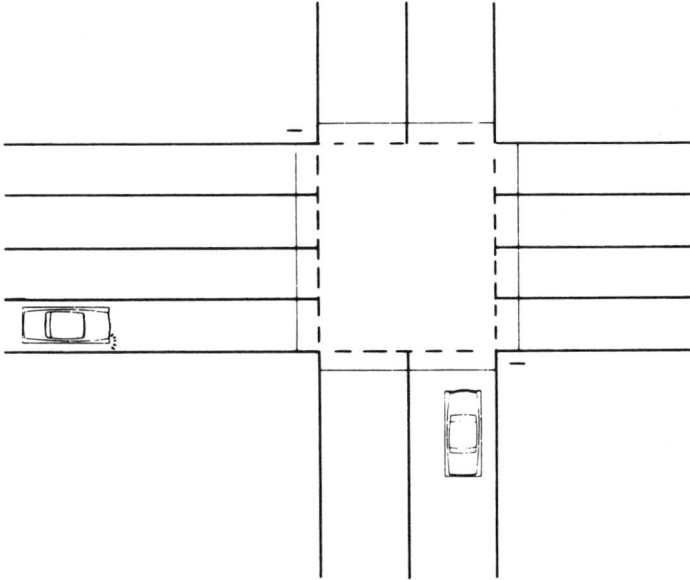

changed lanes and the signal not yet gone off, or the driver may be planning on turning into the service station just beyond the intersection.

Better, by far, to recognize that you are dealing with probabilities—and wait for some additional information before you pull forward. Look out for the "either/or's." Dangerous traps!

The fourth conscious level process is DECISION: deciding to pull away from the stop sign, to wait for some additional information, or some other alternative, based upon what has been perceived, the association with already acquired information/emotion, and the evaluation of the probable predictive consequences. This is the behavioral output of the mental processes.

The decision may, of course, be to do nothing. You may decide to ignore or dismiss what has been perceived. You may decide to search for more information. Or, your mental processes may send some signals to muscles in the physical mechanism—to take action.

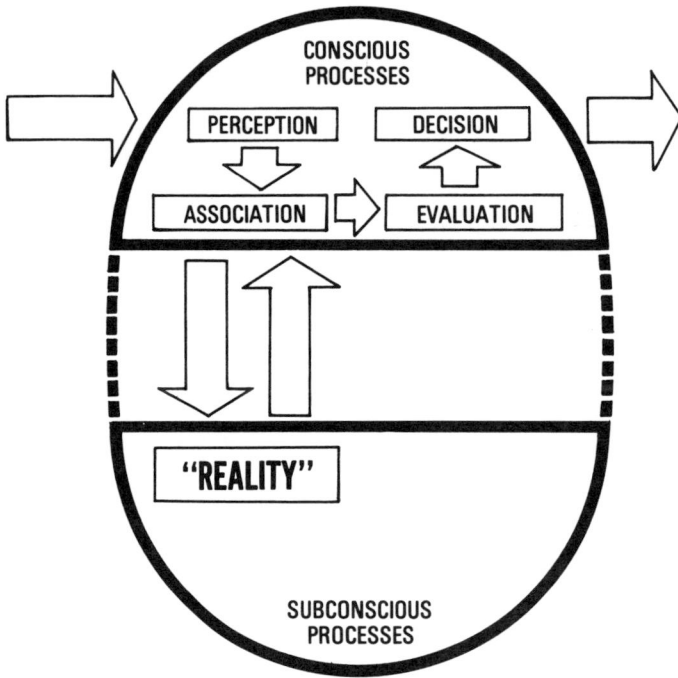

The most important part of all of this is the fact that your decisions are not simply a function of what is now happening—or even of that fraction of what's happening that you are perceiving. The decisions are *primarily* a function of what has already happened—the thoughts and feelings which have cumulatively developed within your mental processes, through the years, into the complex reference system which we will be calling your "REALITY" structure.

A little later we will see just how the "REALITY" system develops. For the present I will simply define it as the total, present time accumulation of data or information—and feelings—which you have acquired about yourself and the world around you. It is your "truth" system, the total "programming" of your computer. But remember that, unlike the electronic computer, your "REALITY" includes what you know and how you **feel** about yourself and your world.

It is this "REALITY" structure which serves as your reference library as you associate and evaluate what you are perceiving. The decisions that you make, the actions you take, the behavioral output of your system, will tend to be consistent with your own, personal, unique "REALITY."

That is a very important principle—one which I will refer to frequently in the pages which follow.

> HUMAN BEHAVIOR TENDS TO
> BE CONSISTENT WITH
> THE INDIVIDUAL'S CURRENTLY
> DOMINANT "REALITY" STRUCTURE.

Perhaps equally important is another principle or "fact of life" about your "truth" system.

> YOUR "REALITY" STRUCTURE IS
> INCOMPLETE AND INACCURATE.

That is why I have put the word "REALITY" in quotation marks—to distinguish the "REALITY" which you have in your mental processes from the REALITY that is actually happening or has actually happened.

You do not, and probably never will, know all that there is to know about anything. No matter how long, or how intensively, we study any subject, there is always more that can be learned. Whether it is something as large as the universe or as small as the atom, the more we learn the more we realize how little we know. Your "REALITY" is incomplete.

Moreover, what you do know—about anything—is never completely accurate. There are distortions in the programming process. What is actually happening in your life does not somehow get "injected" into your "REALITY" system. You can only store, or record, what you are thinking/feeling *about* what is happening—and that is never exactly the same as what is going on in the environment or your physical mechanism.

Can you see that this is happening right now? As you are perceiving words on this page you are associating those words with your already existing "REALITY" and giving them some sort of "meaning." Then, as you evaluate the probable validity and usefulness of the ideas which they represent you are deciding what, if anything, to do with those ideas. All of those conscious processes are different in your system than in any other person who reads the same words on the same page.

If you have ever heard (or read) two eyewitness accounts of an accident or any other happening, you have seen dramatic evidence that people do not record what is happening, but rather what they are thinking/feeling about what is happening. Two people may stand side by side and observe the same event, but their associations will be different, and even more important, the evaluations will be different. They are "programming" their experience files or "REALITY" structure with different inputs.

Alfred Korzybski, creator of the science of General Semantics, expressed this in a very simple way: "The map is not the territory." No matter how detailed a map may be, it is never exactly the same as the territory it is intended to represent.

If you are driving your car from Los Angeles to New York City, it helps a lot to have a map. You know, of course, that the map is incomplete and that it has some inaccuracies. You cannot drive your car down that red line on the paper. It will not surprise you to find a section of highway that has been completed since the map was printed, or curves in the road which are not shown on the map. You *expect* maps to be incomplete and inaccurate.

Your "REALITY" structure is a map of the territory—a map which you have personally designed and manufactured within your own mental processes. You can accomplish a great deal more with that map than you could without it, but you will get to where you want to go more easily and more quickly to the degree that your map is an accurate representation or reflection of the real world—and the real *you!*

Let's look at a simple example of the four conscious mental processes in action. Put yourself into this situation and trace each of the steps in the sequence as though they were happening to you. Suppose that the door to the room in which you are sitting were to open right now and a large, full-grown, healthy-looking Bengal tiger walked in. What do you suppose would happen?

First, you would **perceive** that there had been a change in your environment. Whether that perception is with your eyes, ears, nose, or sense of touch, not much else will happen until you perceive some kind of change.

Then you **associate** what you are perceiving with your own personal, unique "REALITY" about tigers—whatever patterns of information and feeling you have programmed into your experience files.

Next, you **evaluate** the probabilities. What is the likelihood that this is a real live tiger—or might it be some friend dressed up in a tiger costume? Is it probably dangerous? What will it probably do if you sit very still—or if you run for the other door?

Then you **decide** what to do. I cannot predict what that decision would be, because I don't know enough about your "REALITY." Would you run? Yell for help? Talk to the tiger? Sit still?

Several years ago we had a real tiger expert in one of our *PACE* Seminars. Herman Brix, the famour actor who played the role of Tarzan in many films, had worked with a lot of real tigers. Herman told the group that, on the basis of considerable personal experience, *he* would sit very quietly and immediately caution everyone else in the room to do the same. Part of his "REALITY" was that quick movements were very likely to frighten a tiger and cause him to attack.

On the other hand, if a person has never had a negative thought or feeling about tigers, but has seen pictures of friendly ones, has been told that a tiger makes a nice cuddly house pet that likes nothing better than to be scratched behind the ears, we will see a different kind of behavior. That person will perceive the same animal that you and I are seeing, but as he or she associates those perceptual inputs with the very different "REALITY," the evaluations will be different and that person may quite logically, rationally, sensibly walk toward the Bengal tiger with the intent of scratching him behind the ears!

If you were watching that happen, you might think that your friend had gone crazy! "Crazy" behavior is often simply the result of extreme distortions—or incompleteness—in the "REALITY" maps.

When people *knew* that the earth was flat, they behaved as though they lived on a flat earth. That wasn't crazy, was it? It was perfectly logical, rational behavior given the "truth" that the earth was flat. Notice that they did not "think" that the earth was flat; they *knew* that it was! And they felt very deeply about that "truth."

When you were a child you probably knew that there was a Santa Claus or an Easter Bunny—and maybe a Bogey Man, too. The child, too, behaves in a manner that is consistent with his or her "REALITY."

When you see people—adults or children—whose behavior is different from yours, people with different customs, values, religious rituals, or food preferences, it is important to remember that they are behaving in a very logical, "normal" manner on the basis of their different "REALITY" structures. The difference is in the programming, a different map of the same territory.

I want to emphasize once again the importance of the emotional component of those attitude patterns which make up your "REALITY" system. What you know is a very significant aspect of your behavior, but how you *feel* about what you know is even more influential.

Mankind has recognized the importance of the emotions for centuries. In the book of Proverbs (23:7) it is stated quite simply, "As he thinketh in his heart, so is he." Not in the brain, and of course not in the organ which pumps the blood. In the heart of your thinking process—the emotions.

The ancient sages considered the heart—or more commonly the bowels or solar plexus—the control center of human behavior. Aristotle taught his students that the brain was simply a device for the purpose of cooling the blood, and that the behavioral mechanism was in the abdomen.

It is easy to see why this might have been regarded as the "truth" about the human system at one time. Today we understand a little more about the sequence of events which might lead to that conclusion. When you have some thought processes that include the emotional component of fear, the emotional center of your nervous system is activated. The resulting combination of activity in the muscles and glands of the physical mechanism is sensed—felt—in the abdominal area. The butterflies are in the stomach! That, of course, is why emotions came to be called "feelings"—because they can be physically sensed or felt.

The subconscious mental processes

We will concern ourselves with only three kinds of activity which seem to take place most of the time at a predominantly subconscious level in our mental processes. Once again, we are working with a very simplified model of an extremely complex system, but a better understanding of these three functions will contribute a lot to increased effectiveness.

All three of these activities are "un-thinking," automatic, robot-like. While it is possible to affect them—stimulate or re-program them—with deliberate, directed conscious-level thought, they will go right on functioning automatically if we allow them to do so.

The first process is that of managing, guiding, controlling the automatic activities within the physical mechanism and the mental processes.

You were born with some automatic functions already wired into your circuitry—reflexes, for example. When the doctor hits your knee with his little rubber hammer, you do not go through the perceive-associate-evaluate-decide cycle. A reflex loop is activated in the spinal cord, a signal is sent back to the leg muscles to contract, and then when it is all over a message is sent to the brain about what has happened. By the time you perceive it the reflex has completed its cycle.

Breathing is an interesting built-in automatic process. So far as we can tell, you did not learn to breathe. The controlling mechanism or circuitry was built into your system right from the beginning. You do not need to think about breathing for it to happen, and yet if you choose to do so, you can breathe deliberately—consciously. You can decide to take a deep breath or to breathe rapidly. This is one more example of the continuum or scale which extends from the extremes of very conscious to very subconscious levels of your mental system.

Many other activities going on right now in your system are being handled quite efficiently at a subconscious, automatic level: the digestion of your food, adjustment of the level of sugar in your blood, circulation of the blood through the physical mechanism, and countless more.

We also have the ability to "train" the system to perform various functions automatically. Many activities which were not built into the original blueprint and which were once managed quite consciously in your system have now been "moved down" to the more subconscious level where they can be handled automatically.

When you first tried to walk, it was a very deliberate, conscious activity. Over a period of time walking has become so natural and automatic that it seems as though you have always done it that easily.

You can still move the walking skill up the scale a little if you want to do so. But, if you do, you may find yourself walking less smoothly, less effectively. When you have trained your system to handle an activity automatically, you are usually better off letting it flow—not thinking too much about it consciously.

Hitting a golf ball provides an excellent example of

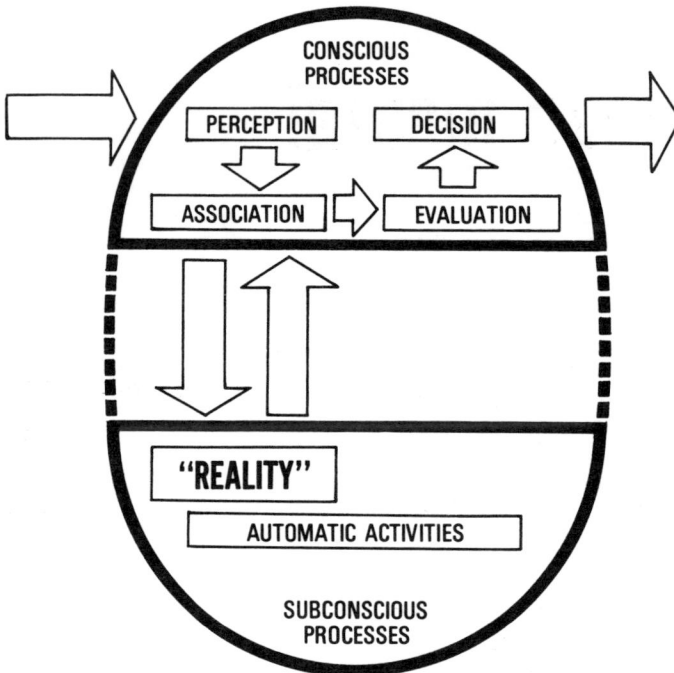

that danger. The professional golfer has trained the system to hit the ball in a natural, free-flowing manner, automatically. When he is playing in a tournament, he is not thinking about keeping his left arm straight, keeping his head down, and all of the other coordination activities which are so important to his success. These activities are all automated. If he starts thinking about them his game is almost certain to suffer.

Think of some other activities of a physical nature which you have trained your system to handle at an automatic, subconscious level. Tying your shoes? Riding a bicycle? Driving a car? What else?

Now look at some of the *mental* activities that you have automated which started out at a very conscious level. Multiplication tables? When you first learned about numbers you made a conscious mental effort to think through the solution to a multiplication problem. Now, when someone says *two times four*, you don't "think" about it at all. The number *eight* simply pops to the surface like a cork. See how differently you react when someone says *thirteen times sixteen.* That takes a little longer, doesn't it?

Most of the activities which you do extremely well are activities or skills which you have automated.

Think of some examples within your own system. Your tennis stroke, vocabulary, rules of grammar or spelling, skiing all fall in this category. The outstanding surgeon has practiced his skill so that it has become automatic. The professional salesperson doesn't just *know* how to prospect, make appointments, present his product or service, and close the sale—he has trained his system to handle all of the skills of high-performance selling easily, spontaneously, automatically.

When you have automated an activity, while you are engaged in that skill, your more conscious processes are free to think about something else. When you are driving your automobile you can think about where you are going and what you are going to do when you get there. I am always impressed with the way Vicky, my secretary, can accurately transcribe dictation and carry on a conversation on the telephone at the same time. There is a closed circuit between her eyes and her fingertips which functions so automatically that she can think about other matters while she is typing and rarely makes a mistake. In fact, she is a lot more likely to make a mistake if she starts to "think" about her typing instead of just letting the system work for her.

So much of our life involves automatically controlled thinking and action that it is difficult to conceive of a human being without that capability. It is not just a convenience, but clearly an essential element of survival.

The second subconscious level process in our model is the storage of information/emotion—the automatic cumulative development of your "REALITY" structure.

All of the thoughts and feelings which occur at the more conscious levels in your thinking are stored or recorded. This is a very important characteristic of your system. Be sure that you grasp this idea. **Whatever is "experienced" at a conscious level is recorded, subconsciously, as experience or "REALITY."**

More often than not, the conscious thought processes have something to do with an event that is actually happening. You record your own distorted version of that event, and it is usually close enough to be a useful map. But not always!

Sometimes you may experience an event or activity *totally* in your imagination. To the degree that it is experienced vividly, it will be recorded in your "REALITY" structure as something which has actually happened to you. It becomes part of your "experience"

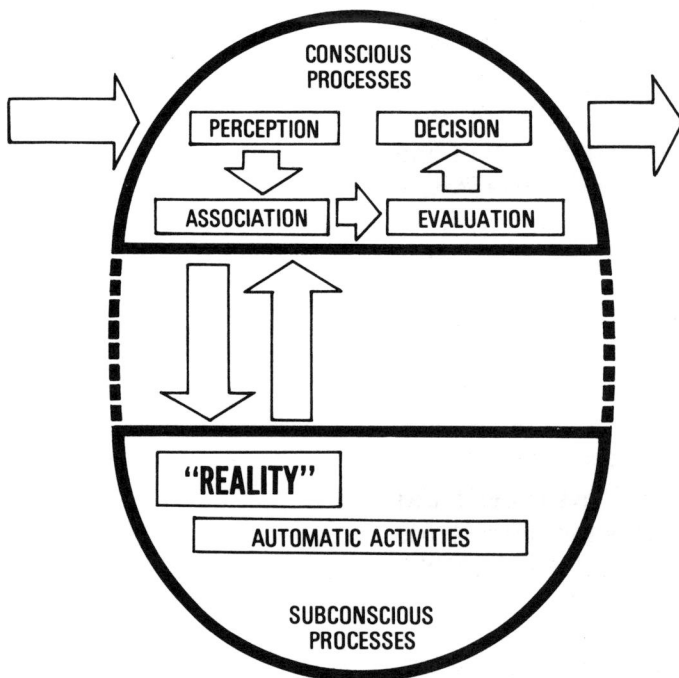

files—the reference file which will guide and direct sub-sequent behavior.

We can express this very important characteristic of the storage process with a simple formula:

$$I \times V = \text{"R"}$$

Imagination times vividness equals "REALITY"!

TO THE DEGREE THAT YOU EXPERIENCE AN EVENT VIVIDLY IN YOUR IMAGINATION, IT IS ACCEPTED AND RECORDED SUBCONSCIOUSLY AS "REALITY"— SOMETHING WHICH HAS ACTUALLY HAPPENED!

At first, this may appear to be a serious weakness in the human system. It is, of course, the chief reason for inaccuracies in the "REALITY" structure, but it need not be regarded as a weakness or fault in the system. Quite the contrary. In fact, it was the recognition and understanding of this quality of the mental processes which led me to realize that deliberate conscious control of the inevitable process of change in human behavior is possible. The basic method for personal growth and development which I will describe in detail in Chapter 10, "Constructive Imagination," is based upon this principle.

I want to increase the probability that this idea is sufficiently clear.

Can you think of a time when you have experienced something so vividly in your imagination that it has become a part of your "REALITY"? Do you recall the surprise you felt when you found that your image of that situation was inaccurate?

This can happen with a dream. Sometimes a dream is so vivid—so real—that you are later quite certain that it actually happened. You not only recall the event that you dreamed about, but all of the emotions seem real, too.

Have you read a book—a novel or perhaps a mystery story—which was so well written that you became a part of the story? It might be more accurate to say that the story became a part of *you.* The author developed such vivid descriptions of the characters, their thoughts, appearance, and activities that you felt that you actually knew them. You knew how they walked, talked, ate and drank, their innermost thoughts and feelings. You may even have felt a tinge of sorrow as you finished the book because you were saying goodbye to some close friends. To some degree that book, and the people in it, became a part of your experience files—your "REALITY."

Then you went to the movie which was made from the book. How did that feel? Uncomfortable? Irritating? "Well, the movie was okay, but it wasn't as good as the book!" This very common reaction was probably at least partly because what you were watching on the screen did not match the way it "really" happened in your mental processes—in your imagination—as you read the book.

Here is another example. Have you listened to a voice on the radio day after day? A newscaster or disc jockey while you rode to work each morning, perhaps. As you heard that voice, you imagined a face to go with it. That is part of the association process.

As the days went by, your image became more vivid, more real. Then you saw his photograph in the newspaper. Did you find yourself thinking that the newspaper made a mistake? "That's not what he looks like at all!" Your imagination did the distorting, not the newspaper.

A very dramatic example of how the imagination can build a "REALITY" which then affects behavior happened in 1938, on Halloween, when the Mercury Radio Theater presented Orson Welles' version of H.G. Wells' story *The War of the Worlds* on the Columbia Broadcasting System.

So vividly and realistically did that radio drama stimulate the imagination of thousands of listeners that there was near panic on the Eastern seaboard—especially in New Jersey and New York. Some of the people who tuned their radios to that broadcast "knew" that we were actually being invaded by hostile, destructive creatures from Mars. Highways were jammed, police switch-boards couldn't handle the incoming calls, people were behaving in a manner that was entirely consistent with their currently dominant "REALITY" about what was happening and what was likely to happen next.

One more illustration with which you may be able to identify: can you recall anything that happened in your family before you were born? I mean *remember* it just as though you had been there watching it happen, even though you know, logically, that you couldn't possibly have seen it happen?

I can remember an incident that happened when my brother, Bill, was about five or six years old. He was playing with Dickie Bancroft who lived down the street. My brother was at the upstairs window and Dickie was standing down below, looking up at Bill. My brother dropped a sharply pointed metal object—a milk bottle cap remover—for Dickie to catch. Dickie missed catching it, but it hit him in the face, about a half-inch from his eye. Blood all over the place and lots of yelling, crying, and furor.

The peculiar part of this is that Bill is ten years older than I am and I couldn't possibly have been there to see that all happen. It seems like it though. I can recall it so vividly that it seems like it is happening all over again.

Of course, the reason is that that story was told dozens, perhaps hundreds, of times when I was a child. Every time my brothers or I were seen playing with a sharp object, Mother would re-play the story about how Dickie Bancroft almost lost an eye. She told it with a lot of vividness and emotion, too. Put that with the lively imagination of a child and it's easy to see how it became a part of my reference file of experiences.

Computer programmers have a simple way of express-ing this idea: *GIGO*. It stands for Garbage In, Garbage Out! If false information is programmed into a computer, we will almost surely get some strange answers from the mechanism. You and I function in much the same way—except that we have the added dimension of emotion which causes many of the false inputs to have an even more profound impact on behavior.

I am not going to attempt to look at the chemical or biological processes which are involved in the storage of your "REALITY" structure. There are still some major gaps in our understanding of the exact electrochemical processes which result in various kinds of "memory" activity. It is a fascinating scientific frontier; once again, the more we learn about it, the more amazingly complex it appears to be.

If that aspect of our search intrigues you, there are some excellent reference books listed in the bibliography at the end of the book.

The third subconscious mental process has to do with **conflict resolution.**

To the degree that there is a conflict, or difference, between what you are perceiving and what you "know" to be "true," creativity and energy are released or activated to resolve the conflict. Your mental system goes to work, automatically, to change what you are perceiving as "wrong" or to revise your "REALITY."

Consider the child who knows that there really is a Santa Claus—and remember, there is a lot of emotion attached to that "truth." Then someone in the neighborhood says, "You don't believe that Santa Claus stuff, do you?" The child's first impulse is to cling to "REALITY," to reject the conflicting input, and perhaps even to expend some energy to force the person who made such a stupid statement to shape up!

Then, as more and more evidence is perceived which

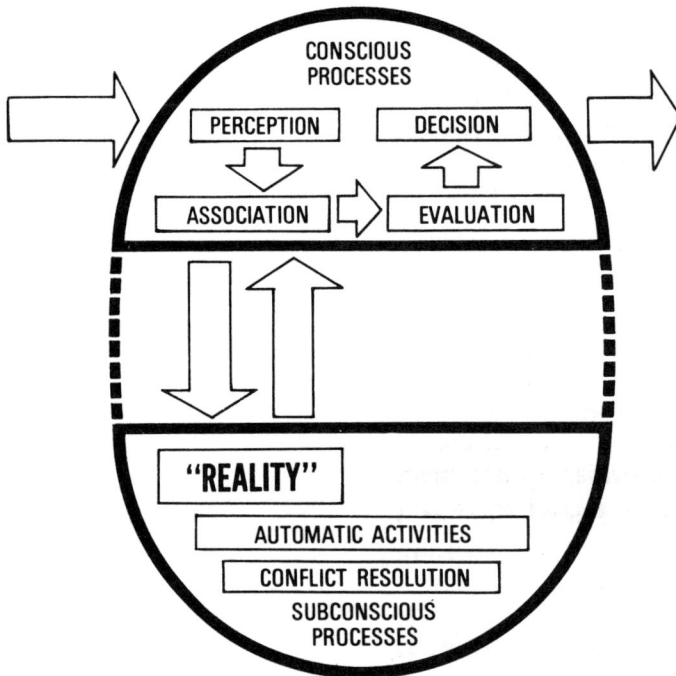

seems to indicate that Santa Claus truly is a myth, the evaluation process slowly begins to change and the "REALITY" structure is re-programmed. The "truth" about Santa Claus is superseded by a new "truth."

Sometimes, when there is a very strong emotional attachment to the earlier "REALITY," the re-programming is aided or assisted by some creative activity at a more subconscious level. One example of such subconscious creative re-programming is found in dream activity. Dreams are not just a way of passing the time while you are asleep. They are thought to perform a very important psychotherapeutic function—like having your own built-in therapist, working while you are asleep with creative psychodrama to help you cope with the conflicts in your life.

Dreams seem to be symbolically related to the upheavals which are happening in your day-to-day world, and if you are deprived of dreams, the deprivation will eventually result in neurotic or even psychotic behavior.

An example of an extreme conflict, with a great deal of emotion, is the sudden, unexpected death of a close loved one—your spouse, parent, child, brother, or sister. That other person had become a very important part of your environmental "REALITY." Then, one day, he (or she) isn't there any more. Your immediate impulse is to cling to your "REALITY," to reject the idea that the person you love is really gone. There must be some mistake! You may feel a strange mixture of emotions as you are confronted with additional evidence that there really has been a death. Along with the grief there will be anger, and then guilt and frustration.

Meanwhile, at a subconscious level in your system, dream activity will be working to help revise the "REALITY" structure so that you can accept what has happened as final, real, and something that you can live with. The creative subconscious re-programming process goes on all the time, not only when you are asleep.

Another application of this same process can be seen in action when you are confronted with a business or personal "problem." When you perceive something that

is not complete or finished, you tend to feel uncomfortable. When something isn't "neat" or the way it is "supposed to be" there is that automatic impulse to get it "fixed."

Look at the illustration on the left.

Do you see a picture? You probably filled in the empty spaces and saw the figure of a dog. That happened at a largely conscious level; the same sort of process occurs continuously in your mental system at a subconscious level.

In *Chapter 17* we will look at some specific steps that you can take to make more productive use of this creative process.

Another application of this third subconscious activity—conflict resolution—can be seen in the goal-seeking function of your system. We will be looking at this area in considerable detail in *Chapter 13*. For the present it is sufficient to note that when you set a goal and program it into your "REALITY" structure, a conflict develops between "the way things are" and "the way things are supposed to be" which stimulates creativity and releases the necessary energy to achieve the goal.

There is one more aspect of the conflict resolution process which we do not yet clearly understand, but which should at least be mentioned.

Sometimes your mental system seems to be able to tap outside sources of information or inspiration through some channel other

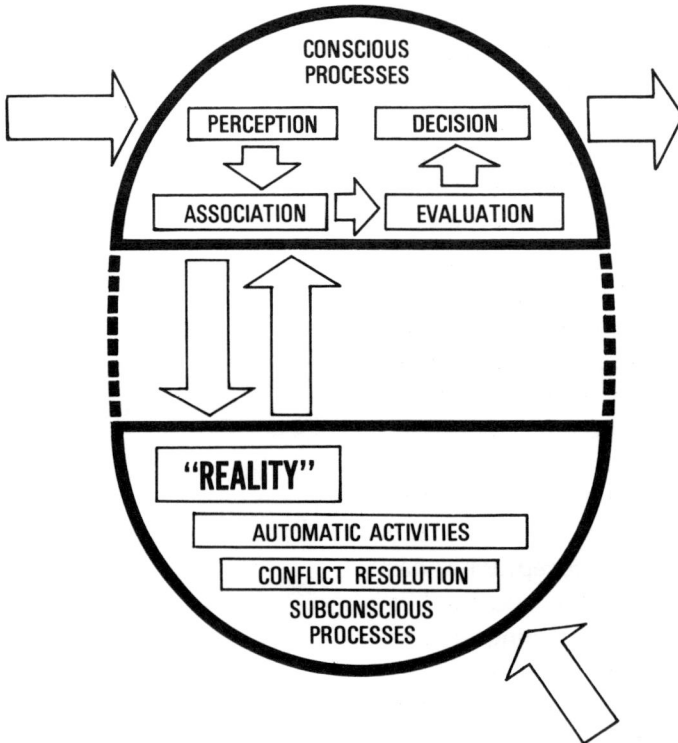

than the conscious process of perception. This may be related to parapsychology—telepathy, clairvoyance etc.—or for some it may seem to have religious or spiritual implications. Carl Jung, the great psychoanalytical theoretician, called it the *Collective Unconscious.*

For lack of a better term, we will simply label this additional input channel the **Eighth Arrow.** A clearer understanding of the nature and function of this flow may well be one of the most exciting frontiers of the next half-century. We will look at it in a little more detail in *Chapter 17.*

The care and feeding of attitudes

Your "REALITY" structure is an intricate network of attitude patterns, countless combinations of what you know and how you feel about yourself and your world. Each attitude pattern is the result of your own conscious thought processes. You were not born with attitudes. You have built every one of them, piece by piece, bit by bit with your thinking, your imagination, and your responses to the events of your life. The conscious mental processes are the programming mechanisms for the subconscious "REALITY."

What are the building blocks with which you have built this complex structure?

There are three media that we use at a conscious level which, together, contribute to the development of attitudes. The most obvious of these, to most people is the VERBAL medium. We think with words. Can you notice that right now you are talking to yourself, inside your head, even while you are reading? That inner dialogue or "self-talk" goes on all the time that you are awake. While you are reading, listening to someone else talking, watching television—even while you are talking to someone else—your self-talk continues at a rate of about three hundred to four hundred words per minute.

Of course, you did not talk to yourself, with words, until your mental system had been programmed with those verbal symbols. In the early stages of your life, before you found out that words existed, your thinking involved only two media.

55

How else do you think, besides with words? Can you observe your thought processes in action and detect what else is happening? You think with images, don't you? You think about a sunset and suddenly you "see" the sunset (maybe a whole series of them) in your "mind's eye." You can think with your mind's ear, too. How does a violin sound, or a fingernail scraping across a chalkboard? Or, you can draw back up to the surface of your thinking the fragrance of a rose, bacon cooking in the frying pan, or an angered skunk. You can think about touching a piece of velvet or sandpaper, tasting a lemon or a chocolate sundae. You can even think about a stomachache, or how it feels to hang upside down.

All these are simply thoughts which make use of sensory information which you have perceived at some time in the past, or which you have experienced in the imagination as though they had been perceived. Now, if you wish to do so, you can use those prior experiences in your present thought processes.

But the second medium of conscious thought goes beyond the sensory area to include abstractions such as the future, personal liberty, or 3:00 P.M. Those ideas are not really sensory inputs, but they certainly are concepts with which you can think. So, we use the label CONCEPTUAL for this second kind of thought.

What is the third level or medium? When you thought of the word "sunset," you triggered your file of sunset experiences. What else was going on in your mental processes?

When you thought of the violin, the fingernail on the chalkboard, the rose, or the skunk, what happened besides the verbal and conceptual thoughts?

One more example: what happens in your system when you read this sentence?

THERE IS A LONG, BLACK SNAKE
OVER THERE IN THE GRASS.

First the words, and there may have been a flood of them going through your thoughts. Then the concepts, the experiences you have had with or about snakes in your past thoughts. And then, of course, the EMOTIONAL medium. The **feelings** which you have trained yourself to have about snakes. Were they warm, affectionate feelings? Fear? Revulsion? Whatever the emotions were, can you see that you were not *born* with them? Oh, you were born with the ability to feel those particular emotions, but you *learned* to associate those feelings with specific items or events.

The emotional medium is the first one that was activated in your thinking. As a child—perhaps even before you were born—you had feelings of security, fear, frustration, joy, and many others. As time went by you began to associate specific emotions with certain people, events, foods, sounds, odors, etc. You were, even at that very young age, developing attitudes. At that point these attitudes were only two-dimensional, but they were the early building blocks of your "REALITY" structure.

Then you were programmed with words. Now you had labels for the experiences, abstractions, and emotions, and you could think on three levels.

The degree to which you can think with words—symbols—is one of the primary factors which separates you from other forms of animal life. If, for some reason, it had not been possible for you to assimilate words into your mental system, your life and your behavior would have been very "animal-like." Even among people who *do* think on a verbal level, there is a remarkable correlation between vocabulary and effective, intelligent behavior.

The three media of thought, **verbal, conceptual,** and **emotional,** are flowing continuously in your mental system—at least during your waking hours.

Any one of the three media may initiate a sequence or stream of thought, but the other two join in right away. One of the three may be dominant for a while, but all three are there to some degree at all times. "Self-talk," then, is not entirely verbal as it might, at first, seem.

There is a very important reason for looking so carefully at all three dimensions of your thinking. Those three-dimensional thoughts are not fleeting impressions which occur and then evaporate or disappear! The automatic subconscious storage process records each thought as a new experience in the "REALITY" structure. Every thought that you have makes its contribution—reinforcing, modifying, adjusting the existing patterns of information and emotion.

We can think of an attitude as the way that we "lean," toward or away from something—a positive inclination or a negative inclination. Notice that I am not classifying attitudes as *good* or *bad*. What is important to our discussion is the degree to which the emotional component of the attitude pattern is positive or negative. Whether the behavior which results is useful, profitable, and productive or the opposite is an entirely separate question. A very positive attitude about sweets might be unhealthy for a diabetic, and an attitude with a strong negative emotional component might be very desirable if the attitude is about heroin.

Check this out in your own system. See if you can get acquainted with your own attitude in the following areas. How do you lean: toward or away from? In some cases there may be only a slight, almost imperceptible inclination; in others it will be stronger and easier to identify. To what degree is your attitude positive or negative about:

Sailboats.
Foreign cars.
Ten-week-old kittens.
Spinach.
Making speeches to large groups of people.
Drinking buttermilk.
Remembering people's names.
Mowing the lawn.
Eating a horsemeat steak.
People with different colored skins.

The Catholic Church.
Money.
People who smoke.
People who do not smoke.
Policemen.

The list could go on indefinitely. As you look at each item can you sense the "REALITY" at work in your mental system? Can you feel the emotional component that you have programmed as a part of your "truth" about that aspect of yourself or the world around you?

Remember that each of the countless attitudes which you now have has been developed, programmed, adjusted, and reinforced by *you.* They are all the result of your own three-dimensional self-talk.

NO ONE ELSE CAN DEVELOP AN
ATTITUDE WITHIN YOUR SYSTEM.
ONLY *YOU* CAN DO *THAT!*

It may help to portray an attitude pattern visually. Picture it like a scale that a chemist might have in his laboratory, with a positive side and a negative side.

Every three-dimensional—verbal-conceptual-emotional— thought is like a small weight or rock, automatically deposited on one side of the scale or the other, depending on whether the emotional component is positive or negative. The weight, or mass, of the rock is a function of the intensity of the emotion. One thought about a particular subject (one rock) does not have much impact, unless there is a very strong emotion involved. But a constant flow of weights to one side of the scale will result in a firmly held attitude and, of course, corresponding behavior.

Let's look, once again, at the area of public speaking. When the child is still functioning at the emotional/ conceptual level of thinking and is first introduced to the world of words, he finds an exciting new frontier. Each time that he learns to say a new word he has a very positive feeling about his success. He senses approval and encouragement from his parents and other important people in his environment—**positive reinforcement.**

Before long he has learned lots of words and he enjoys using them to communicate his desires and frustrations to others. Words are serving his needs very well. He piles a pretty good stack of rocks on the positive side of the "talking scale."

Then he may begin to encounter some new messages from the people in his environment.

"Shhh, Johnny. You musn't talk all the time."

"Be quiet, Johnny!"

"If you're going to talk, talk, talk, go in the other room."

"I'll give you a quarter if you'll be quiet for five minutes."

"Shut up!"

We cannot predict with absolute certainty what the effect of these messages will be. We are only dealing with probabilities. It is not what other people are saying that will build Johnny's attitude, it is what *he* is saying to *himself* that counts. But there is certainly a distinct possibility that he may not feel as enthusiastic about the business of expressing himself with words as he has been. Now his thoughts may begin to put some rocks on the negative side of the scale.

Next, he may be required to learn—and recite—a poem or a Bible verse. How he feels about standing up in front of a group of strangers to recite is going to have a further effect on his "REALITY." When he enters school there are more opportunities (or requirements) to express himself, to his teacher and his classmates. In each instance his thoughts—particularly the emotional dimension—will further modify the attitude. It's not hard to see how he might come to "know" that "public speaking is really hard." Or, "I just can't stand up in front of a group of people and talk!"

With that kind of attitude, how likely is the adult Johnny to enroll in a public speaking course? Not very! He will behave in a manner that is consistent with his "REALITY." If he *is* called upon to stand up and express his opinion, he probably won't do it very well, even though he has all of the *potential* that he needs to do a terrific job.

Let's observe another attitude pattern as it develops in a little girl. Mary is six years old. This afternoon she is playing at the home of her best friend, Cindy. Near the end of the afternoon, Cindy says, "Why don't you call your mother and ask her if you can stay over for dinner?"

Mary is about to pick up the telephone when Cindy changes her mind. "No, you'd better not. Maybe you can come to dinner tomorrow, but you'd better not stay tonight. We're having *spinach*!"

Now, we're going to assume that this is the first time in her life that Mary has ever heard that word. What do you suppose is going to happen in her mental processes? Here is the first input in the development of a brand-new attitude. Her "spinach scale" is completely empty, never been used, never had anything deposited on either side.

As Mary perceives that word for the very first time, she perceives along with it a tone of voice and a facial

expression. The word is new, but the tone and the grimace are familiar. As she associates what she is perceiving with her prior experiences she is very likely to interpret the message as meaning that Cindy doesn't like spinach (whatever that is).

But Mary's evaluation of the significance of this event to *her* will also include another association. How dependable is Cindy's judgment about whether foods are good or bad? If Mary already "knows" that Cindy doesn't like fried chicken or chocolate ice cream, then Cindy's negative message about spinach may be converted to a positive rock to go on Mary's attitude scale.

What Cindy says—and how she says it—does not put a rock on Mary's scale. Only Mary's own self-talk can do that!

We will make another assumption for the purpose of our example—that Mary has a very positive attitude about Cindy's credibility regarding foods that do or do not taste good. If that is the case, then when Mary perceives the negative expression and tone of voice, she is very probably going to think, "Whatever that spinach stuff is, it must be pretty awful!"

Along with the words, she will have some conceptual processes—visual imagery, taste, odor—in her imagination, and of course, the emotional input, too. The three-dimensional rock clunks onto her new spinach attitude scale.

That one input doesn't form much of an attitude. But a few days later, Mary overhears her big brother talking with one of his friends about the food in the school cafeteria. "Yeah, usually the food's pretty good at school," he says. "But twice a week they have *spinach*!"

There's that tone of voice again. As Mary associates what she hears with her already existing "REALITY," she may think to herself, "David doesn't like spinach either. It must be pretty bad!" Once again, notice that her brother did not put the rock on her scale. Mary's own verbal/conceptual/emotional thought process made the deposit.

She may also perceive some positive information about spinach. As Mary watches the cartoons on tele-

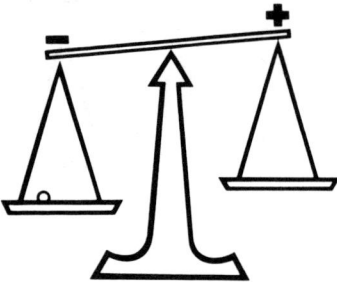

vision, she may learn that Popeye eats a lot of spinach, apparently likes it, and that it makes him strong.

Chances are that she will put that input on the positive side of her scale.

Then, one evening while she is playing on the living room floor, she hears an exchange between her parents. Dad is sitting in his favorite chair in the living room, reading a magazine. Mom steps out of the kitchen and says, "Charlie, we're having broiled chicken for dinner. Would you rather have spinach or broccoli?"

Now Mary's father likes both spinach and broccoli. But since he had spinach for lunch, he says, "Let's have the broccoli, honey. I don't feel like spinach tonight." What are the probabilities with respect to Mary's balance scale in the spinach department?

Notice that Dad didn't say, "I don't like spinach." Nor did he say, "Spinach tastes awful." But it is not what he says that will determine what happens to Mary's attitude pattern. It's what *she* says to herself that counts. As she hears her father's reply and associates it with what she already knows/feels about spinach, she may very well evaluate the significance of what she has heard with, "Hmmm, Daddy doesn't like that spinach stuff either!"—at the same time reaffirming the imagery and the emotions already attached to that word.

Clunk!

In this case the rock is bigger, heavier. The weight of the rock is determined by the emotional impact, and Mary's admiration and love for her Dad adds an extra intensity to this input.

A few nights later as Mary sits down to dinner she is delighted to see that the family is having hamburger steak tonight. There are some french-fried potatoes on her plate, too, and over on the other side there's a pile of green stuff.

"What's that?" inquires Mary.

"Oh, that's spinach, honey." Mother's reply is friendly and encouraging. *"You'll love it!"*

"I don't want any." **(Clunk!)**

"Sure you do, Mary. Spinach is delicious, and it's so good for you!"

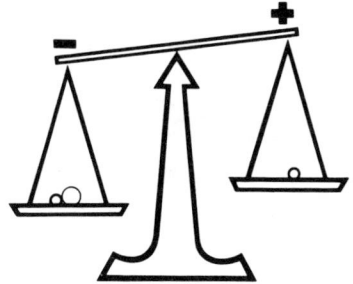

"I don't like it." **(Clunk!)**

"But you've never had any before. Just try a little and see how good it is."

"I don't care if I haven't tried it. I don't like it and I don't want any!" **(Clunk!)**

Now father steps in. *"I don't want to hear any more conversation. You just eat that spinach."*

"Daddy, I hate spinach. It's awful. I don't want any and I'm not going to eat it." **(Clunk!)**

"You'll sit there until it's all gone!"

"I may throw up!!" **(Clunk!)**

And that is just possible.

Notice that every time Mary reaffirmed her dislike for spinach she was not just talking to her parents, she was also talking to her own "REALITY" structure. As the dialogue progressed, the emotions became more intense and the rocks got heavier and heavier.

Without intending to do so, and without realizing that they were doing so, Mom and Dad virtually insisted that Mary develop a full-fledged hatred for spinach. They did not program her mental system; she did that.

ATTITUDE ("REALITY")

BEHAVIOR (yours or others)

But their behavior certainly played a role in the development of that attitude.

Now, whether or not Mary likes spinach is not the most important question in her life. I offer this illustration simply because it is pretty easy to see that she was not born liking or disliking spinach. This and other food preferences were acquired, learned.

The same principle applies to much more significant areas of your "REALITY" structure which control the effectiveness level of your behavior.

As an attitude begins to develop, it tends to be self-reinforcing. To the degree that you lean either toward or away from something, you tend to further strengthen and reinforce that inclination. A negative attitude tends to become more negative—a positive attitude more positive.

Here is how the self-reinforcing cycle works.

First of all, your behavior tends to reflect—to be consistent with—your attitudes or "REALITY." Your expectancy when you enter into any situation will either enhance or limit your ability to function well, effectively. When you lift a bite of spinach toward your mouth, what you *expect* will influence how it tastes. In fact, your expectancy will govern whether you choose to put the spinach in your mouth to begin with. When you go into an interview, stand up to make a speech, or call someone on the telephone, how you expect that event to proceed will have a lot to do with how it actually does proceed. I call this the SURE ENOUGH! effect—a short, convenient label for the phenomenon of the self-fulfilling prophecy.

There are actually two stages to the SURE ENOUGH! effect. First, your expectancy either helps or hinders the flow of your potential; second, what you expect is communicated to others in subtle ways and they tend to respond in a manner which helps to create the outcome which you expected.

Look what happens if you waken in the morning, reach over to turn off the alarm, and think to yourself, "Oh boy, this is going to be a miserable day!" You can just about bet that it will be. Not only will your negative emotions limit your ability to function well, but everywhere you go you will be telling others—with your facial expressions, posture, and tone of voice—that you have decided this day is going to be awful. Usually, people will pitch in and help make the day miserable for you. Or, you go into the sales interview "knowing" that this person will be a very difficult prospect. SURE ENOUGH! he will be difficult. A lot more difficult than he would have been had you entered into the interview with a more positive expectancy.

And, fortunately, the SURE ENOUGH! effect works at least as well in the positive direction. When you waken in the morning with an optimistic feeling about the day, your abilities and skills flow much more smoothly and effectively. Everywhere you go on a day like that, people will find it easier to respond to you with cheerfulness, openness, and warmth. To the degree that you expect success in an interview, tennis game, or any situation which involves other people, your expectancy will be contagious and will have a very powerful impact on the event.

Then comes the self-talk process. As you perceive what is happening, associate what you are perceiving with your "REALITY" about such matters and evaluate its significance, your conscious thoughts tend to further reinforce the already existing "truth." Your verbal/conceptual/emotional self-talk process compares what you perceive to be happening with "what is supposed to happen in cases like this." To the degree that there is a match, you are likely to think, "That figures. Just what I would have expected." Your existing attitude or "REALITY" has been reinforced.

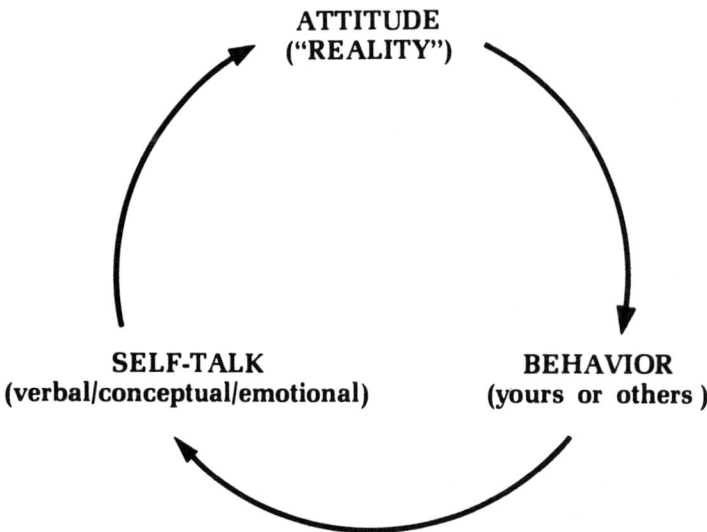

ATTITUDE
("REALITY")

SELF-TALK
(verbal/conceptual/emotional)

BEHAVIOR
(yours or others)

To the degree that what you are perceiving seems to conflict with your attitude, there is a tendency to think, "How did that happen? That's not 'normal.' An exception to the rule." Again your existing "truth" has been reinforced.

Here is an example. Betty "knows" that she just cannot bake cakes. She feels pretty good about her cooking generally, but her image of her ability to bake cakes is tilted way over to the negative side.

As a rule, Betty behaves in a manner that is consistent with that "REALITY." Most of the time she just doesn't bake cakes—why should she, when they always turn out so badly? If there is a special birthday in the family and she summons all her courage and tries her very best to bake a cake that is edible, it is nearly always a disaster. Her grim determination causes her to misread the directions, stir the batter too long, or set the oven at the wrong temperature.

Then, as Betty looks at the drooping result of her valiant effort, she thinks, "I knew it. Just my luck! I might as well face it, I can't bake cakes!" **Clunk!** Another big negative rock just reinforced her already existing attitude.

What would her reaction have been if the cake had turned out well? What kind of self-talk would she have engaged in as she perceived an attractive, light-textured, tasty cake? And associated it with her "REALITY" about her ability in that area?

That depends a lot on how far the scale is already tipped, doesn't it? If the existing attitude is only slightly negative, she might think, "Hmmm, maybe I *can* bake cakes after all. I sure do feel good about *this* one!" Moreover, if that scale is only tipped a little, she may even accept the compliments she receives and use them to drop some more rocks on the positive side.

However, the more that particular attitude scale has been tipped to the negative side—the more certain Betty is that she is not a cake-baker—the more likely she is to look at the beautiful cake she has produced and think, "What a lucky break. Somehow this one isn't as bad as usual." **Clunk!** When the family praises her creation, she will reject the compliments and remind herself that baking an edible cake is not like her. **Clunk!** She might say, "If it's good, it's not my fault. Give the credit to Duncan Hines." **Clunk!** She may even decide to "quit while she's ahead" and get all future cakes at the local bakery. **Clunk!**

Betty doesn't react only to her own baking activities. When she is at Helen's house for a bridge game and Helen serves coffee and a cake that she has baked, Betty again has a self-talk opportunity. Here, too, she is almost certain to reinforce the existing pattern.

If Helen's cake is heavy and dry, Betty is likely to

think, "Poor Helen. She bakes cakes the way I do. I know just how she must feel." **Clunk!**

If Helen's cake is outstanding, Betty may say to herself—and to everyone else—"I wish that I could bake a cake like this." **Clunk!**

That's right, a wish is a negative rock. One of the biggest, heaviest rocks you can drop on the negative side. Think about that. When Mary thinks, "I wish that I could bake a cake like this," what is the rest of the sentence? ".....but I can't, and I know that I never will be able to." We tend to use wishes for those areas in which only a miracle could make something happen. "If it's up to me, there's no chance that any change for the better will take place. It could only happen if the genie grants my wish. It could only happen by magic or if somehow the laws of the universe are set aside."

There's a big difference between a "wish" and a "goal." "I want to" or "I plan to," are a lot different from "I wish I could." Next time you catch yourself wishing for something, see if it feels any different to rephrase your thought as a "want to" or a goal or a plan. That simple difference in approach will open the door to some constructive action, instead of waiting for your wish to be granted.

Take a few minutes now to play with this self-reinforcing concept. Be sure that you grasp it thoroughly before we go on. Go through the example that we have just observed, in reverse. If Betty has a more positive attitude about her ability to bake cakes, how will she behave? What will her self-talk be in each of these four instances;

    1. If she bakes a poor cake?

    2. If she bakes a good one?

    3. If a friend bakes a poor one?

    4. If a friend bakes a good one?

Do you see that the same tendency for self-reinforcement happens on the positive side, too?

Whether or not it is true with people, it is certainly true with attitudes that the rich get richer and the poor get poorer!

Now, see how this same principle applies to some specific areas in your own life. Pick out a few attitudes that are important in your profession, in your family, or in social areas. Identify some attitudes that you have which are positive, and some which are negative, and note that in each case, to the degree that the attitude is already tilted—in either direction—it tends to "feed" on itself, to grow, and to have a more and more powerful effect on your behavior in that area.

Remember, though, that while there is a strong *tendency* for attitudes to continue to build in the same direction that they are now leaning, it is not inevitable. If that were absolutely predictable, there would be no reason for this book. The normal, natural flow of your conscious thought processes tends to reinforce or re-affirm the already existing "truths" which you have adopted, but it is also possible for you to decide to direct your thinking, deliberately, to build the kind of attitudes which will serve you better.

In that connection, it may be useful at this point to look at what I call the "rock exchange exercise." All day long you are on the sending and receiving end of a lot of rocks—a lot of messages and signals which stimulate the self-talk process and are deposited on the positive or negative side of various scales. As your awareness of this exchange increases, notice that it is very much to your benefit to keep the messages that you send to others on a positive channel. You cannot be sure what the other person will do with what you are saying to him, but if it appears to be a sincere positive expression it is likely to be received and accepted as such.

It may be even more important to recognize that when you are on the receiving end, you can decide which side of the scale is going to get each new input. Even though the message that you are receiving from someone else appears to be very negative, your self-talk can respond to that rock in a positive way and use it to reinforce the positive side of that attitude scale.

Look at how this might apply in a family situation. Teen-age daughter Susan is on her way to her bedroom to do some homework after dinner. As she goes through the kitchen, she notices that her mother is scraping the dishes and getting them ready to wash. Susan is not in a very big hurry to get to her homework, so she says, "Can I help you with the dishes, Mom?"

There are a lot of ways her mother may respond to that offer—some very positive reactions and some that are not so positive. Let's assume for this example that her response is one of shock: "Can you *what?* I can't believe my ears! What's come over you?" Looks like a big, heavy negative rock, doesn't it? It wouldn't be any surprise if Susan says, "Forget it. I'm sorry I asked," and goes on to her room.

Why on earth would Mother react so negatively to an offer of help? That's easy, isn't it? Mother has an image of Susan as a part of her "REALITY" structure. Based upon her observation of her daughter for the past sixteen years, Mother "knows" that Susan is thoughtless, self-centered, inconsiderate, and immature. She has been *wishing* that Susan would grow up, but it has never occurred to her to reinforce mature behavior when it happens. So, when she perceives her daughter offering to be helpful, she associates that action with what she "knows" about Susan; the evaluation is, "That's not like her," and Mother behaves accordingly.

On her way to her bedroom, Susan's thoughts and feelings about the incident will probably further reinforce the idea that offering to be helpful is a waste of time.

To the degree that Susan's mother understands the concept that we are exploring, she is much more likely to simply accept Susan's offer with appreciation. "Sure, honey, thanks. I really appreciate your help." No big fanfare, just a pleasant, loving thank-you. Even if it is the very first time that Susan has ever offered her help, it will be a lot more profitable if her mother accepts and reinforces the kind of behavior which she admires than if she expresses her shock and reinforces the past behavior.

If Susan has a grasp of this rock exchange idea, she will know that even though her mother's amazement is a pretty negative message, she is not required to put it on the negative side of her scale. If she wants to, she can reply with, "Oh, I don't know. I guess this is just my day to be helpful. Would you like me to dry the dishes?" In other words, it will be in Susan's self-interest, in the long run, to grow up in spite of Mother!

One of the reasons this idea is especially important to you right now is that as you put to work in your day-to-day life what you are learning in this book, you are almost certain to encounter some reactions of surprise—or even shock—from other people. Your family, friends, people that you work with are going to notice changes in your behavior, and they may give you a "That's not like you" reaction. Welcome those responses and put them on the positive side of your scales. They are rewarding evidence that what you are doing is working!

The importance of childhood conditioning

A remarkable amount of learning takes place in the first few years of a child's life. While we usually think of that learning process as it relates to acquiring *information,* many habits are also formed during that period. Not just habits like brushing our teeth or washing our hands before a meal, but all sorts of skills, attitudes and habits of thinking/feeling.

Because of the emotional attachment, dependency, and love for the parents, the messages (rocks) which a child receives in the early years have a much higher *probability* of being processed and accepted into the "REALITY" structure without question or reservation.

If a child's parents repeatedly tell him how clumsy he is, the youngster is much more likely to accept the negative rocks (messages from experts) and begin to know/feel that he is uncoordinated than if the exchange were between two adults. Still, the attitude is the result of the child's own conscious thoughts and feelings—in response to the messages from the parents.

The development of those patterns may be "motivated" either positively or negatively—with pleasure or with pain, promises or fear. Actually, the emotional impetus is a matter of degree, and falls somewhere along a continuum or scale ranging from the very negative to the very positive.

We tend to move toward those activities, events or things which we expect (on the basis of prior experience) will bring pleasure or reward of some kind. And, of course, we tend to avoid or move away from activities which we associate with discomfort or pain (physical or emotional).

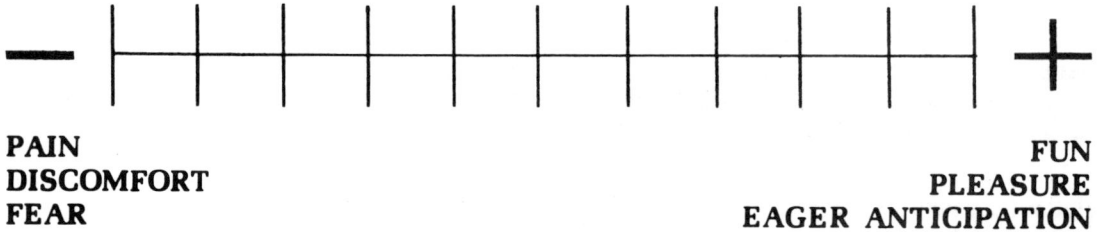

$$-\ \ |\!-\!|\!-\!|\!-\!|\!-\!|\!-\!|\!-\!|\!-\!|\!-\!|\!-\!|\!-\!|\!-\!|\ \ +$$

PAIN   **FUN**
DISCOMFORT   **PLEASURE**
FEAR   **EAGER ANTICIPATION**

This principle applies to you now, but it applied even more when you were small. As a child, your emotional channel of thinking was an even more significant part of your system than it is today—the key part of your thought processes at that stage of your life.

We can categorize those patterns which have developed through repeated association with a positive emotion as **constructive** patterns, and those which are built with negative emotions as **restrictive** patterns.

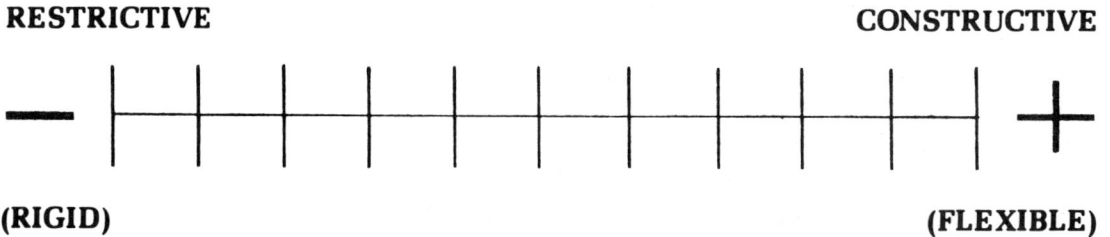

RESTRICTIVE   **CONSTRUCTIVE**

$$-\ \ |\!-\!|\!-\!|\!-\!|\!-\!|\!-\!|\!-\!|\!-\!|\!-\!|\!-\!|\!-\!|\!-\!|\ \ +$$

(RIGID)   **(FLEXIBLE)**

The constructive patterns tend to be more flexible—more easily changed or adjusted—while restrictive patterns are more rigid.

Let's see how a constructive pattern develops with a simple example of a physical coordination skill: walking.

For a variety of reasons, a child *wants* to learn how to walk. Most of the other people in his environment are doing it, it seems to get them from place to place a lot faster than crawling, it looks like it would be fun, and besides, Mom and Dad seem to get a kick out of holding his hands and showing him how to shift his balance and move his feet.

Next, the child acquires some *information* about how to walk. Some of the inputs are the result of what he is perceiving in his environment—watching people walk, being shown how to take a step. We can call this kind of informational input *training.*

The child also learns a lot about walking from the trial-and-error-and-success process. When he falls down, since he is so small it's not a very painful impact. He just picks himself up and tries again, correcting for the error. As he is able to take a step or two without falling, he reinforces the kind of coordination and balance which led to the success. He uses both the failures and the successes to do an increasingly effective job of walking.

As he acquires more and more information about the skill of walking, and uses that information *repetitiously,* a pattern begins to develop at a more subconscious level in his mental processes. What has been happening at a very conscious, deliberately directed level now is automated—becomes an increasingly subconscious, constructive pattern.

There are three steps, then, to the development of a constructive pattern:

1. A positive feeling about the activity or object.
2. Acquiring information through:
   A. Training (inputs from the environment).
   B. Experience (trial-and-error-and-success).
3. Repetition.

Take a few minutes right now to trace this simple three-step process as it applied to you when you learned how to:

- Drive an automobile.
- Play tennis.
- Tie your shoelaces.
- Operate a typewriter.
- Knit.

You can readily think of many other coordination patterns as well. See if you can recall the kind of emotion you had about a skill when you first started to think about it. Look back at the ways that you acquired information from the environment, how you learned from your experiences, and how the repetitious use of that information gradually automated the skill.

Now, think about how the same constructive sequence helped you to learn some patterns of a mental nature, such as:

- The multiplication tables.
- Rules of grammar or spelling.
- Vocabulary.
- Speaking a foreign language.
- Sending and receiving Morse code.

How about some attitude patterns about such aspects of your life as:

- Silk fabric.
- Sunsets.
- Your own savings account.
- Your favorite kind of music.

As you think through the conditioning process with which these patterns have developed, you will note that the amount of feeling that you have in each area varies a lot. Get acquainted with those emotional leanings.

The **restrictive** conditioning process includes the same three stages or steps, with one very important difference. The emotional component in restrictive conditioning is *negative* instead of positive. This sequence correlates information with a negative feeling—anger, frustration, hate, envy, disgust, or, most frequently, fear—repeatedly.

The repeated association of a negative emotion with some aspect of your self or your environment builds a restrictive pattern. We saw that happen with Mary as she programmed herself with the "truth" that "spinach is awful!" Another way that she might express such a pattern would be, "I can't eat spinach!" Restrictive patterns which involve a "can't" are called **inhibitive** patterns. Others which involve a "have to" are called **compulsive** patterns. Both inhibitive and compulsive patterns are restrictive, and the great majority of them are formed and maintained with some sort of "OR ELSE!"

What other inhibitive patterns can you recognize in yourself? How about these:

- Crossing the street in the middle of the block.
- Public speaking.
- Drawing or painting pictures.
- Eating horsemeat steaks.
- Buttermilk.
- Wetting your pants.

Look for a few compulsive patterns, too. Do you have any of these:

- Being on time for appointments.
- Going to church.
- Eat everything on your plate.
- Answer the telephone when it rings.

Can you see that each of these patterns is the result of the repetitious "depositing" of information with a negative emotional exponent. Whether the result of a perceived message such as "Don't do that!", "You have to do that!" or "You can't do that!" or repeated association with similar activities or objects to which you had already attached a negative feeling, as you have repeatedly added negative rocks to that scale the attitude has become more and more a controlling part of your "REALITY" system.

Let's look at a compulsive pattern in the process of development.

Johnny, age six, runs out to play baseball with the kids in the neighborhood. As he zips through the kitchen toward the back door Mom says, "Be sure that you're home by five o'clock, Johnny, so you can be ready for dinner when Daddy gets home."

"Okay, Mom. See ya later."

When is Johnny likely to come home? Probably when the game is over, or when it gets dark, when he gets hungry, or is kicked out of the game, when all the other kids have gone home, he's hurt, or he hears his mother calling him. This doesn't mean that Johnny didn't hear his mother tell him when to come home. Nor does it mean that he is deliberately disobeying his mother. It means that he is thoroughly engrossed in the game and the concept of time is, by comparison, both abstract and unimportant.

So, he comes bouncing happily into the house at six o'clock, and bounces right into an explosion!

"Where have you been? Do you know what time it is? Did you hear me tell you to be home at five o'clock? When we tell you to be home at a certain time, we expect you to be home at that time!"

The first rock has just been deposited on Johnny's punctuality scale. We cannot be absolutely *certain* which side he will put it on, but there is a very high probability that it will go on the negative side of the scale. The importance of being on time has been related to the negative emotion of fear—fear of the consequences of being late.

Next day, Johnny comes home from school, runs upstairs to change his clothes and get his baseball mitt, and heads out the back door to find his playmates. As he leaves, Mom gives him a reminder, "Now you be sure to be home by five o'clock, young man. You know what's going to happen if you're late!"

"Okay, Mom. I'll remember."

When will Johnny start home from the baseball game this time? Probably when the game is over or it's dark or something else happens to break his complete concentration on the game. But this time, as soon as he starts for home, he will think, "Oh, wow! I wonder what time it is. I hope I'm not late again!"

But he *is* late again. This time as he walks into the house he really gets the whole avalanche. Shouting, berating, physical punishment, sent to his room without dinner, and threats about what will happen to him if he ever does this again. An exaggeration? Maybe, but not by much.

Each time that lateness results in physical or emotional discomfort or pain, Johnny's self-talk will deposit another rock on the scale. Soon, he will know (and feel very strongly) that, "You have to be on time. . . . . . OR ELSE!"

The **have to,** or compulsive, pattern is now a part of Johnny's "truth" system and it will have a powerful impact on his behavior. Often it will seem to be a useful pattern—being on time is courteous and considerate. But with Johnny punctuality is not a matter of thoughtfulness, it has become a compulsion.

Imagine this situation. John is now an adult businessman, and he is driving his car through city traffic on his way to an appointment set for three o'clock this afternoon. It is now twenty minutes before three. John is only about ten minutes from the office toward which he is headed. The appointment is not a matter of life and death, but it is more than a casual "drop in when you're out this way."

Now John's car is approaching a railroad grade crossing. Just before he gets there the gate comes down and the bell starts ringing. There are cars on both sides of his car, and more behind him—and now the crossing gate is down in front of his automobile. As John looks down the track he can see a switch engine approaching, pulling a string of 130 freight cars. *Slowly.*

When fifteen freight cars have passed the crossing, the engineer stops, gets down out of the engine, and walks back to talk with the brakeman. Then he walks back to his engine and begins to shuffle the freight cars onto the appropriate sidings. Back and forth he goes. Four boxcars to that siding, a refrigerator car over there, two gondolas over there.

It is ten minutes past three, and there is no indication that the train is going to get out of the way so that John can proceed to his appointment. What do you suppose is going on in his system? What is he thinking? How is he **feeling**? What is happening in his physical mechanism?

All of that will be directly a function of the degree to which John has taught himself that "You have to be on time—OR ELSE!" To the degree that this compulsive pattern has become a part of John's "REALITY" structure, he will be feeling an emotion called **anxiety.**

Anxiety is a kind of low-intensity fear, but without a specific focus on exactly what is threatening the person who is feeling it. When someone points a gun at you, what you feel is *fear.* You know exactly what you are afraid of. Anxiety involves the same physical symptoms, the same organic changes in the physical mechanism, but you can't really put your finger on why you are afraid.

When you violate a restrictive pattern which you have adopted as a part of your "REALITY" structure, the anxiety that you feel is a fear of the OR ELSE! Of course, John is no longer afraid of being spanked, sent to his room, or deprived of his dinner. He simply knows that when he is late, something terrible is sure to happen! So he stews and frets and suffers very much the same sort of physical symptoms he would experience if he noticed a big tarantula spider walking across the seat of his car.

Not only is the anxiety likely to be damaging to his physical health, but let's see what happens to the effectiveness of John's behavior. What will he do when the gate crossing goes up? Gun his engine? Lay a little rubber on the street? He will probably dart in and out of traffic, exceed the speed limit, not quite stop at the boulevard stop sign, try to beat the traffic light, and yell at anyone who obstructs his progress. When he arrives at his destination, he will be in no condition to do what he has come there to do. He may spend the first ten minutes explaining why he is so late and begging forgiveness for his transgression. Whatever potential he may have to function well in this interview is not going to be flowing very freely or spontaneously. The brakes are on!

Notice that John feels anxiety whenever he is late, whether it is due to some condition over which he has no control—an accident—or on purpose. The train was beyond his control, but lateness stimulated anxiety. Suppose the battery had finally run down in his electric watch. When he checked his watch he thought that he had plenty of time, so he would be in no hurry driving to the appointment. Then, when he is almost there, he notices that the digital clock on the front of the local bank says it is 3:20! He is late by accident, but he is late—and the anxiety will be just as intense.

What will happen if John *decides* to be late? He

knows that if he stays in his office until three o'clock he can close a very large sale which will mean a big commission for him. If he leaves he will definitely lose that sale. Yet there is no way for him to contact the person with whom he has the three o'clock appointment. So, in order to make the sale, he decides to be late for the appointment. Even though it is clearly his decision, for what he considers to be a good, logical reason, the anxiety will be the same.

Of course, punctuality is a socially desirable habit. I am not suggesting for a moment that people should be completely carefree about time. It is the compulsion—the HAVE TO, OR ELSE!—which can be so damaging to your effectiveness and to your health.

It is possible to make it a habit to be on time for appointments as a result of constructive conditioning. If a person associates punctuality with positive feelings, repeatedly, there will be a consistent inclination to be on time, but without the anxiety when the pattern is violated. If a person with a constructive attitude about punctuality were to be delayed by the freight train, what would the reaction be? A momentary feeling of disappointment, perhaps, followed immediately by a recognition—and acceptance—of the fact that this situation was beyond the person's control.

The waiting time while the train moves back and forth might be used to prepare for the appointment or some other productive activity. When the crossing gate goes up, this person will probably pull into the nearest service station to call and see if it is still convenient to keep the appointment or re-set it to another time.

Now let's look back at *why* Johnny became a compulsive punctual—why did the pattern develop in the first place?

The pattern was developed, built, and reinforced within Johnny's own mental processes, programmed with his own conscious-level self-talk activity. Still, it is not entirely reasonable for him to ignore the messages from the environment, his perception of which initiated the thought/feeling sequence which dropped the rocks on the scale. While it is possible that his thinking might have responded to those messages in a different, more positive, way, his age and emotional attachment to the sources of those messages rendered that pretty unlikely.

Why did his parents react so violently to Johnny's behavior when he got home late for dinner? If you were to ask them about that, they would probably explain it all quite logically: "So that he will grow up with an understanding of the very important role which time plays in our modern society." Or, "It is simply not convenient to fix a separate dinner for each member of the family if they all choose to come home at a different time." Those sound like very sensible reasons, don't they? They are actually rationalizations, attempts to make irrational behavior seem to be rational.

You can bet that Mom and Dad did *not* arrive at a consensus decision, after lengthy discussion, that "because of the social importance of time and the inconvenience to the family when people are late for dinner, every time that Johnny comes home late we will lose our tempers, scream, yell, and beat the dickens out of the child." If you were to watch a film or videotape of the parents' behavior when Johnny arrived late, you would see something very much like a Dr. Jekyll/Mr. Hyde transformation. A sweet, gentle, loving mother suddenly turned into a witch! A warm, understanding father suddenly looking and acting for all the world like a monster!

What is happening is not a result of cold logic, or loving parental guidance and training. It is a function of the parents' own restrictive patterns. If Johnny learns that "you *have to* be on time, OR ELSE!" it is almost certain that either Mom or Dad (probably both) is compulsive about punctuality. The "transfer" of the pattern from one generation to the next is the product of a secondary effect of the restrictive pattern on the parents' behavior.

We have already seen that when you violate a restrictive pattern you will feel anxiety. The amount or intensity of the anxiety will be proportional to the amount of fear that was involved in the original conditioning process. The compulsive punctual will be anxious when late for an appointment. A person with an inhibitive pattern about nudity ("you can't be naked in front of other people—OR ELSE!") will feel anxious if he or she disrobes in front of another person.

There is a secondary reaction. You will also feel anxiety—usually somewhat less intensely—when someone else violates one of *your* restrictive, fear-conditioned patterns in your presence. The compulsively punctual person will not only be very upset when he is late, but will also feel anxious when someone else is late for an appointment with him! In fact, there will even be a feeling of anxiety when he knows that *someone else* is being late for an appointment with *another person.* Even though he is not directly involved in the situation at all, if he knows that someone is being late he will feel uncomfortable.

The person with an inhibitive pattern about nudity will not only feel anxiety if naked in the presence of others, but will feel a similar anxiety if others take off their clothes.

When Johnny came home late for dinner, he was not just inconveniencing his parents; he was violating one of their restrictive patterns. Their predictable response was one of anxiety. So, they struck out at what they regarded as the cause of the uncomfortable feeling— Johnny. Most child abuse, whether or not it is severe enough to be regarded as a crime by the various governmental agencies, is a direct result of this process.

I hope it is clear that I am not suggesting "permissiveness" in the sense of an absence of training, coaching, rules, or discipline. Rather, I am suggesting that it is to the best interest of both the parents and the child to administer those rules with love and acceptance rather than anger or hatred.

Certainly there are many areas of your life which are more significant than punctuality. I have used this pattern to illustrate the process simply because it is such a common compulsion in our present culture. Take time to see how the same framework applies to other areas such as those I have listed on page 77.

There is another very important adverse effect restrictive patterns can have on your behavior. Restrictive conditioning limits your awareness of alternatives. If you "know" that you *can't* do something, it will be difficult, if not impossible, for you to even look at or consider that course of action. In some cases, that might be just exactly the best thing to do.

The **compulsive** pattern is even more limiting. The *have to* restricts you to only one possible alternative—everything else is unthinkable. Many restrictive patterns are not purely inhibitive or compulsive. A little of both are involved in the attitude. You *have to* be on time—you *can't* be late! You *can't* run around naked—you *have to* wear clothes! But in every case, the awareness of the available alternatives is restricted by the pattern.

Restrictive patterns can also be formed later on in life; they do not all develop in early childhood. In your early years you were more susceptible, receptive, inclined to accept the "or else!" messages without question. However, if you are confronted with a brand-new experience in your adult years and, for whatever reason, you associate that activity or object with pain, fear, disgust, or other negative emotions—repeatedly—the result will be a restrictive attitude pattern.

You tend to act like yourself

Of the many thousands of attitude patterns which you have acquired or developed through the years, some are clearly related to your "self." What kind of person are you? What abilities do you have? How well do you use those abilities? What do you like to do? Are you patient, warm, understanding, enthusiastic? In hundreds of interrelated areas you have developed "truths" about yourself, each a combination of information and feeling.

That part of your "REALITY" structure—your self image—is the core of the entire system, certainly the most important complex of attitudes which you have built into your mental processes.

Yet this vital central image or concept, like everything else in your "REALITY" structure, is both incomplete and inaccurate! You do not know all that there is to know about yourself, and you never will. No matter how much time and effort you spend studying your physical and mental systems, there will always be more to learn. What you do (or will) know about yourself is distorted. The thought processes which have built, strengthened, and adjusted the self image have not recorded a completely accurate impression of the real you. You have been recording—for future reference—what you have been thinking and feeling about yourself, and sometimes that has been very different from what was really happening.

CHAPTER

9

Can you identify some of the self-talk you have mentally digested over the years which has related directly to you? What are some of the three-dimensional thought processes (words, experiences, and emotions) which have built incomplete and distorted patterns about you which are now a part of your "truth" system? How about some of these:

- Well, some people have artistic talent and some don't. I guess when they were handing out the artistic abilities I just got passed by. I can't draw a straight line!
- Why am I so clumsy? I always seem to goof everything up.
- Me, run for office in our club? You've got to be kidding. That would involve standing up in front of people and speaking. I can't even lead a group in silent prayer!
- She has such good taste in clothes. I wish that I did.
- Oh, I've always had a terrible temper. I guess it's the Irish in me.
- As soon as he walked in I recognized him, but I couldn't think of his name no matter how hard I tried. I really have a lousy memory!

Can you see how the words trigger the experiences and the emotional response? You can almost feel the rock clunking into place.

Check out some of the other self-talk that you have been programming into your self image. Take a few minutes to challenge the "truths" about you which you have been reaffirming and reinforcing. Are they accurate representations of your true talent and abilities—your real potential?

Notice that in some cases the self-talk may have changed from an honest expression of emotional discomfort to a more "rational" explanation. Instead of, "I feel afraid when I stand up in front of a lot of people to make a speech," you may find yourself thinking, "I just don't have any *ability* in that area."

The tragedy is that over a period of time, with continued repetition of that sort of self-talk, you will come to *believe* what you have been telling yourself. You get to the point where you "know" that you were shorted in the original manufacturing process, and if that is the "truth" of the matter, then it would certainly be a waste of time to take a public-speaking course or join the Toastmasters Club.

The clincher will be, "I can't help it. That's just the way I am!" Or, "I wish I could get up in front of people and give a speech." Either of these thought sequences will lock up whatever potential may exist by making it seem impossible that any change could be made—unless there's a miracle!

As you review some of your favorite self-talk exercises—about your self—notice that many are quite positive. Look at the difference in your behavior—and achievement—in those areas of your life in which you have formed the habit of positive self-talk.

Your self-image is a composite of many, many attitude structures—each of which is a combination of what you "know" and how you feel about that aspect of yourself.

This simplified diagram may help you to visualize the relationship between the self-image, behavior, and your potential. In each sector you have adopted a "truth" about yourself, complete with an emotional pattern about that "truth." Your potential is probably far greater in each area than you have realized.

That is not *necessarily* the case, however. It is possible for a person to have adopted a self-image in a particular area which is greater than the actual potential which that person possesses. I am sure that you have known people, for example, who were *sure* that they were fine singers, but they couldn't carry a tune if their lives depended upon it. They had a physical impairment which simply made it impossible for them to detect the difference between

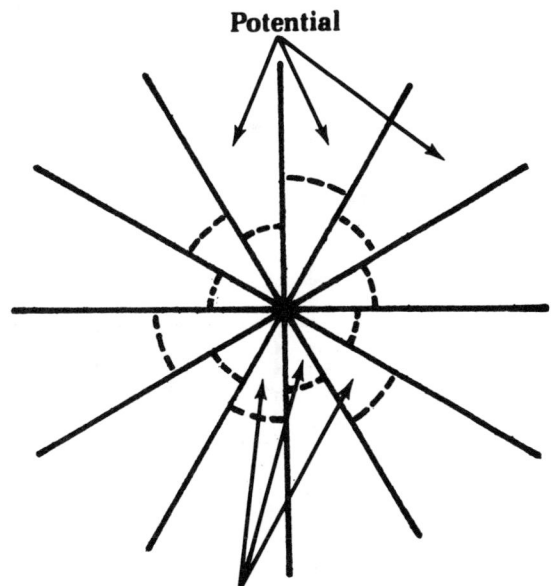

Potential

What You Know About Yourself

adjacent tones on a scale. But their "REALITY" was that they were very good harmonizers, and whenever a group started to sing they always joined in!

While that kind of situation can, and does, happen, it is much more rare than the reverse. Most of the time people have a great deal more potential than they recognize and accept, and that is the primary direction with which we will be working. The important point is that you do not tend to behave on the basis of your *potential.*

You tend to behave in a manner that is consistent with your self image. You tend to act like your "self." Picture this as though you had a regulating mechanism within your mental processes which functions very much like a thermostat. This is *your* **Effectiveness Regulator.**

Instead of a temperature setting, the *Effectiveness Regulator* has your self-image as the standard or controlling input. Then, just as the thermostat functions to keep the heat level in the room within a range of the temperature setting, the *Effectiveness Regulator* tends to keep your behavior within a range of the self-image setting.

In nearly every area of your system, there is more potential than you are using. You do not behave in accordance with the potential that you have—you behave in accordance with your "REALITY" about yourself.

The vertical scale on our Regulator diagram which represents your potential is constantly changing. As you acquire additional information or skill—take a golf lesson or learn how to close a sale—your potential increases. That doesn't necessarily mean that you will behave more effectively; it just means that the information part of your potential package has been expanded. As the years go by, your potential may diminish in certain

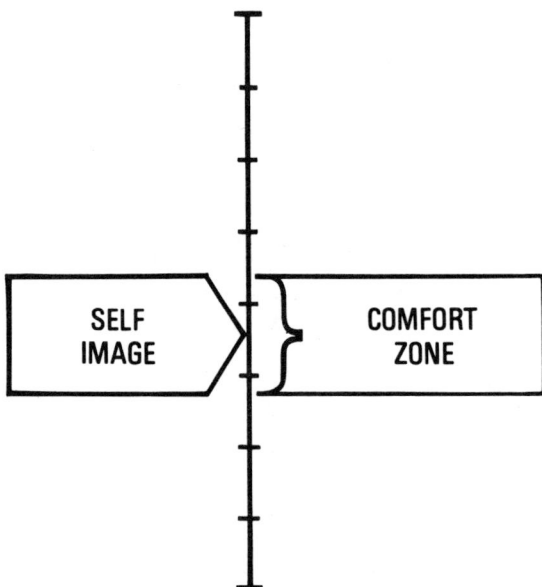

areas because the original physical equipment is beginning to wear out.

Our concern is with the degree to which you are using whatever potential you possess right now in a particular area. You may also want to increase that potential, but let's see how the *Effectiveness Regulator* works.

With a thermostat, when the temperature in the room gets to the edge of the thermal range, an electrical signal is sent to the furnace or the air-conditioner to turn on or off. Then, as the temperature in the room changes, those electrical signals continue to respond to the changes and keep the temperature within the range.

Instead of electrical signals, your *Effectiveness Regulator* uses tension signals to keep you within the *Comfort Zone.* As your behavior gets close to the edge of that zone, you begin to feel uncomfortable, uneasy. Things are not happening the way that they are supposed to happen. The discrepancy between what you are observing and the way that you expect yourself to behave in such situations creates tension within your system.

To the degree that your behavior deviates from the *Comfort Zone,* you tend to want to "get back to acting like yourself."

It's easy to see the *Regulator* at work in the life of a golfer. If you play that game you may be able to empathize with a golfing friend of mine. Jerry enjoys the game, most of the time. He plays at least once a week, sometimes more often than that. And for a long time he has been shooting in the mid-nineties. On a particularly good day he might come in with a ninety-one, or occasionally he will barely break one hundred.

Over a period of time Jerry has begun to think of himself as a mid-nineties golfer. His self-talk process reaffirms that "truth" at every opportunity. It has become a very real part of his self-image, and the setting on his golfing *Effectiveness Regulator.*

If you were to watch Jerry play a game of golf, you would sense immediately that he has the potential to be a much better player. He has the physical equipment

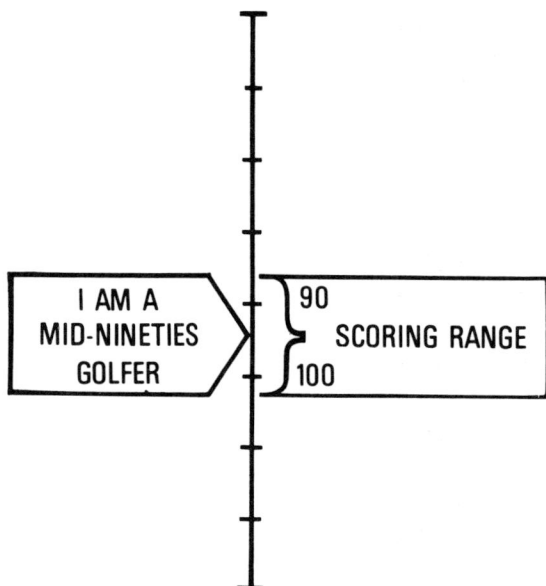

that he needs. He has taken many lessons from the club professional and has spent hours on the driving range practicing what he has learned. And he is certainly highly motivated to get his score down.

You can see the potential breaking through from time to time as Jerry plays. Sometimes his drives are straight, long, climbing beauties—right down the middle of the fairway. Sometimes his approach shots have just the right loft and back-spin to land on the green and stop near the cup. And sometimes he putts like a professional.

But not always.

If Jerry starts his game well, using the knowledge and skills he has acquired in a natural, free-flowing manner, he might finish the first nine holes with a 44. But then, as he tallies up his score for the first half of his game, what do you suppose his reaction is?

"Wow! If I keep on playing like that for the back nine I'll have the best score I've ever had!"

Then, instead of continuing to play in a relaxed, effective way, Jerry will "try hard" to hit the ball well. On the last half of his game he will have a score of 51. *Back in his Comfort Zone!*

Another day the same principle might apply to Jerry's game in the other direction. If he has a score of fifty-one on the first nine holes, he will nearly always "settle down" and play a better game on the second half. By the time he gets back to the clubhouse, his score is nearly always in the mid-90s. Then his self-talk goes to work again to reaffirm his self image: "No matter how I play, I seem to end up in the mid-90s.

If he *does* get out of his Comfort Zone with an eighty-eight (or a hundred and one) he is quite naturally inclined to see that score as a fluke, an exception to his "normal" game.

Does this mean that Jerry is inevitably destined to stay in the mid-nineties? Of course not! It just means that the natural tendency of the system is to continue to reinforce existing attitudes, and to behave in a manner that is consistent with those attitudes. Getting out of the ruts is possible—even easy—but it requires an understanding of the system and some consciously directed effort to change the setting on the *Regulator.*

Here's another example of the *Regulator* at work—this time with a professional salesperson.

Marty has been with his company for five years. His monthly sales volume hovers around $10,000 per month. With a commission percentage of 20 per cent, that gives him an income of about $2,000 monthly. With all sorts of "logic," Marty has "made up his mind" that he is a $2,000 a month salesperson. He has a great deal more *potential* than that (which gives his sales manager a constant feeling of frustration!) but even with the fluctuations of season and the economy, his sales volume stays within a pretty narrow range. Automatically, his system does whatever is necessary to keep him acting like himself.

Then one month a lot of proposals that Marty has been working on result in sales all at once. His gross production for the month adds up to $18,500 and his commission check for $3,700 is the biggest monthly check he's ever received!

Now what happens? I expect we would all like to think that Marty's reaction will be, "Well, now that I know that it is possible, I'll sell that much every month." Wouldn't it be nice if he just accepts that as his new standard and continues to produce at the higher level?

But what actually happens in the real world, almost without exception, is that Marty will spend the next couple of months "correcting for the error."

He will get his files in order, do some research at the library, re-work his sales presentation (the one that just made him more money than he has ever made before), or spend a lot of time calling on unlikely prospects. One

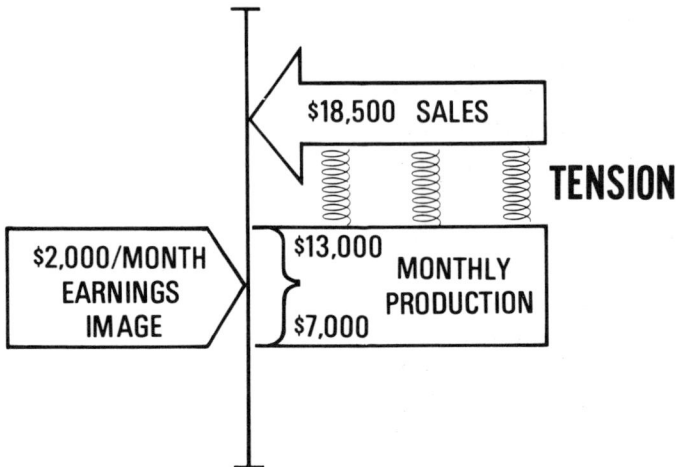

very common action which will get him back into his Comfort Zone is to take a "well-earned" vacation. After all, if he earned all that money he must have been working terribly hard. How else could he have produced such extraordinary volume?

Marty's sales for the next few months will be somewhat below his normal level, and he will very likely end up the year with earnings of about $24,000.

Won't that excellent month have *some* effect on Marty's image? Of course. But we cannot predict that effect with any certainty. Remember that the only event which ever has a direct effect on Marty's self image is Marty's own conscious level self-talk process. It is not what is *happening* with his sales, but what he is thinking and feeling *about* what he *perceives* to be happening that will change the self image.

He may reinforce the already existing image by seeing the excellent month as an exception to his normal production, or he might see it as progress toward a more consistent use of his potential. Which direction his thinking takes—and the degree to which it will move in that direction—will be a function of how strongly attached he is to his present "REALITY."

Unless Marty understands some of the principles we are exploring together in this book, it is very likely that as he associates the outstanding monthly performance with his existing "REALITY"—the "truth" which he has developed and accepted about his sales ability—he will find some "reasons" why it happened which have little or nothing to do with his professional ability. He knows it won't last, and sure enough, it doesn't!

The *Effectiveness Regulator* concept helps to explain why "will power" is so ineffective and sometimes destructive. Will power is the teeth-gritting, fist-clenching, determined effort to change one's behavior—the deliberate, conscious attempt to move outside the Comfort Zone. Of course it is possible to do that. You do have the capacity to act in a manner that is not "like you." But the tension that kind of action produces within your system is very uncomfortable, and the net result of the self-talk which is stimulated by that discomfort will probably be to *lower* the self-image setting on the *Regulator*.

If you have a negative attitude about buttermilk, you can exercise your will power and force yourself to drink a glassful. That is certainly not your "normal" behavior with respect to buttermilk, but you can do it. But, after it is gone, do you suppose that you will like it any better? That will depend upon how negative your attitude was before you drank the glassful, won't it?

DRINK A GLASS OF BUTTERMILK

TENSION

BUTTERMILK IS TERRIBLE

AVOID BUTTERMILK WHENEVER POSSIBLE

If the scale was tipped pretty far toward the negative side, you will find yourself wondering why you are doing this, and with each sip you will reaffirm the "truth" that "buttermilk is awful!"

Trying hard to behave differently doesn't work. In fact, it may even have a backlash effect. If you want to get the temperature to a higher level in the room that you are in right now, it doesn't make a lot of sense to leave the thermostat set where it is and build a fire in the fireplace. The thermostat, sensing the temperature rise from the fire, will send a signal to the air conditioner to turn on. Then you will have cold air coming from the ducts in the wall and hot air from the fireplace—a very inefficient conflict in the system. It would be a lot simpler to just change the setting on the

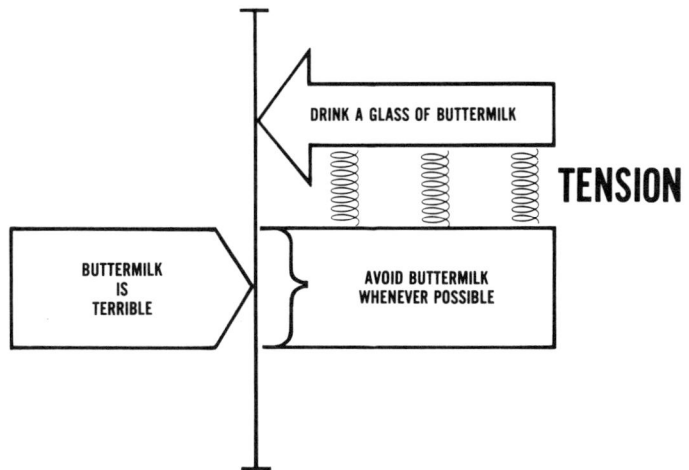

thermostat to a warmer level and let the automatic mechanism work for you.

With the *Effectiveness Regulator*, too, it is much easier and more efficient to simply adjust the setting than to try hard to change your behavior.

> ALL LASTING, CONSTRUCTIVE CHANGE IN HUMAN BEHAVIOR STARTS ON THE INSIDE—WITH A CHANGED IMAGE OF "REALITY"!

Constructive imagination

The more that an attitude is inclined toward the positive or negative, the more that it is *likely* to become stronger in that same direction. The more rocks you have piled on one side of the scale, the more probable that subsequent rocks will be deposited on the same side. Attitude patterns *tend* to be self-reinforcing.

They *tend* to be, but if you want to do so you can break into that self-reinforcing cycle that we talked about in Chapter Seven and deliberately guide it in the direction you want it to go. You can deposit some heavily weighted rocks on the positive side of whatever scales you want to work on. There is no way to *remove* the negative inputs, but there *is* a simple way of adding new experiences to those patterns you would like to change. There is a procedure with which you can re-set your *Effectiveness Regulator* in the direction of your real potential.

Of course, you have been re-setting that *Regulator* all of your life. It has been a constant, flowing process ever since you were born. Every thought which you have experienced at a conscious level in your mental processes has moved your self-image in one direction or the other to some degree. The technique which I call **Constructive Imagination** is simply a way of guiding and managing that process a little more deliberately, intentionally, consciously.

With *Constructive Imagination* you can quickly and easily bring about the changes that you *want* to make in your self-image—and the behavioral changes follow automatically.

There is nothing mystical about this process. It is not a "magical secret key to the mysterious power of the subconscious." *Constructive Imagination* is a practical, proven application of the principles of human behavior that we have reviewed in the preceding chapters to the exciting project of releasing your potential and becoming more nearly the person you are capable of being.

There are five basic principles which led me to the realization that *Constructive Imagination* is a valid, useful method; five aspects of human behavior which can be observed and tested and which lead directly to a dependable formula which you can start using immediately to guide your life in the direction that you want it to go.

I believe that these five "premises" are so important to what follows that I want to review them to be sure that they are clear. Think them through thoroughly. If there is any question or reservation in your acceptance of these five principles, please go back over their development in previous chapters. Dig more deeply into them and see exactly how they apply to your own personal experience.

1 EVERY HUMAN BEING TENDS TO BEHAVE IN A MANNER THAT IS CONSISTENT WITH HIS CURRENTLY DOMINANT, SUBCONSCIOUS "REALITY" STRUCTURE, WHICH IS ALWAYS SOMEWHAT INCOMPLETE AND INACCURATE.

Your decisions and actions—and mine, and everyone else's—tend to "make sense" on the basis of what we know and feel about ourselves and the world around us. Every person behaves "normally" considering the kind of "truth" he has accepted or digested into his "REALITY" structure.

Natives in a primitive tribe who "know" that it is forbidden to cross a certain river, and that to do so causes death, tend to stay on this side of the river. So powerfully does this principle operate that a member of the tribe who defies the taboo, perhaps to escape tribal justice for another crime, will often literally drop dead when he reaches the opposite bank of the river.

So long as people "knew" that we could not possibly get from here to the moon, not much was done to develop the materials and technology to make it happen.

I once ordered a shrimp salad and a glass of milk in a coffee shop in a small town in the mid-western part of the U.S. The waitress refused to take my order to the kitchen, because she "knew" that milk and shrimp, eaten together, were poisonous. That was the "truth" in her mental system and nothing that I could say was about to change her mind. She was going to help me to live longer by protecting me from a suicidal act.

My "REALITY" was different, and after a friendly discussion with the manager, I did get the milk and the shrimp salad; he brought it himself. You should have seen the expression on the waitress' face as I ate my lunch. It was all she could do to even look my way. I'm sure that she did not expect me to get out of the restaurant alive.

> **YOUR "REALITY" STRUCTURE IS THE *CUMULATIVE* RESULT OF THE EXPERIENCES WHICH HAVE TAKEN PLACE IN YOUR MENTAL PROCESSES.**

2

Each verbal-conceptual-emotional thought process makes a lasting contribution to the attitude patterns which make up the "REALITY" structure and nothing is ever lost or erased. Once a thought has been "programmed" or stored in the experience files—your "truth" system—it is a permanent part of that system. It may not be easily accessible to recall, but the attitude has been affected and your behavior will reflect that change from that moment on. The only exception to this is the actual physical deterioration or destruction of part of the brain.

Psychotherapy or psychoanalysis does not erase or eliminate information, impressions, or feelings from the mental system. Change in the "REALITY" structure results from the acquisition of *additional* inputs.

Did you at one time "know" that there was a Santa Claus or a Tooth Fairy? If you no longer listen for reindeer on the roof on Christmas Eve, or put your used teeth under the pillow to be exchanged for a coin, it is not because anything has been *deleted* from your "REALITY"! Somewhere along the line you have adopted some new, more accurate (more verifiable) information.

You are constantly *building* upon what you know and feel about yourself and your world. And, of course, as that structure changes, behavior changes right along with it.

3   YOU BUILD YOUR OWN, UNIQUE "REALITY" STRUCTURE WITH YOUR OWN THOUGHTS AND FEELINGS—YOUR OWN MENTAL PROCESSES.

Your mother or father did not "give" you your "REALITY" system. Nor did society, or the neighborhood in which you were raised or a church or any other "they." You have built it, step by step, piece by piece with your own thoughts and feelings.

That is not to say that one's environment—including the people who are a part of it—is completely unimportant. The world around you—the environment—is part of the whole person system. But what you have *done* with the constant stream of signals, messages, stimuli which have come to you from your environment is what is important! It is those experiences that you have dwelt upon, those about which you have felt deeply, those images and ideas which you have accepted, digested, adopted into your own unique, personal "REALITY" structure which are determining your behavior.

Have you been puzzled when children brought up in the same family—the same environment—develop such different personalities? There are a lot of reasons for this, of course. Part of the answer is in the different genetic patterns—each child starts off with a different blueprint. A very important element is the fact that no two children ever grow up in exactly the same environment. The first child in the family is, for a while, an only child who then may have the opportunity to adjust to the presence of a brother or sister. With each succeeding child there is at least a chance that the parents will be somewhat wiser and more mature, that the family's income will be higher and the house, food and clothing a little better.

So, there are differences in the environment. Even identical twins, with the same genetic endowment, do not receive identical inputs from their environments.

Still, the way in which a child (or an adult) will respond to a particular situation is neither predetermined nor predictable. We can guess, estimate, evaluate the probabilities, and sometimes we will be close. More often we will be far from accurate.

There are many classic stories of brothers who have gravitated to different ends of the spectrum of society from the same early childhood environments. One may have become a judge; his brother, a hardened criminal. It would, I think, take a good deal of stretching to fit such very real happenings into the idea that behavior is purely a function of heredity and environment. The other critically important element is what you decide to do with what you have inherited and what you encounter in your world.

Some years ago I saw a sign hanging on the wall of a business office:

> IF AT FIRST YOU DON'T SUCCEED
> .... FIX THE BLAME FAST!

Sometimes that is pretty tempting, isn't it? But the fact is that your present patterns of behavior are a function of the patterns of "REALITY" which *you* have programmed into your mental system with your own thought processes.

4
TO THE DEGREE THAT YOU EXPERIENCE AN EVENT VIVIDLY IN THE IMAGINATION, IT IS STORED AS A "REAL" HAPPENING.

In a *PACE* Seminar recently I asked how many in the group liked buttermilk. A few hands went up—some more vigorously than others. I got more hands when I asked how many had a negative attitude about buttermilk.

Then I asked how many of those who did not like buttermilk had never tasted it. One woman reluctantly raised her hand.

"Why don't you like it, Audrey?" I asked.

"Well," she replied, "I just know it doesn't taste good. It reminds me of something that has spoiled."

Audrey had never had any physical contact with buttermilk in her life. But she had certainly tasted it in her imagination! She had experienced it so vividly, repeatedly, in her imagination that now she **knew** that she didn't like it. She **felt** so strongly about it that when I offered her some of my buttermilk at the dinner table that evening, she hardly wanted to look at it, let alone taste it!

Have you ever eaten fried rattlesnake meat? Parachuted to earth from an airplane? Floated through space in a gravity-free environment? Can you feel your vivid imagination at work as you project yourself into those experiences mentally?

How about the time that you were absolutely certain that you had mailed a letter? You could remember dropping it into the mailbox; if someone had offered a wager you would have bet that it was well on its way.

And you would have lost the bet! Do you recall how surprised you were to find that letter in your pocket? You had so vividly experienced the process of mailing it—in your imagination—that you *knew* you had done it.

THE MOST IMPORTANT PART OF YOUR "REALITY" IS THE EMOTIONAL COMPONENT—HOW YOU FEEL ABOUT WHAT YOU "KNOW."

5

I was puzzled for a long time about why "positive thinking" didn't always seem to work. Lots of people told me that it was foolishness, a waste of time, very superficial. Yet others claimed that most of what they had achieved in their adult lives could be traced to the practice of positive thinking!

I was fascinated with the idea that a system which evoked such mixed reactions should have been around for so long—the oldest form of psychological folk medicine. It was part of the ancient Egyptian culture. Variations can be found in philosophical writings of the Orient, Europe, and the New World. Early in this century many thousands adopted Emil Coué's system of repeating each morning, "Every day in every way I am getting better and better." And a lot of people *did* get better. Dr. Norman Vincent Peale's classic, *The Power of Positive Thinking,* has been acclaimed by many as a major aid to their health and happiness. How can so many people of similar intelligence be so divided on the issue of positive thinking?

Like most puzzles, the solution is pretty simple after you see it. The difference in results—and therefore the enthusiasm of the person who has tried thinking more positively—is a function of how the individual interpreted and practiced what the author suggested. To the degree that one thinks of positive thinking as a verbal exercise, little or nothing will happen. As the other two media of thought—conceptual and emotional—are involved, by accident or intent, changes in behavior will result. "As he thinketh *in his heart,* so is he!"

I found that many people who read a self-improvement book assume that all that is necessary is for them to say the words over and over again to themselves. Somehow they have gained the impression that thinking the words, "I am happy, I am happy, I am happy," will work like a magic incantation. If they think these words often enough, happiness will search them out and move into their systems. When that doesn't happen they are understandably disappointed and inclined to regard the whole idea as a fraud. "I tried it. It didn't work for me!"

That's not unreasonable, is it? After all, they have done what they were told to do (as they understood it at least). They have thought a lot of happy thoughts, and where has it gotten them?

Others, reading the same book, respond differently. Because of different habits of thinking or a different understanding of what the author suggests that they do, they go further. Instead of just repeating positive sentences in their thoughts, they allow those words to trigger an experience in the imagination to match the words. And then, they let the positive emotions that go with that experience flow through the system.

And their whole life changes!

Words are important in the thinking process, but when it comes to changing the attitudes which control and guide your behavior, experiences are much more important. Most important is the emotional dimension.

Constructive Imagination is not in the area of positive thinking. It deals, instead, with *the power of positive* **feeling!**

Applying this technique in your own life is simply a matter of repeatedly experiencing, in your imagination, the information, images and feelings which you want to have become the dominant, controlling patterns in your "REALITY" structure.

Does it sound too easy? Don't let that stop you. Sometimes the puzzles which seem the most complex turn out to have the simplest solutions. The best thing about *Constructive Imagination* is that it *works!* In fact, as we look carefully at the specific way to practice this technique, I believe that you will discover that you have been using *Constructive Imagination* without realizing it, in exactly those areas in which you are making the best use of your potential.

Over the years I have had a unique opportunity to observe *Constructive Imagination* in action. Many thousands of adults and teen-agers who have attended *PACE* Seminars and Conferences have seen fit to share with me their own personal experiences, the many ways in which they have successfully used this powerful method. Because of my special interest in this area of human behavior, I have been particularly aware of many other examples of both the positive and the negative impact that one's self-talk can have on performance. Newspapers, magazines, books, and news and sporting events on television provide a constant stream of dramatic illustrations of the importance of the attitude dimension and the use of imagination as a preparatory exercise.

It has been particularly fascinating to me to see the wide spectrum of human behavior to which *Constructive Imagination* can be productively applied.

The broad area of physical coordination is perhaps the easiest area in which to watch results happen. Whether in individual sports like high-jumping, gymnastics, or diving, or in team efforts such as football, baseball, or hockey, the top performer knows that physical conditioning and skill training are important, but in the final analysis his ability to use the potential he has developed will depend upon attitude—how well he has prepared his mental/emotional system to allow all of that potential to flow.

Olympic and professional athletes spend a lot of time practicing their skills in the imagination, and at the same time, building an attitude of confidence in their abilities to handle the pressure of a highly competitive contest.

Watch the Olympic high diving competition on your television set. At first it may seem that you are watching a purely physical competition. The muscles have been trained and conditioned with hours of practice and exercises. At the same time, though, the mental system has undergone equally extensive preparation. Each dive has been practiced repeatedly in the imagination to build the necessary confidence to handle intense competitive pressures. As the athlete stands on the high board, you will notice a moment's pause just before starting the sequence of action. One last run-through in the imagination. One final reminder to the mental and physical systems, and then the performance. The training and conditioning are there, and the quality of the dive will be as good as the athlete's ability to *let* the system do what it has been trained and prepared to do.

As top athletes like Gene Littler, John Brodie, Tom Gorman, and many others have attended *PACE* programs, I have nearly always asked the question, "Do you ever practice your skill in your imagination?" The answer is always, "Of course. I do it all the time!" Very often the next sentence is, "Everybody does that." Not so! The habit of practicing in the imagination is one of the key activities which separates the high performer from the multitude of other people who have similar potential but use only a small fraction of it.

If you are having difficulty with your golf game, your tennis stroke, bowling, or skiing, use your imagination regularly to further develop both your coordination and your confidence. Pick out the exact area that needs improvement and go through the procedure in the next chapter to stimulate successful experience and emotions in your mental system. You will be surprised how quickly you will see results.

Many teachers and coaches are now using *Constructive Imagination* to help students learn a new skill more quickly, or to help team members to use more of their abilities. Payton Jordan, the great track coach at Stanford University and leader of the American track team in the 1968 Olympics in Mexico City, has made extensive use of *Constructive Imagination* and credits it with being a major contributor to the successes which he and his teams have achieved. John Ralston, one of the nation's top football coaches, who took Stanford's football team to Rose Bowl victories in 1971 and 1972, attended a *PACE* Seminar in 1968 and has applied this system not only at a college level but also with the Denver Broncos in the National Football League.

When you take lessons in skiing, golf, tennis, or other sports, it is increasingly likely that the teaching pro will show you how to perform a particular skill, and then tell you to "go home and practice that over and over again in your imagination until it has become a natural, flowing action." Be sure, though, that you *experience* the activity in your imagination—do not observe yourself doing it as though you were a spectator. Only in that way will you be reinforcing the neural-muscular circuits and sequences which build automatic coordination—and the confidence to let that coordination flow.

One of the primary obstacles to progress in learning how to ski is the emotion of fear. Fear of falling, fear of looking clumsy, fear of physical pain can easily block the productive use of whatever knowledge you may have about how to get down the hill. The first time a child tries to roller-skate or ride a bicycle you can see the same process working. At first the child and the bicycle are separate systems—not working together at all. Then comes that magic moment when the two systems become as one; the child and the bicycle are together in a single, flowing system. The skier and the skis merge into a smoothly functioning combination. You can reach that point of "letting it happen" much sooner by augmenting your actual physical practicing with the mental rehearsal of *Constructive Imagination*

Many flight instructors now make use of this technique to help their students learn to fly an airplane more quickly. After a lesson in which the student has gone through the actual process of taking off, landing, or another phase of the learning sequence, he is told to go home and practice what he has learned again and again before the next lesson. His "homework" includes sitting quietly in a chair in his own living room, with his eyes closed, experiencing the process of flying the airplane in his imagination. As he does this, he not only reinforces the information he has acquired and builds the coordination patterns needed for that particular maneuver, he also creates a feeling of confidence and enthusiasm which comes from a series of successful experiences. It all adds up to a much faster learning process than would otherwise be possible.

As we discussed the application of *Constructive Imagination* to the project of learning how to fly in a *PACE* Seminar several years ago, one of the executives in the group said, "Sure, that works. It's exactly what I have done every time I have tested a new aircraft." The speaker was Scott Crossfield, the famous engineering test pilot who first tested the X-15 rocket plane for North American Aviation. Scott went on to say that while a new plane was still being designed, he would familiarize himself with the controls and expected performance capability of the craft and practice flying it in his imagination. Often he would make suggestions to the engineering department on ways they might improve the design, based upon his "experience" with the plane.

Most important, though, was the fact that when the time finally came for the new aircraft to be rolled out, and for Scott to climb into the cockpit for the first test flight, he had already logged a lot of hours in the pilot's seat. Scott Crossfield expressed it this way, "Even though it was the first time I had actually flown the plane, I felt as though I were at the controls of a familiar 'old friend.' There were always some surprises, but not nearly as many as I would have had if I hadn't spent hours preparing for the real experience with imagined experience."

Another student in one of our Seminars related this dramatic personal experience with the purposeful use of imagined experience. Bill had been in the infantry on the·front lines in the Korean conflict. A mortar shell exploded a short distance behind his position. He was given emergency treatment in a field hospital and then transferred to Tokyo for major surgery to get the shrapnel out of his back. When he awoke from the anesthesia, there were sandbags piled around him on the bed, and straps across him; the nurse cautioned him to lie very still. The surgery had involved his spinal column and the doctor warned him that if he moved there was a pretty good chance that he would be paralyzed from the waist down for the rest of his life!

For weeks he lay very still in his hospital bed, moving

almost no muscles other than those controlling his eye-balls and his jaw.

He could watch television or listen to the radio. If he wanted to read, there was a rack over his bed where the nurse could put a book or magazine for him to read. After just a day or two Bill had an idea. He had always wanted to learn how to type, and had never progressed beyond the two-finger hunt-and-peck system. It occurred to him that this was an ideal opportunity to study the keyboard and memorize it so that when he was released from the hospital he could take typing lessons and learn more quickly.

One of the nurses was able to find a typing textbook in the hospital library, and she propped it up in the rack over his bed so that he could study it whenever he wanted to spend a few minutes with it. In just a few days, Bill had memorized the positions of each letter on the typewriter keyboard, and he had also committed to memory which finger should be used to strike each key. He could close his eyes and imagine that his fingers were on the typewriter and that he was reaching over with the little finger of his left hand and hitting the "a" key. Then, in his imagination, he would see the letter "a" appear on the paper that was in the machine. Next, he would imagine that the index finger of his left hand reached down to the right and hit the "b" key, and so on through the entire alphabet.

Now he could type his name—in his imagination. He could type "The quick brown fox jumps over the lazy dog." Lying there in the hospital bed, he practiced typing for fifteen or twenty minutes at a time, several times each day—without moving a muscle. He typed imaginary letters, paragraphs from magazine articles, and sometimes, while the television set was on, he would imagine himself typing what someone was saying on the tube.

Even though Bill was not aware of any muscular activity, he was training and reinforcing the mental circuits which would coordinate the muscles used in the actual typing process.

When he was able to move around again, Bill went through an extensive program of physical therapy to get his muscles back into shape. He practically had to learn how to walk all over again, did a lot of weight lifting and other muscle building exercises. Finally, when he felt that his hands and arms were working pretty well, he went into the hospital office and asked one of the typists if he could use his typewriter for a few minutes. "Sure, help yourself," was the reply. "I'll take a break for a few minutes."

So, Bill sat down at the desk, put a sheet of paper into the typewriter and copied some material from a book he had brought with him. He timed himself. It was his very first attempt to use his new touch typing skill, and he typed fifty-five words per minute—and with no errors—he hadn't been practicing any mistakes!

Checking into a hospital for delicate spinal surgery is hardly the best way to learn how to operate a typewriter, but Bill's experience provides a graphic example of how *Constructive Imagination* can be applied to coordination skills.

Here is another instance, this time from the Viet Nam War. Before Air Force Colonel George Hall was shot down over North Viet Nam, he had played a lot of golf. He had a four-stroke handicap, which classes him among the better amateur golfers. Colonel Hall spent seven years as a prisoner of war, and each day he played at least eighteen holes of golf *in his imagination.* Stroke by stroke, hole by hole, he would play various courses which he had actually played in past years.

Of course, his intention was simply to occupy his mind—to escape, mentally, from the horrors of the "Hanoi Hilton." The extra bonus which Colonel Hall hadn't counted on was the way that his imagined golf games maintained his proficiency. When he returned to the U.S. in 1973 he shot three practice rounds and then entered the Pro-Am preliminary to the Greater New Orleans Open with his old golfing buddy, Orville Moody. In spite of the seven years without actually playing golf, Colonel Hall shot par golf. He had at least maintained, perhaps improved, his performance level by constructively using his imagination every day that he was in prison!

Do you take shorthand? If so, the chances are that your imagination helped you to develop that skill. If you play a musical instrument, try playing it in your spare moments in your imagination. Professional musicians do that a lot, and that is one of the primary reasons that they are so good!

You have used *Constructive Imagination* in a lot of areas which have had little to do with muscular coordination. When you study a foreign language, one of the best ways to develop fluency is to practice having conversations in that second language, in your imagination. Experience the process of ordering a meal, getting a hotel room, asking for directions. As you project yourself into those actual situations and practice them again and again, you will find the words flowing more easily and automatically.

One of the best ways to prepare for that staff meeting—or the directors' meeting—you are going to conduct tomorrow morning is to have the meeting several times in your head before it happens. That doesn't mean memorizing a prepared script—just walking through the meeting's agenda a few times so that you feel comfortable with it and can more easily keep the meeting on track.

The professional public speaker uses this idea regularly. When he arrives at a hotel where he is to deliver an address to a large banquet meeting, he checks in, gets his bags to his room and then goes directly to the meeting room where the banquet is to be held that evening. Once he has familiarized himself with the room layout— where the speakers' table will be placed, the position of the microphone and how his audience will be seated in the room—he will relax, shower, and dress while he is imagining the experience of presenting his ideas to that group in that room. Then, when he is introduced and steps forward to speak, he's "doing it again."

The professional salesperson understands this method and uses it to prepare for a sales presentation. In fact, it is one of the key ingredients in the successful salesperson's formula. Every spare minute is used to practice handling objections, answering questions, asking for the order under all sorts of conditions. It's a lot easier to do anything the hundredth time, even if the first ninety-nine times you have done it in your imagination.

Most of the time the professional artist has the painting "in mind" before putting it on the canvas. The sculptor has a clear image of what his statue is going to look like before starting to chip away at the block of stone. When Michelangelo was asked how he could possibly produce such beauty from a cold piece of marble, he is said to have replied, "The statue is already *in* the marble. All that I do is cut away the part that doesn't belong there." I believe that what he was really saying was that the statue already existed in his vivid creative imagination. Then, with his hammer and chisel he transferred it to the marble.

Before you have a dinner party do you have it several times in your imagination? If you have not done that in the past, try it next time. Go through the entire sequence of the party from the arrival of the first guest, through each step in your plan until the guests have all gone home. You may find that it helps you to remember to do some things you would have forgotten, and you will surely find that you are more relaxed and able to enjoy the evening as a gracious host or hostess.

Here is another example of *Constructive Imagination* as it was applied to a rather extreme situation. During one of our Seminars in the early sixties, one of the wives in the group took me aside during a break to ask me a question. Could this technique be helpful, Helen wondered, in overcoming a fear of high places? She told me that for years she had not been able to go above the second floor of a building. "I know that it doesn't make any sense, but I have an overpowering fear. I'm not even sure what I'm afraid of, but I just cannot force myself to go above the second floor."

When they were married, her husband had not known of her phobia. When they checked into the beautiful resort hotel for their honeymoon, he told her that he had arranged for a luxurious suite on the top floor of the hotel. After he had registered, as they went toward the elevator, Helen summoned her courage to tell him that she simply would not go higher than the second floor! He arranged for another room, but that was only one of hundreds of difficult and sometimes embarrassing situations in which she had found herself. Department stores, the dentist's office, even visiting friends who lived in apartment houses presented insurmountable problems.

I encouraged her to try *Constructive Imagination*—to test it and see what would happen. We spent a few minutes discussing a specific sequence which she could use. I suggested that at first she should imagine herself climbing the stairs from the second to the third floor, feeling very calm and secure, relaxed every step of the way. Then, when she could get to the third floor comfortably in her imagination, I recommended that she spend some time just being there in her thoughts, strengthening the positive feelings of comfort and peace of mind. Then it would be possible for her to go on up to another floor and then another.

The next time that I saw Helen was four years later. I was speaking at a national convention of young chief executives in San Francisco. Her husband, Bob, was a member of the organization and they were both at the meeting. One evening I was invited to join several couples for dinner at one of the fine Chinese restaurants in the area and I was especially delighted to find that Helen and Bob were among the group. It wasn't until we were seated at our table and studying the complex menu, that I realized that our table was right next to a floor-to-ceiling window—on the seventh floor of the building! And there was Helen, the lovely lady who had not been able to go above the second floor of a building, sitting right next to the window.

I leaned over and told her that I thought she looked very relaxed and at ease, considering the fact that we were on the seventh floor. "I wondered if you would remember," she said. Then she told me that she had followed my suggestions, and that within a few short months she had built a new, confident attitude about high places. Helen said that at first she could only go a few steps, even in her imagination. But as she went through the exercise again and again she finally got to the point where she could feel completely at ease as she imagined herself climbing all the way to the third floor. Then, she practiced taking the elevator to the third floor, walking around and even looking out the window. After she had reaffirmed her feelings of confidence many times, she went to a downtown department store, took the elevator to the third floor, and discovered that she really did feel safe. Going through the same sequence with the fourth floor was a lot quicker and easier and by the time she had progressed to the sixth floor the entire situation had been resolved.

Of course, Helen had applied *Constructive Imagination* to many other areas of her life, but she told me that this was the application which had meant the most to her. Bob smiled as he leaned across the table to tell me that it had meant a lot to him, too. Their room while they were at the convention was on the twelfth floor of the hotel!

How to use constructive imagination

There are six sequential steps to follow in applying *Constructive Imagination* to your life. First, here is a quick summary of them, then we will examine each step in more complete detail.

1. **Select** areas in which you have potential which is being limited by negatively inclined attitude patterns.
2. **Evaluate** whether it will be to your advantage to use more of your potential in those areas.
3. **Define** each area clearly, identify the positive emotion you would like to have about that part of yourself and build the kind of self-description you would like to have become accurate about you.
4. **Design** a triggering verbal affirmation for each characteristic or skill you have selected.
5. **Use** the affirmations repeatedly to stimulate the experiencing and feeling—in the imagination—of the kind of behavior and emotion you want to have become your real, normal habit.
6. **Allow** the changed images to guide your behavior in the new directions that you have decided upon.

First, identify some areas in which you can recognize that you have some potential that you are not fully using. Try to pick segments of your day-to-day behavior which are probably being limited by negatively inclined attitude patterns—departments of your life in which you are driving with the brakes partly set.

It would be very difficult—perhaps impossible—to measure exactly how much potential you have in a particular area, but it is a lot easier to decide whether there is a gap between your potential and your performance.

Do you know more about how to organize your time than you act like you know? How about remembering people's names—do you have more knowledge and ability to remember than your behavior would indicate? If you play golf or tennis or some other active sport, perhaps you can see that all you have learned and practiced sometimes seems to get clogged up. How do you feel about public speaking? Are you as patient with your children as you know how to be?

If you have a vocation or profession, pick out three or four areas which relate to that part of your life. If you are a student, consider that to be your profession at this time. If you are managing a household then that is your professional sector. On page 263 you will find a list of some "thought starters." You will probably think of many others that are not on that list, but it will help you to clarify the sort of characteristics you want to select.

From the same list, choose three or four aspects of your family and social life in which you think that you could function more effectively. Then, turn your attention to more personal characteristics and skills. Pick out three or four of those departments that you would like to further strengthen.

As you scan the list, see if you can really get in touch with your emotions. How do you **feel** about each of those sectors? How do you feel about **yourself**? Select areas in which it appears to you that the emotional part of your attitude pattern is negative.

Write down the characteristics and skills that you choose on page 264. Be sure that you have a balanced list—about the same number in each of the three categories. It may seem at first as though you could achieve results faster if you were to focus all your attention on a single area, but it doesn't work that way. Centering your efforts on just one department of your system can (and usually does) create some undesirable distortions. Growth is more stable and lasting as it applies to the whole person.

Now that you have listed some areas in which you can see a clear difference between your potential and your performance, you are ready for the second step. Think carefully about each characteristic you have selected, with this question in mind: "Would it be to my advantage, profit, self-interest to use more of my potential in this area?" If, by whatever means, it were possible for you to function more effectively in that particular department of your life, would it help you to do what you want to do, achieve what you want to achieve, live a more fulfilling, happy life?

If it appears to you that such a change would make an extreme difference, put a "5" in the box by that line on page 264. If the difference in your future would be very small, put a "1" in the box, and if the change in your life would be somewhere in between those extremes, grade it accordingly. If you cannot see any profit at all that would result from using more of your potential in one of the sectors that you have selected, eliminate it and find another to put in its place.

In some cases there may be both advantages and disadvantages which would result from a change in your behavior. List them on a piece of paper and then evaluate what, in your judgment, would be the net result.

Constructive Imagination will only work within the framework of your potential, and in those areas in which you perceive a possible change to be to your self interest. This method will not set aside the laws of the universe. It can take you far beyond what you now consider to be your limitations, though, and it has done that for many thousands of people.

You may have heard the expression, "Anything the mind of Man can conceive and believe, Man can achieve." I regard that statement as untrue, and potentially very dangerous. I have worked with people in mental institutions who could conceive and believe that they could step off the roof of a very tall building and float gently to the ground below. That sort of "belief" can be very hazardous to your health! The suggestion that the idea only applies to "normal" people compounds the danger by encouraging an attempt to judge "normalcy."

Distorted maps of the territory are perilous, whether the distortions are positive or negative. With all the books and courses that promote positive thinking, it would be easy to conclude that anything positive is good and anything negative is bad, but life is not that simple. Some negative attitudes may help you to live longer, and some positive thinking can get you into a heap of trouble!

Now we're ready to move on to the third stage in applying *Constructive Imagination.*

Exactly what kind of information would you like to have become the controlling, managing "REALITY" in your mental system in each of the areas that you have selected? If you could create the kind of self image in that department which would be most advantageous to you, what would it be?

To develop this information to the point that it will be useful, it will help to give some careful thought to each segment on your self image that you have listed on page 264. Use the kind of form shown on page 265 for this purpose.

First, clearly define the pattern that you would like to strengthen. Don't look it up in the dictionary; think it through and decide just what *you* mean by that characteristic that you have decided to work on. A sentence or two will be sufficient in most cases. The purpose of this activity is to be sure that you have a clear understanding of what you really want to develop.

Also, what kind of emotion (or emotions) would you like to have with respect to that activity or event? What kind of feelings would be most advantageous for you to have become your automatic, spontaneous response to that part of your life? In some instances it may be helpful to identify the negative emotion which is now attached to the area, but that is not ordinarily a necessary step.

Write out how you would like to be able to describe yourself in that area. If you were to become just the kind of person you would really like to be with respect to that kind of behavior, how would you describe you? Sometimes it helps to think about someone else that you know who is extremely effective in that particular area. If you were telling someone about that person, what would you say?

Here is an example of what I am suggesting. If you were to decide that sometimes you don't concentrate as well as you would like—that you have the ability, but often when you are trying to concentrate on something your mind wanders off to other matters—you might put that on your list. Then ask yourself how important that is to you. How profitable would it be to you to be able to maintain good concentration when you want to do so?

After you have "graded" concentration in terms of its value to you, turn to the three "fine tuning" questions. First, how would you define concentration? I believe that most people think of the ability to concentrate as a teeth-gritting, will-power activity—something that you can only do if you really work at it. As you think this through and work out a functional definition of concentration at its best, I think that you will find yourself using words like "fascination," "absorption," "engrossed." The harder you *try* to devote your attention to something, the more easily you will be distracted. It is when you find something (or someone) fascinating that your attention is riveted. Concentration at its best is effortless.

So, your definition might be something like: "the ability to become thoroughly engrossed in a project or activity, to find what I am doing so fascinating that I just don't notice what else is going on."

Notice, that is not *the* definition of the word "concentration." You may very well come up with a better, more useful definition for yourself. It is important that you identify just what it is that **you** want to develop and strengthen.

Next, what kind of emotion would you like to have as a part of your "REALITY" about concentration? Instead of feeling frustrated or irritated when it is important that you devote your attention to a specific area, how would you like to feel? Enthusiastic, excited, eager to get started? The kind of positive anticipation that you feel about anything that you do well?

Now, if you were to become the kind of person you would really like to be in that area, how would you describe yourself? It may help to think of an example that you have observed. When have you seen a person in complete, total, effortless concentration? A child watching a television set? A fisherman watching his fly-line? You might want to be able to think of yourself as a person who easily and quickly allows your attention to become focused or engrossed in an activity or another person. Look at page 266 to see how I have completed this stage of the project.

Here is another example. You have decided that you have more potential as a public speaker than you are using—because of a limiting emotional pattern. In the area of public speaking, you have been driving with the brakes partly set.

You have rated public speaking as a "4" in importance or value to your future achievement and happiness.

On page 267 I have completed the definition, identified the desired positive emotion and the kind of description one might want to have become an accurate self-appraisal in this area.

Now we have arrived at the very important fourth step in your project—designing the verbal affirmation for each area that you have selected. Remember that the purpose of the affirmation is to set into motion the experiencing of the kind of behavior which the affirmation represents—in the imagination—and the feeling of the emotion which you wish to cultivate with respect to that behavior.

On page 269 write out a simple, positive verbal affirmation for each characteristic or skill you have selected. When you have completed that part of your project, you have the first part of your own personal, unique tool kit with which to start releasing the brakes that are limiting your effectiveness.

In order that the affirmation may stimulate the kind of constructive imagery and positive feeling that you want to develop as a part of your "REALITY" structure, it is vitally important that the affirmation be worded correctly. On page 270 are ten rules to follow as you design each of the affirmations for your "tool kit." Be sure to study each rule very carefully so that you understand the reason why it is important. Then, when you have written out an affirmation, check it against each of the ten design rules to be doubly sure that it is properly worded.

There is another discomfort that you may find yourself feeling as you construct your affirmations. It may seem as though you are lying to yourself. The affirmations are certainly not *true,* so they must be *false*!

It is important that you recognize and feel comfortable with the fact that your affirmations are not in the category of "true or false." They are *tools* which you are designing and constructing for the purpose of building a new structure of attitudes. That new structure will be a more accurate, more honest, more complete image or representation of the real you, but the tools with which you build it are just that: neither true nor false, just tools.

If someone were to ask you if a particular hammer is true or false, you would see immediately that it was a nonsense question. Hammers are not true or false. A more rational question would be, "Is this hammer well designed, well balanced and well constructed to do a good job of building something?" That question can be tested and checked. And so, with an affirmation, we are much more concerned with the design and construction than with the present accuracy of the statement. If your affirmations were already accurate representations of your behavior, you would not have any need for them. On the other hand, from the standpoint of your true potential, the affirmations are a lot more accurate or "truthful" than some of the things you have been telling yourself in the past!

Don't get caught in the "lying to myself" trap. Our purpose is to build a more accurate self image, and in order to do that we need some images of effectiveness in the form of present tense affirmations.

Now let's look at the fifth stage in our project—the programming of the affirmations.

The actual process of depositing or digesting new positive inputs into your "REALITY" structure involves the use of all three media with which you think—**verbal, conceptual,** and **emotional.** In terms of subsequent behavior, the verbal medium is the least important, but it is a very convenient and effective way of triggering the other two, more important levels of thought.

Experiencing (conceptualizing) the kind of behavior represented by the verbal affirmation is much more important, and the most important part of the whole process is the emotional medium.

The programming sequence can, I think, best be explained with an example. Let's use something quite familiar—an attitude which is probably already a part of your system.

Please repeat the following sentence two or three times in your thoughts—not out loud, just in your thinking. The sentence is, "I enjoy eating an apple." As you repeat those words in your mental system, let yourself experience the activity which they describe. In your imagination your hand reaches out toward a bowl of fruit, selects a shiny, ripe, red apple and holds it up in front of you. Mmmmm, that really looks delicious. Now, still in your imagination, open your mouth and bite into the apple. It's a juicy one! Can you taste it? Feel the texture of the fruit as you chew it? Hear the crunching sound? Smell the fragrance?

Now let yourself feel the emotion—the pleasant feeling you have as you chew, taste, swallow and take another bite.

Some people find it easier to put themselves into the experience of an affirmation with their eyes closed. You may want to try an image with your eyes open and then try the same one with eyes closed to see whether blocking out the visual distractions enhances the vividness of the experience. If you found the apple exercise the least bit difficult, go back and try it again until it flows easily.

That is all there is to the programming process. Repeat the words of the verbal affirmation, let yourself experience the kind of behavior represented by those words, and feel the positive emotion that goes with functioning well in that area.

Here is an extremely important point. In order for the three-step programming process to have any effect on your "REALITY" structure, it is absolutely essential that you be a participant, not a spectator. You must *experience* the behavior represented by the affirmation, not observe it!

That means putting yourself into the action—doing it, not "watching" yourself. That is why I have carefully avoided using the expressions, "Picture yourself" and "Visualize." If you watch yourself as though you were looking at a motion picture on a screen, it may be an interesting pastime, but it will *not* revise any patterns in your "REALITY" structure!

The effect of *Constructive Imagination* is to bridge or supersede old patterns with new *experiences*. Fortunately, your storage system is so designed that to the degree that you experience an event with vividness in your imagination, it becomes a part of your subconscious collection of "the way I have done things." As you slip out of the action and become a spectator, all you are doing is increasing the number of times that "I have watched someone do things that way."

What is the most important part of the programming process? Right! **The emotional input.** As you think IN YOUR HEART so are you. As you experience the affirmation, let your positive emotions flow. Feel the warm glow, the enthusiasm, the pride, joy, sense of accomplishment. Let that feeling bubble up inside of you with all the richness and depth you can muster.

Think back for a moment to the time that you saw **The Sound of Music** or **South Pacific**. The words were important. The actions of the players added great meaning to the words. But the *music* gave it the feeling and lasting impact. In the process of *Constructive Imagination,* the emotional dimension is the music—the part that gives rich meaning and lasting impact to the experiences.

Now let's see how this same three-step programming sequence applies to the example on page 266.

An appropriate affirmation for the further development of your ability to concentrate might be, "It is easy for me to focus my attention and become fascinated with a project or activity." Now think of a situation either in your job or family or social activity in which it would be to your advantage to be able to concentrate your attention on something that is happening. It might be an activity like balancing your bank statement, filling out some reports for your employer, or studying a textbook. Put yourself right into the scene, sitting at your desk, perhaps, and let yourself become engrossed in the project that you are working on—so involved in it that you lose track of time and think only about what you are doing.

Use as many of your senses in your imagined experience as you can. Feel the book or papers in your hands, see the printing on the pages, hear the sound of a page turning. Then let yourself feel good about the fact that you can concentrate so completely when you want to do so. Get a sense of personal satisfaction about being that kind of person.

As you can see, this need not be a long, involved, time-consuming task. If you wanted to practice your tennis serve or speaking a foreign language, you might devote several minutes to repeated practicing of the skill. But reinforcing an attitude pattern is a quick, one-two-three deposit of a positive experience rock on your scale. Read the verbal affirmation, experience the behavior, and feel the positive emotion about being that kind of person.

Here is another example. Let's see how this would work with the public speaking area that is on page 267. An appropriate affirmation might be, "I have an enthusiastic, conversational style of public speaking and I enjoy the excitement of sharing ideas with large groups of people."

If you have any difficulty experiencing that kind of attitude and behavior in your imagination, try identifying with someone you know who is an outstanding public speaker—someone like Art Linkletter, Bill Gove, Billy Graham, or any other top professional. Think about what must be going on in that person's mental system as he stands in front of a large audience presenting some ideas which he believes in and thinks are very important. What is he thinking—**feeling**? Remember that he has hundreds, perhaps thousands, of very successful public speaking experiences programmed into his "REALITY" files. Can you sense the eager anticipation, the positive, enthusiastic, warm excitement that he is feeling?

The purpose of projecting yourself into that person's reaction to the situation is only to get in touch with the positive emotions—not so that you will imitate his style, delivery or vocabulary. Your objective is to become the enthusiastic, well-organized, fascinating public speaker that only *you* are capable of being.

Occasionally, a participant in one of our *PACE* Seminars says, "But I just can't *imagine* myself giving a good speech (or concentrating or remembering names, etc.)!" One of the wonderful characteristics of your system—all human systems—is the ability to imagine anything for which you have the pieces with which to construct the image. If you know what a polar bear looks like—either from having seen one at a zoo or having seen a picture of a polar bear—and if you know what the color pink looks like, then you can imagine a pink polar bear.

If you have ever been really absorbed or fascinated with something, and you know what it is to study for an examination, then you can put those two experiences together in your imagination if you want to do so, and you can imagine what it is like to concentrate on the book you are studying for the examination.

If you have ever expressed yourself in a forceful, enthusiastic manner to one or two people, and if you have ever been on a stage or platform and looked out at a large group of people, then you can—if you want to— imagine how it would feel to express yourself easily and confidently while standing before a large group.

Just remember that whether or not you have ever experienced a particular behavior in a specific situation, if you have the elements available with which to create the experience in your imagination, you can do so.

It is not necessary for you to have any faith or belief in order for *Constructive Imagination* to work for you. Some books or courses which deal with "positive thinking" suggest that the system they present will work providing you have enough faith. That provides a very convenient escape hatch—if the method doesn't work, then you must not have had enough faith!

Fortunately, belief and faith play no part at all in *Constructive Imagination.* They may develop as a result of its use, but they are not needed to practice it with success. If they happen to be present, they do no harm, but they are not required. I have seen many people who have attended *PACE* programs try *Constructive Imagination* with a great deal of skepticism and *dis*-belief. Each time I have felt a special kind of excitement as they have come to me and said, "This technique really *does* work! Not only do I feel some changes, but other people have noticed them, too!"

Like the hammer, the way to build something is to use the tool. The only way to avoid getting results is to leave the hammer in the tool box. But it is impossible to leave your imagination in the tool box. You have been using it all your life to build and reinforce patterns of "REALITY." Now, instead of using this powerful tool on a haphazard basis, put it to work for yourself deliberately, purposefully, to build just the kind of guidance mechanism you want to have in charge of your behavior.

There is one particular time in each day when *Constructive Imagination* will have an especially powerful impact on your mental system. One time in each twenty-four hour period when the thoughts and feelings that you are experiencing at a conscious level are most easily accepted and made a part of your "REALITY" structure. That very important time is just before you fall asleep, whether it's at night or any other time. Even just before you take a nap is a good programming time, but the very best period is just prior to your regular "night's sleep."

As you are relaxing, getting ready to fall asleep, you become more receptive to suggestion—more suggestible. As your conscious mental processes begin to "turn down" you are less inclined to question the "validity" of the images that you are experiencing. The evaluation process is not as questioning or challenging. You will find it easier to project yourself into the experiences represented by your affirmations; they will seem more real, more acceptable.

It may also be that when you work with your affirmations just before sleeping, you provide your subconscious creative processes with the necessary stimulus to re-program your "REALITY" structure while the conscious processes are "turned off." It would appear that dream activity is often directly related to the thoughts and feelings one has just prior to falling asleep, whether those thoughts are stimulated by your positive affirmations or by the negative images of the late news on television.

If you are a parent, particularly if your child has not yet reached the teen years, here is a very simple exercise with which you can test the importance of the conscious thoughts and feelings just before sleep. If you will try this for just a few days you will see dramatic results in the outlook and behavior of your youngster.

Each night when your child is ready for bed, take a few minutes to sit on the edge of the bed and talk about something pleasant. Gently, easily guide the child's final thoughts and feelings for the day into a positive direction. That does not mean to get the child so excited that he or she cannot go to sleep; just be sure that good feelings about himself and his world (or hers) are uppermost in the thinking process. Then tell that beautiful little person how much you love him or her, plant a goodnight kiss, and go back to what you were doing.

As with everything else that you do, how effectively you handle this time with your child will depend a lot on how you feel about doing it. If you see it as a nuisance, an interruption of something that is a lot more important, then it will be of little value. Look forward to those three or four minutes as a special time. If there is a question about whether you or your mate are going to handle the goodnights, it should be a question of who "gets to," not who "has got to."

Have you ever noticed the difference in a child's behavior in the first three weeks of December? At first it might seem to be the result of a conscious effort to "be good" in order to get more Christmas presents. I think what is really happening is that when a youngster falls asleep each night thinking about the wonderful, exciting presents, Christmas tree, turkey, visit to relatives, or whatever plans he knows are being made, it is almost certain that he will wake up with increased enthusiasm and a more positive outlook on life. The same sort of thing happens just before a camping trip or vacation—providing that the child expects the trip to be enjoyable.

It may help to focus this idea more sharply if we look at the other end of the spectrum for a moment. The time to scream, yell and berate your child is *not* just before sleep time. Knowing how important the emotional dimension of one's thinking is in those early years, it is clearly not to either the child's or your benefit to send him to sleep with an avalanche of negative rocks about himself and his world!

Help the people that you care about to fall asleep feeling good about life. And, of course, that includes **you**!

Here, then, is the specific, step-by-step process to follow to program your own personal affirmations into your "REALITY" structure. Keep your list of verbal affirmations on or in the table beside your bed. Just before you turn out the light to go to sleep, get out the list and read the first affirmation. It is not necessary to read it aloud; just read the words to yourself.

Then, think of a situation related to that affirmation and let yourself experience, in your imagination, being that kind of person—behaving that way—in such a situation. You may want to think of an experience you have had in the past that you didn't handle well. Re-play that experience, this time handling it very effectively. Or you can use a situation which you have observed, re-casting yourself as one of the principal characters in the scene and *experiencing* the action instead of watching it.

Let the positive emotion flow through your system. Feel good about being that kind of person. Revel in the enthusiasm, joy, excitement that you feel as you behave effectively, as you feel your potential being productively applied. Feel the satisfaction as you know that you are releasing your brakes!

Read—experience—feel. The entire process takes between five and ten seconds per affirmation. Even if you have as many as thirty affirmations on your list and you spend ten seconds on each, that is a total investment of five minutes. That will probably be the most important five minutes of the day from the standpoint of your future achievement and happiness.

Then, turn off the light and go on to sleep. Do *not* experience your affirmations and then watch the late news. Fall asleep with the positive knowledge that you are growing, becoming, guiding your own future.

The next best time in each twenty-four-hour day to work with your affirmations is first thing in the morning when you wake up. That is also a time when your system is relaxed and more receptive to the imagined experiences you want to digest into your "REALITY" structure. When the alarm goes off, sit on the edge of the bed, reach for the page of affirmations and quickly read, experience, and feel each one on the list. It's a terrific way to start out each day with some positive feelings about yourself and the other people whose lives you will touch.

The next best time to work with your affirmations is any time. Carry a set with you on a piece of paper or on cards. There are many times during each day when you will find that you are doing something quite automatically and your conscious mental processes are free to work with your affirmations if you want to do so. When you are driving a car, washing dishes, cleaning the garage, taking a walk, riding your bicycle or going to the bathroom, you can easily let your thoughts reinforce some positive imagery. Every time that you deliberately, purposefully deposit another rock on the positive side of one of those scales it will have an impact on your subsequent behavior.

Now let's look at the sixth step in the application of *Constructive Imagination.* Allow the changed images to guide your behavior in the new directions that you have decided upon. The key word here is **allow**. *Constructive Imagination* will work best for you if you will *allow* it to work. As you are reviewing your affirmations each day and adjusting your self image in the direction of greater accuracy and increased effectiveness, go right on acting like yourself while the self is changing.

If it has been your style in the past to get things done by gritting your teeth and exerting a lot of "will power" then this may take a little practice, but it will be well worth the effort. While you are re-programming the setting on the *Effectiveness Regulator,* go right on behaving in a natural, free-flowing manner. I am *not* suggesting that you go sit under a tree and wait for some kind of magical transformation to happen, but it is equally important that you not work with your affirmations and then *try hard* to make them happen. That conscious effort will simply impair your progress and can even have a reverse effect in many instances, diminishing performance instead of improving it.

Have you ever tried hard to do well on an examination? If you play golf, you may recall times when you have tried very hard to hit a long ball off the tee. Those were probably the times that you topped the ball or ended up in the rough. What happens when you use your will power to try to remember the name of a song, or of a person you see coming across the room toward you? Perhaps you can recall the time that you were up very late one night and you knew that you had an important meeting early the next morning. If you tried hard to get to sleep, the chances are that you didn't get much rest that night.

Change in the human system is ordinarily a gradual process. There are, of course, exceptions to that rule—sometimes a person will undergo a very sudden and profound change in outlook, values, and behavior. Such instant conversions are rare, and even more rare are those which continue over a period of time. Lasting change in your behavior is more likely to resemble the way a ship or an airplane changes course. When you turn the helm on a ship, the craft begins to turn right away, but it also continues to move forward in the direction that it has been going. If you let it, your change process will begin very quickly too, but some of the old patterns of behavior will still be there for a while. Lasting, constructive change in human behavior is the result of a changed *image,* and that change is a process, not an instantaneous event.

Let's carry the ship example one step further. If you have an autopilot on your ship it will keep you on a preset course automatically. You can set the autopilot for 180 degrees, bring the ship to that heading, and turn on the automatic mechanism; the ship will stay on that course. If the wind or currents deflect the vessel from the heading you have set into the autopilot, servomotors are activated which will turn the rudder and correct for the error—bring you back to the 180 degree heading.

If you want to change course, there are essentially two ways to do so. You can turn the wheel manually, overriding the autopilot, until the ship is headed in the new direction. That won't be easy, because you will be struggling against the force of the autopilot's correctional motors. When you reach the new course, you will find it necessary to continue to hold the wheel firmly, not only fighting the winds and currents, but also the force of the automatic mechanism which is working to get the ship back to the original course of 180 degrees. If you release the wheel, the ship will immediately turn back toward that heading.

The other way to change course is to use the automatic mechanism. Re-set the autopilot to the new heading and let it work for you instead of working against it.

Your *Effectiveness Regulator* is a lot like the autopilot. The self-image functions as the course which you have programmed into the automatic device, and the *Regulator* tends to keep you on course—acting like your self. You can certainly override the *Regulator* with a conscious determination to behave differently. You can exercise your will power and temporarily move outside of the Comfort Zone, but it will require constant conscious effort and create uncomfortable tensions until you get back to acting like yourself.

It is a lot easier—and a lot healthier—to simply re-set the *Regulator* and let it work for you. As you modify the attitude patterns which make up your self image, you go right on acting like yourself as the self changes.

The only kind of "will power" that need be involved in the use of *Constructive Imagination* is the tremendous *power* that comes from deciding that you *will* work with your affirmations each day. Then stay out of your way to allow the growth process to proceed.

The high performance syndrome

Until very recently, most of the emphasis in the study of human behavior has been directed toward illness instead of health. Certainly an understanding of "mental illness" is important, and helping people whose "REALITY" system has become so distorted that it is difficult for them to function in society is equally vital. However, it seems to me that understanding healthy, high performance behavior is much *more* important.

In each of the next six chapters I want to explore a symptom of wellness—behavior patterns which seem to be common denominators of excellence. People who are using a great deal of their potential—in all walks of life—have developed these characteristics or qualities to a high degree, by accident or by intent.

Each one of these patterns is a releaser. As you understand them more clearly and learn how to strengthen and reinforce them, you will have your hands on some very simple and direct ways to release your brakes. As we look at them, remember that in each case we are primarily concerned with the emotional dimension—the degree to which your feelings are positively or negatively inclined. To the degree that negative feelings predominate, the brakes are on and little potential is flowing. To the degree that your emotional inclination is positive, the abilities and skills you possess tend to flow easily and productively.

Study each of these characteristics carefully, and selfishly. How does each one apply to you, personally?

CHAPTER

12

Where are you now in each of these departments? Most important, what would the impact be on your life if you were to further strengthen any or all of these patterns?

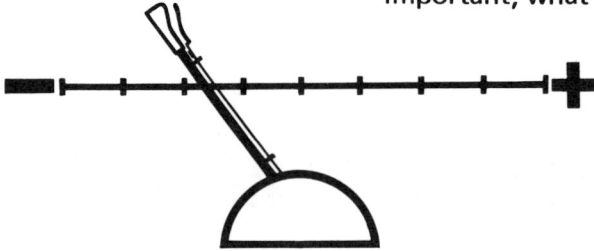

We will also look at two other practical applications of each of the six high performance patterns—ways in which you can strengthen them in the groups of which you are a part and useful approaches for helping other people that you care about to grow and release their potentials.

Groups of people have personalities very much like those of individuals. Whenever two or more people get together, in a family, an athletic team, department, branch office or a company, a new personality emerges—the group personality. The collection of individual people becomes an organism made up of organisms—an epi-organism—which has patterns of thought and behavior, a self image, goals, tensions and an effectiveness level. The epi-organism tends to function about as effectively as the attitudes within the group will permit.

Think of some of the groups to which you belong. Your family, bowling team, country club, company, neighborhood or various clubs or associations. Can you see that each of those groups has a lot more potential than it is using? Can you see that it would be to your advantage—to your self interest—if those groups were to become more effective? It's a lot more fun to be a part of a winning team, and when the group is functioning effectively it is much easier for you to focus your attention on what you want to achieve and make it happen more easily.

So, we will look at some steps that you can take—right away—to help your family, your company, or any other group to function better, to use more of its potential.

The third area in which you can put these releasing mechanisms to work is in your role as a "people grower." As a parent, a manager, a mate, and in many other areas of your life, there are people who are looking to you for leadership, guidance, inspiration. There are people who admire you and see you as a "role model"—a person they want to be more like.

If you want to do so, there are some very simple ways in which you can help those people to grow, to expand their horizons, to become more nearly the kind of people they are truly capable of being. Of course, this turns out to be in your own self-interest, too! It is a lot easier to live and work with effective people.

As we examine methods which you can use to facilitate and nurture the growth process of other people, notice the very important difference between "getting someone else shaped up," and "helping someone to grow and to become the person he or she wants to be." Getting someone else shaped up is a manipulative process, usually involving coercion (force, pain, threats, fear), the goal of which is to force (or bribe) that person into behaving the way you think that he or she should behave. As soon as you find yourself with thoughts involving "should," "ought to," "had better," "must," or "have to," you know that you are in the process of doing some shaping up.

Helping another person to grow means helping that person to unfold, to release the negative emotional braking mechanisms which are limiting his or her effectiveness. This approach might be expressed with two simple questions: "What do you want to accomplish?" and "How can I help you?" But remember that help is only help when the person being helped sees it that way! When you find yourself thinking, "I know what's best for this person and I'm going to help him whether he likes it or not," you are probably moving in a dangerous direction.

How goals release potential

For a person to have a goal structure is not just desirable; it is *essential*. Essential to the survival of the system. The extreme negative end of this continuum is death!

People who do not have goals—for whatever reason—literally, physically die. We see this all too frequently when the retired person who has lived a dynamic, achieving life neglects to set new goals when crossing the retirement threshold and is gone in just a few months.

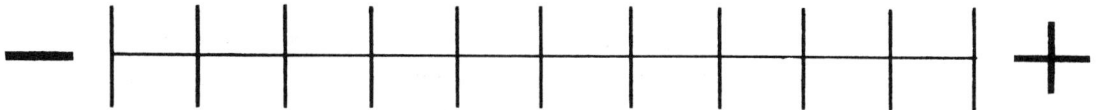

$$-\!\!\!+\!\!+\!\!+\!\!+\!\!+\!\!+\!\!+\!\!+\!\!+\!\!+\!\!+\!\!+$$

**NO
GOALS**

**COMMITMENT TO
CLEAR, SPECIFIC,
EXCITING GOALS**

Sometimes an elderly couple demonstrates this principle. They have been married for many years; one dies and the survivor does not develop new interests and objectives. We may have a second funeral much sooner than anyone expected.

Much evidence of the importance of a sense of future purpose has been seen in prisons, prisoner of war camps, and concentration camps. Even in such horrible environments, those who survive tend to be those who have specific, personally meaningful goals.

Often, in less grim situations, people set "default"

135

goals. Such objectives are not deliberately, consciously set, but whatever becomes the "uppermost thought" functions as a goal. You move toward whatever you dwell on, think about, imagine and feel strongly about—whether it is something that you have *decided* to set as a goal or something that you allow to become a primary focal point of your thinking because you have not fulfilled the system's need for a goal structure. I have known people who behave as though they had set the goal of failing. Of course, they did not sit down with pencil and paper and write that out as something they wanted to achieve. But because they have neglected to set specific, positive goals, and instead spend a lot of time worrying about failing, imagining it and thinking about all of the dire consequences they will suffer if it should happen, it becomes the uppermost thought and they have all the creativity and energy needed to fail!

If your primary goal is to "get through the day," then you will have just as much creativity, awareness, and energy as you need to get through the day—and not an ounce more. If you dwell on illness, chances are that you will find a way of getting sick. The "accident-prone" person has spent a lot of time thinking about and worrying about having accidents, until it has become a part of the person's "REALITY" that he is the kind of person who has a lot of them. Sure enough! Even the bum on skid row has goals, and all of the creativity, awareness and energy he needs to achieve them.

In our earlier discussion of the Subconscious Mental Processes (page 52) I suggested that part of the Conflict Resolution activity of your mental system is related to the achievement of your goals. When a goal is digested or assimilated into your "REALITY" structure, it becomes a part of "the way things are supposed to be." It is the conflict or disparity between that "REALITY" and your perception of "the way things are" which stimulates the creativity, expands the awareness and releases the energy needed to change the environment—"the way things are"—in the direction of the goal—"the way things are supposed to be."

To understand how this works, and how you can work *with* it, it will help to look once again at the Effectiveness Regulator.

Part of your Self Image is the "REALITY" that you have about "your kind of environment." You have adopted an overall image of what kind of world you "belong" in. The kind of dwelling, car, club, social activities, vacation trip, recreation and cultural events which are familiar and which you know how to handle, how to relate to. Your environmental Comfort Zone is the kind of world in which you feel at ease, relatively free of tension—not necessarily comfortable in the sense of luxury but rather in the sense of a minimum of uncomfortable tension in your physical system.

Think about your Comfort Zone for a moment. Probably the mid-point is when you are sitting in your favorite chair in your own living room, alone, with the hi-fi playing your favorite music. A complete feeling of belongingness. If you want to do so, you can kick off your shoes, put your feet on the coffee table, say anything you want to say, do anything you want to do without stopping to think about it.

If you go to a neighbor's home, you will still be in your Comfort Zone, but not quite as totally at ease and spontaneous. When you go to a party over on the other side of town, at a house you've never visited before, some people there whom you know and others you've never met, you may be a little more inclined to think before you speak, a little more tense in the unfamiliar situation.

Have you ever been out of your Comfort Zone?

Think about some times when you have been very up tight because you were "out of place"—in an environment that was so unfamiliar that you didn't quite know how to handle it.

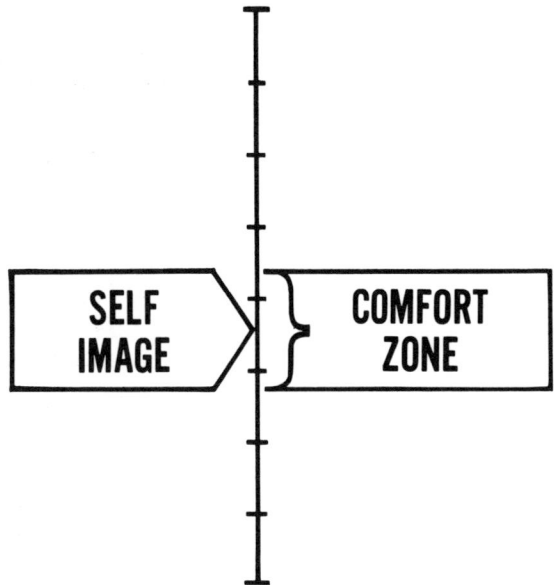

How about the first day on a new job? Or when you are being interviewed for a new job? The personnel manager feels very much at home, but the applicant may be feeling a lot of tension—out of the Comfort Zone. How do you feel in a hospital? If you are part of the medical profession, the hospital may be an integral part of your Comfort Zone, but if not, you may feel very much out of place when you are there, even if it is only to visit a friend.

How do you feel in a courtroom, or a prison? How about the first day of basic training in the Service? Think of specific times when you have personally been out of your Comfort Zone. Recall how it felt. What did you feel like doing about the situation?

Sometimes when people travel in foreign countries they find themselves out of the Comfort Zone. Different language, different foods, different customs may create some tension in the system. But if we are there because we have *decided* to go—if it is a trip we have wanted to take—then it is an adventure. Adventure is the deliberate, volitional movement out of one's Comfort Zone. We still feel the tension from being in a strange, unfamiliar environment, but it becomes a positive, exciting, stimulating tension.

Camping is another example of adventure, the intentional, deliberate venturing out of our "normal" world. Very often, even though the camping trip is voluntary, as soon as we make camp we set about energetically and creatively to make the campsite a little more like home. Some people even take a camper, trailer or motorhome—their portable Comfort Zone!

But, whether it is a vacation trip to a foreign country or a camping trip to the mountains, when your adventure is finished and you walk in the front door of your own Comfort Zone, how does it feel? Even if you weren't aware of the tension in your system which resulted from being out of your Comfort Zone, you can sense the release of that tension as you return to the familiar environment.

We can reduce this to a very simple, but very important, principle:

PEOPLE TEND TO MOVE TOWARD—OR RE-CREATE— THEIR COMFORT ZONE

Think of some "real world" situations which illustrate this idea, not only in your own life, but in circumstances where you have had the opportunity to observe others. If you served in some branch of the armed forces, you probably felt the tension that came with being out of your element. When some people reported to their first training assignment they were out of their Comfort Zone in the direction of much greater luxury than they had ever experienced. Tension! Since it wasn't possible to "get out," they did what they could to make the barracks a little more like home. Others found the service environment pretty shabby, but the impulse was the same—make it a little more like "my world" is supposed to be.

Another graphic and all-too-common example may be seen in government slum-clearance projects. When a slum area is cleared, the rats and roaches killed, and a new housing project built, the people who have been living in the slum move in and convert the new buildings into a new slum. That doesn't mean that there is any-thing "wrong" with the people in the housing project. They are behaving in a perfectly normal, predictable manner. If anyone should be criticized it is the people in charge of the government agencies who, because of their ignorance of this simple principle, continue to pour our tax dollars into projects which are doomed to failure before they begin.

Look at this slum situation in reverse—that may help to make it clearer. If you were to be moved into a slum tenement room, complete with the rats, bugs, smells, and filth, would you find it easy to simply adjust to your new environment? Or would you set about quick-ly, creatively, and energetically to change the environ-ment to more nearly resemble your Comfort Zone? Your first impulse would be to get out, but if that were not possible for some reason, can you see that you would find some ways to make the place a little more like home? If you find yourself thinking, "But that would be changing things in the right direction," think again. It would simply be changing things in *your* direction.

Here is another, less extreme example which you can observe in the suburbs of any city. Have you ever visited a new housing tract, just after it has been completed? By housing tract I mean a development of homes built by the same builder with very similar floor plans and appearance. As you drove through that tract you noticed the great similarity of the houses and lots. Returning two years later, what did you find? The houses which were so much alike in the beginning aren't alike any more. Each family has moved into their home and the creativity and energy have flowed to change the property so that it conforms to that family's Comfort Zone. One house has been improved, added onto, landscaped, painted, maintained. The next house looks like a disaster area. The front yard is all weeds; the paint is peeling; the back yard has three automobiles in various stages of being dismantled and reassembled. As you move down the block you see that some families consider the inside to be very important; others have spent time only on maintaining or improving the exterior. For some, the back yard is the part which should look nice; for others the back doesn't matter at all, but the front yard is manicured. Each family has developed their own idea of how a home is supposed to be, and they will display all the creativity and energy necessary to bring their property to that level. It may be tempting to think that the appearance of the property is related to the earnings or economic level of the family. Not so! You will find families of very meager means in homes which are neat, clean and kept up, and some with much higher incomes who seem to make a hobby of destroying the house they live in.

Some years ago the Bureau of Indian Affairs took pity on the poor Navajo Indians in Arizona, because the Indian families were living in hogans, the traditional (and very practical) dwelling of that tribe. The government experts decided that some of our tax money should be spent on giving the Indian families "proper" housing. Many houses were built, concrete block buildings with several bedrooms, modern plumbing, electricity, and modern conveniences. The Indians were very appreciative and began immediately to use the new houses which the government had built for them—to store their grain and house their livestock. They went right on living in their Comfort Zone—the hogan.

I'm sure you will be able to think of many more examples of this principle in action, both in events which you have observed and read about and in your own life. Take a few minutes and see if you can recall times that you have been out of your Comfort Zone and what you did to recreate it.

There is a corollary principle which flows from the idea that it is unpleasant to move out of the Comfort Zone.

PEOPLE TEND TO RESIST MOVING TOWARD THE UNFAMILIAR

If you see that your present course is taking you toward unfamiliar territory, toward activities, events or an environment which you are not sure that you can handle, you will tend to dig in your heels and find creative ways to change course or resist moving in that direction.

For example, you may have decided that you want a promotion to a position of greater responsibility (and earnings) within your company. However, so long as that new position is outside of your Comfort Zone—so long as it is unfamiliar territory—you will find all sorts of ways of resisting progress in that direction and avoiding opportunities which would take you there.

But how about progress? People *do* change. If everyone always moved toward their Comfort Zone or re-created it, things would always stay the same! Not at all. There is no contradiction between this principle and the fact that we do see change, growth, progress in both individuals and groups. The solution to that apparent dilemma lies in the principle we looked at at the end of Chapter 9 (page 94).

> ALL LASTING CONSTRUCTIVE
> CHANGE IN HUMAN BEHAVIOR
> STARTS ON THE INSIDE—WITH A
> CHANGED IMAGE OF "REALITY"!

As the "REALITY"—the self image—changes, the Comfort Zone changes, too. Then, you find yourself in an environment which *used* to be your kind of world, but in which you now feel out of place. Setting a goal and programming it into your "REALITY" structure has the effect of deliberately creating a positive, magnetic tension in the system, turning on the creative ideas, releasing the energy and broadening awareness of the opportunities which will take you toward the goal.

See if this idea triggers some examples from your own experiences:

> YESTERDAY'S DREAMS ARE
> TODAY'S NECESSITIES

What can you think of that was once a vague fantasy, but now seems like an essential part of your world? Actually, there are three stages in this sequence. The first stage is, "Why on earth would anyone waste money on one of those things?" Then, a little later, you find yourself thinking, "Hmmm, those things aren't so bad. I wonder how it would be to have one." Then, when it has become a part of your Comfort Zone, you wonder, "How can anyone live a normal life without one of these?"

Can you trace those three steps with a car? Or a washing machine, dishwasher, second telephone, air conditioning, color television? How about the kind of house or apartment that you are living in right now?

What has happened in each of those examples is simply an adjustment of your self image, and a corresponding change in your Comfort Zone. As you have thought about, dwelt on, imagined how it would be if that change were to be made in your environment, your image of "the way things are supposed to be" shifted, releasing the creativity and energy necessary to change the environment. Not only are yesterday's dreams today's necessities, but—

TODAY'S DREAMS ARE TOMORROW'S OPPORTUNITIES

The goals you set today, and program into your "REALITY" structure, will expand your awareness of the opportunities that are available to help you achieve those goals.

In our discussion of the Conscious Mental Processes, I suggested that only a fraction of what is happening in your environment is perceived. It is possible for you to look directly at an object and not see it. Your visual system is working properly, but there is a screening or filtering system in the central nervous system (the Reticular Activating System) which allows only the significant stimuli—the "important" information—to reach a conscious level of awareness.

Here is a simple example of this phenomenon which you can test right now. If you are wearing a watch, don't look at it, but think about the following questions.

1. What color is the face of your watch?
2. Does the brand name appear on the face?
3. What is the name?
4. Is it above or below the center?
5. Is there any other writing on the face?
6. How many numbers are there around the outside of the watch?
7. Are they Roman numerals or regular Arabic numbers?
8. Does your watch have a second hand?

Look at your watch and see how you scored. If you didn't answer all the questions correctly, don't be surprised. Most people don't. Even though you look at your watch frequently, there are some things about it that are not very important, and you just haven't seen them.

Now, without looking at your watch again, do you know what time it is? Even though you were just examining it in great detail, you may not have seen the time. For the moment, that was not important.

> **PEOPLE TEND TO *PAY* ATTENTION TO WHAT IS HAPPENING IN THEIR ENVIRONMENT IN DIRECT PROPORTION TO ITS *VALUE* TO THEM**

You have seen this principle at work in many ways. Sometimes it applies to the way that we communicate with each other. Have your children ever looked directly at you and not heard a word you said? Or have you ever looked directly at someone and "turned him off"?

When I was very young we would often take a drive in the family car down through the hills of Missouri. We weren't going anyplace in particular, just taking whatever road looked as if it might be interesting. Someone would say, "Let's turn to the right here, Dad, and see where this road will take us." After several such random turns we would often realize that we were completely lost.

Then one of us would say, "Let's head for home, I'm hungry." Now, the entire situation changed. Up to that point, whatever road signs there were had just disappeared! They had been there, and we had probably looked right at them, but we had not *seen* them. But now that we had all decided to head for home, the road signs, and any other information or signals which would help us to get there, leaped out at us. When you have a destination in mind, the road signs that will help you to get there stand out very clearly. When you have a clearly defined goal structure, the opportunities which will make it possible for you to achieve those goals become more apparent.

Have you ever seen someone walk right by what seemed to you to be a golden opportunity? Chances are that the person just didn't see it, because for that person, it *wasn't* an opportunity. A lot of people go through their entire lives as though they were "taking a drive." Wandering aimlessly, taking whatever direction seems to look appealing at the moment—and more often than not, getting lost.

It is also important to note that setting a goal and programming it into your "REALITY" structure does not guarantee its achievement—it only increases the *probability* that you will achieve the goal. The "guarantee" works in the opposite direction. If you do *not* set a goal, there is a built-in guarantee that you will *not* achieve it!

This principle was expressed beautifully in the song "Happy Talk" from the great Rodgers and Hammerstein musical, *South Pacific.* Remember the words, "You got to have a dream. If you don't have a dream, how you going to have a dream come true?"

If you don't have a goal it is very unlikely that you will achieve it, and if you should happen to accidentally achieve something which is outside of your goal structure—outside of your Comfort Zone—you will nearly always scurry back to where you "belong" very quickly.

You have probably seen many examples of this in newspaper and magazine articles. News stories about people who have either won a lottery or inherited great wealth unexpectedly. After the initial shock and elation, they will almost always set about creatively and energetically to "correct for the error." In no time at all, the money is gone and the person is back in his Comfort Zone again.

Sometimes this happens in companies or other organizations. The sales manager, for example, leaves the company for some reason. The president decides that the logical choice for promotion to that position is the person with the highest sales volume in the company—the best salesperson. Sounds reasonable, doesn't it? After all, that person knows more about how to sell our product or service than anyone else in the company. Who is better equipped to run the sales department?

And yet, that decision could be a disaster. It will depend on the self image of that person. If he has had the goal of being promoted to the position of sales manager, and has been projecting himself into that role, mentally practicing handling all of the various responsibilities and activities of the sales manager, he may move into the new office, feel very much at home, and handle things extremely well. On the other hand, if he still has the self image of a highly productive salesperson, the president may discover that he now has lost the sales volume of his best producer, and the recruiting, training, forecasting, holding sales meetings and many other vital tasks are being handled poorly if at all. When someone is plunged into a situation which is outside of his Comfort Zone, it will result in a lot of unnecessary—and unhealthy—tension, and in many cases the person will find creative ways to get back to where he "belongs" as quickly as possible.

Let's get back to you again. Here are six simple rules to follow as you set and use your own personal goals. You will find a project kit starting on page 272 which will help you to focus your attention on this very important releasing mechanism. Do it right now—not one of these days when you have some spare time!

1. BALANCE: Select three or four goals in each of the three categories on page 272, and write them down on page 273. Be sure that you do not put all of your goals in just one department of your life. Identify some changes that you want to make in the vocational sector—earnings, position, sales volume—in your personal or family life—home, car, vacation trip—and in your community, through your church, political party, service club or other organization. There is a "thought starter" list on page 272 to give you some ideas of what kind of goals might fit into each of the three categories.

You will probably think of others which are not on the list at all, but it will get you started.

2. CONSISTENT: As you write down your goals on page 273, be sure that each one is consistent with the overall Comfort Zone that you are developing with this list, and with the goals of other people with whom you live and work. I like to think of a goal structure as a kind of jigsaw puzzle. Each goal is a piece in the puzzle; when they are all fitted together, they make up a picture of the Comfort Zone in which you want to "feel at home." Notice that we are not setting short-range, mid-range and long-range goals, but one, balanced, consistent list which represents the next plateau toward which you are reaching. You need to achieve some more immediate objectives to reach your goals, and you know that as you accomplish those which you are listing now, you will reset new, higher goals. But the present list should fit together to form a picture which makes sense to **you**. The kind of house, car, job, club, travel, recreation, hobbies, etc., which all add up to the life style that you want to have become your way of living.

3. CONSTRUCTIVE: Your goals should all be within your reach, but not within your grasp. High enough to turn you on, stimulate excitement and enthusiasm in your emotional system whenever you think about them, but not so high that they seem ludicrous, impossible, unimaginable. Only you can decide what *constructive* means for you with each goal on your list. Most people are inclined to "play it safe" and set their goals too low. *Don't sell yourself short.* You have a tremendous amount of potential that you have never tapped, and your goal list is going to help to release that potential. There are also hazards, though, in setting your goals too high. If a goal is beyond your reach—so high that you simply cannot project yourself into it and imagine it as an already accomplished part of your world—setting that goal will have little or no effect on your progress.

4. SPECIFIC: Be sure that you define each goal on your list in considerable detail. There may not be enough room on page 274. If not, use extra pages for this purpose. It is not enough to have a goal of "a house." What is the style, how many rooms, what kind of floor plan, landscaping, price tag? What are some of the special extras about that home that are very important to you? Do you want an entertaining area, a special kind of kitchen, a swimming pool? If you have a goal of an automobile on your list, decide on the make, model, body style, color, and any other details that are important to you. Go to the dealer for a brochure so you can see a detailed picture of just what that car looks like. If you have a vacation trip on your list, decide where you want to go and just how long you want to spend in each city or country. Get some travel folders. Look through *National Geographic* magazines. The more specific the goal is, the easier it will be for you to project yourself into it and experience it as an integral part of your Comfort Zone in your imagination.

5. CONFIDENTIAL: Discuss your goals *only* with those individuals who are going to be directly involved in the attainment or enjoyment of them. If you have a house goal, get the whole family involved in setting it. Be sure that everyone who is going to live in that home is tuned in to the specific image. Not only will you achieve the goal faster, but when you move in it will be a happier day for everyone if they *all* are moving into their Comfort Zones. But don't make the mistake of telling every person you know about your house goal. Many people are so certain *they* cannot do anything about their lot in life, that they will feel resentment and envy toward anyone else who thinks that he can improve his environment. You will invite an avalanche of negative rocks that you certainly don't need. If you have a goal of being promoted to a new position in your organization, discuss that goal only with those who are directly concerned. Your mate, of course, and probably your immediate superior—your boss. But don't tell all of the other people with whom you work, or play golf. You run too high a risk of attracting the negative inputs.

6. PRESENT TENSE: After you have decided upon your goals, defined them very clearly and specifically, and checked to be sure that they are consistent with each other and with the goals of the groups of which you are a part, translate each one into a simple, brief, positive, present tense affirmation. Use the same rules (page 270) that you used for wording the other affirmations you have already constructed. Here, again, the purpose of the verbal affirmation is to trigger the experiencing of the goal as an already accomplished fact. These new affirmations will now become a part of your complete "tool kit," to be programmed into your "REALITY" structure each day. As you repeat the verbal affirmation in your thinking—"We are all enjoying living in our new, modern home in the hills"— allow yourself to *experience* in your imagination how it feels to be living in that new home. Be there in your imagination and let the positive emotions flow. Remember: setting and using goals is a familiarization project. As it becomes possible for you to experience the accomplished goal in your imagination, comfortably, the brakes are released and your potential to achieve that goal will flow much more easily and spontaneously.

Setting goals and programming them into your "REALITY" structure does not eliminate the need for planning, organizing, and all the other activities which may be involved in reaching your objectives. But the use of *Constructive Imagination* to "digest" your goals has the effect of making it all happen more quickly and easily.

The releasing mechanism of goal direction applies to the group personality or epi-organism in very much the same manner as with your own individual behavior. By encouraging and helping your team to set and use goals you make an important contribution to the achievement of that group, and thus to your own progress as well.

Groups, like individuals, must have goals or they die. Some sense of purpose is essential to the continued existence of every epi-organism, whether it is a marriage, a company, or a nation. To the degree that the goals of the group are clear, specific, and become a part of the group's "REALITY" structure—"the way things are supposed to be for *us*"—the creativity, awareness, and energy flow to bring about those objectives.

Picture this situation. Six people are sitting in a boat in the middle of a lake. Each person has an oar, and they are all paddling frantically in an effort to get to shore. It would seem they should have a common sense of purpose, but each one has a different idea of which part of the shore to head for—so the boat just goes around in circles and no one gets anywhere! Wouldn't it make sense to stop for a moment, communicate, decide upon a destination that all six people can "buy" and then pull *together* to reach their goal?

I am constantly amazed at the number of married couples who have never had any discussion about "our goals." I believe this is one reason for the increasing rate of separations and divorces. In today's fast-moving world there is an even greater need for clearly set common goals within a family unit. In a rural society personal goals and family goals are almost built into the life style. Not so for most of us today.

Have a family conference from time to time for the specific purpose of discussing what the family's goals are. Such areas as where we live, changes we want to make in our home, the family car, vacation trips and other objectives which affect everyone in the family lend themselves to an open discussion. Keep communicating until everyone in the group feels a real sense of personal commitment to the achievement of the goal.

The same process works in a company or in a department within the company. As each member of the group feels a sense of personal dedication to the group's goals, it becomes possible for that person to align his or her own goals with those of the epi-organism. Then we all get where we want to go much faster and easier. Commitment is an important part of this structure. To the degree that each person in the team has a "want to" attitude about the group's goal structure, the potential which exists within the group tends to flow. If some in the group see the goals as "have to's," the brakes are applied and progress inhibited. Thus, management's responsibility is not only to see that goals are set, but also that they are communicated throughout the organizational system. The communicating will be most productive if it is designed to *sell* the goals, not simply to inform everyone of what they are.

Think of the difference between a bar of ordinary gray iron and a magnet. They look just alike, and they are made up of the same kind of atoms. But in the iron bar the molecular domains are "pointed" in many different directions—randomly. In the magnet the molecular domains are more coherent—pointed more nearly in the same direction. The magnet, simply because of its internal alignment, has an extra added power. So will your team. Anything you can do to encourage or bring about the establishment of a coherent, specific goal structure in a group to which you belong will help that epi-organism to function more effectively. That, in turn, will help you to achieve your own goals more easily.

There are specific steps that you can take to encourage the setting of group goals.

First, recognize that such action is likely to be taken only to the degree that the members of the group see it to be in their self interest to do so. If setting group goals is an unfamiliar exercise, there will be a tendency to resist it. Your task is to sell those involved that it will be a valuable (and safe) step for them to take.

An initial step which is often useful is simply to ask the question, "What are our goals?" Keep on asking, gently but firmly, until you either get an answer or there is a recognition or acknowledgment that, "We don't have any, and maybe we should set some!"

Or, write out what you think might be a productive goal structure for the group. Ask each person to review your list and comment on what he or she thinks should be changed. Then invite everyone to get together for the purpose of discussing and setting a list of goals which all can agree on and work toward.

Another idea: give each person in the group a copy of *Release Your Brakes!* with the suggestion that you would like to discuss the idea of group goals with them after they have read the book.

Or, ask each person in your group to think carefully about one specific goal that your group should have, write it down and give it to you. This will start some very productive thought processes which can then lead to a group discussion of the goals which all of the members have contributed. Another way to phrase that opening question is, "If we were to become the kind of company (family, association, etc.) that you would like to see us become, what would be one of the major changes that would happen?"

Remember that your group is certainly going to be different a year from now than it is today. The direction that change will take can be left to chance—you can "cope" with what is happening—or you can take the initiative and decide where you want to go. There is no guarantee that your group will achieve the goals you set—only a guarantee that you will *not* achieve the ones you *don't* set!

Let's turn our attention to people-growing. What can you do to help another person with whom you live or work to set and use goals as a releasing device?

First of all, recognize that you cannot *force* someone to set goals and develop the kind of personal commitment to them which will produce positive results. You can discuss, encourage, offer your opinion, share your own experience, sell the idea, but *pushing* won't work. In fact, if you tell someone that he *has to* set goals it may actually stimulate a "push back" reaction—a determination to *not* set goals, followed by a list of creative rationalizations about why goals aren't all that important.

Ask questions: *"What are your goals?" "What are some of the things you want to accomplish?" "Where would you like to be a year from now?"* Encourage the person to do some thinking about the future and then offer some suggestions about how to work with those objectives—how to dwell on them and program them into the mental system.

As the people who look to you for leadership see that you are goal-directed they will be inclined to follow your example. Let it be known that you have a very specific idea about where you are headed; that you think about your goals frequently, plan your time and effort accordingly, and fully expect to achieve them. You won't need to disclose the exact nature of your personal goals to others, but when they are achieved you can discuss them. The fact that you are setting, using, and achieving goals will stimulate your associates and your family members to do likewise.

Self-esteem—a foundation for effective behavior

You are an extremely valuable, worthwhile, significant person.

What is your reaction as you think about that? How do you **feel** about your worthiness and importance as a human being? That feeling—your level of self-esteem—is one of the most fundamental and vital attitude structures in your "REALITY" system. High self-esteem is an almost universal common denominator of excellence—a releasing mechanism that allows your potential to flow easily and freely.

You have developed a pattern of "truth" about your value as a part of your self-image, and you tend to behave in a manner that is consistent with that attitude. Your self-esteem began to develop in the early years of your life. When you were very small you got a lot of messages and signals from parents and other experts about what kind of person you were. Some of those signals were very positive, loving, encouraging, and reinforcing. *"I love you." "You're a great kid!" "I'm glad you're a part of our family."*

Some of the messages from those very important people in your childhood may not have been so positive. *"Pick up your feet, clumsy!" "What did you do a stupid thing like that for?"*

But, here's an important point. It was not just what *kind* of messages you received, but what you *did* with those messages that counted. Look at that very care-

CHAPTER

14

fully. It was not what those other people, those "experts," those authority figures *said* to you that counted nearly so much as what you were *thinking and feeling within yourself* about what you were perceiving. That is what built your level of self-esteem. Your own unique personal feeling of worthiness was started in those early years with your own programming process; you have been building and revising it ever since with your conscious-level thoughts and feelings about yourself. Your present level of self-esteem is the cumulative result of the positive and negative rocks which your thoughts and feelings have deposited on that scale since you were born.

Feelings of worthiness, value

Feelings of insignificance, uselessness

Self-esteem is a matter of degree. You don't either have it or not have it. You are somewhere on a scale or continuum, ranging from the very negative to the very positive—from low to high self-esteem. The person who excels, the high performance person, tends to function most of the time toward the upper end of the scale—most of the time feels a very real, honest, positive sense of personal worth and value.

The person at the low end of the scale is convinced that he is worthless, insignificant, unlikable. He is unsure of his abilities, eager to stay close to home—to do things that are familiar and easy. He "knows" there isn't much chance that he will do anything very useful, is uncomfortable when given a compliment or praise, feels little control over his future, and is sure things will get worse in the future. Unfortunately, there are a great many people in this world who live with that kind of self-image—who genuinely, honestly, deeply *feel* that way about themselves. Negative as it may be, it's "the way things are" for a lot of people. It's easy enough to see how that kind of "REALITY" applies the brakes to a person's effectiveness.

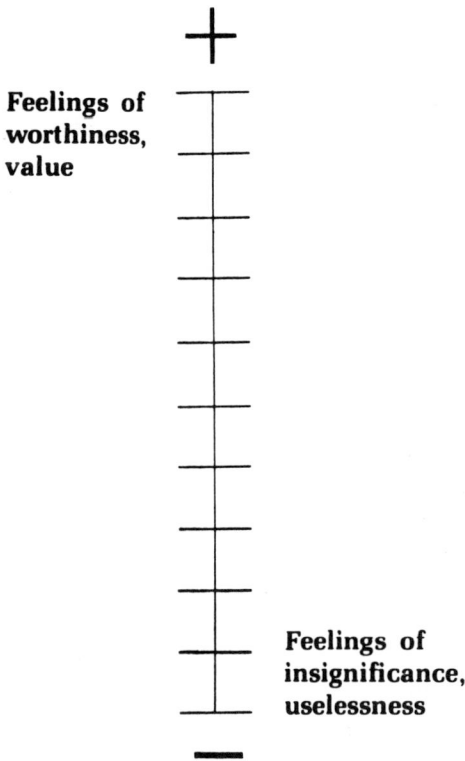

As you reflect on how it must feel to have such a low level of self-esteem, think about the kinds of messages or signals that a person might receive from his environment, from other significant human beings, that might stimulate the thoughts and feelings at a conscious level which cumulatively would develop into that sort of self-image profile—the kinds of self-talk or inner thought processes which would build such a negative "REALITY" about one's self.

Now let's turn to a more positive self-esteem level. How does a person at the high end of this scale deeply, honestly feel down inside about the self? Valuable. Important. Worthy of respect and consideration. Able to influence others. The high-self-esteem person enjoys new and challenging tasks and expects things to go well in the future. That's a little more refreshing and, I hope, a little easier for you to identify with.

Note that self-esteem is not quite the same as self-confidence. You may have a great deal of confidence in yourself in a particular area, or with respect to a particular activity, even though your overall level of self-esteem is rather low. On the other hand, a person can have a very high self-esteem level and still lack confidence in specific departments such as public speaking or painting pictures. *Self-confidence* is more narrowly focused on a particular skill or type of situation. *Self-esteem* is a deeper feeling that you have about yourself, about your value as a person.

If you have a solid base of self-esteem, it is much more likely that you will develop confidence in your ability to handle various skills and circumstances.

Right now, you are somewhere on the scale of zero to one hundred—negative to positive—self-esteem. Ask yourself for a moment whether it might be profitable, worthwhile, desirable to move up that scale—to move in the direction of a more accurate, more valid, more honest appraisal of the real worth, value, significance that you do have. If you can accept the possibility that you may genuinely *be* a very worthy, valuable human being, then might it not be valuable to take some deliberate action steps to move in the direction of greater self-acceptance—a more honest feeling of self-worth?

Here are some ways to do that—some simple techniques or methods that you can put into action right away that will take you in that direction.

The first is simply a practical application of Constructive Imagination. Build a positive affirmation about your worthiness and include it in your list of images that you are reinforcing every day. Define exactly what self-esteem means to *you;* then translate it into an affirmation. An example is, "I like and respect myself. I am a worthy, valuable person." As you work with that affirmation, let yourself experience—in your imagination—how it feels to be in a real situation, *knowing* that you are worthwhile, valuable, and significant. It might be a staff meeting, a party, an outing with your family, or a sales interview. Project yourself into that event and let the *feeling* of self-esteem flow through your system.

You can re-experience an event in which you felt very good about yourself, reinforcing that positive experience. Or think of a situation in which you felt badly about the way you handled things and re-live it in your imagination on a more positive level. Handle the entire scene well, and let *yourself* feel good about *you.* Feel the warm, joyful glow of pride and satisfaction.

Another way to move up the self-esteem scale is to decide that you are going to spend a little more time dwelling on your successes—the things you feel *good* about having done—and less time wallowing in errors and failures. When you do a good job, feel good about it! Not only does that increase the probability that you will repeat that excellent performance, but it also helps you to feel better about yourself as a person. When things go badly (they will still do that), avoid the temptation to wallow in the error or failure. There's a world of difference between *having failed* and *being a failure*—a lot of difference between *having done something badly* and *being bad!*

There is a pair of very useful words which can serve as an "anti-wallowing" device if you want to use them. Nothing magical about them, but they can very easily help you to shift gears from berating yourself and wallowing in the error to a more positive kind of programming.

NEXT TIME

When something goes badly, recognize what has happened—acknowledge the error—and then shift into the thought about how you will handle that kind of situation should it ever happen again. I am not suggesting at all that it is desirable or useful to *ignore* your errors or failures. Certainly you will occasionally stub your toe or do something that just doesn't work out very well. There will be times when you will not close the sale or you will not make the part exactly according to specifications. You may say something to one of your children (or to your mate) that you realize later wasn't really what you wanted to say, or the way that you wanted to say it. When that happens, you have a choice. You can wallow in the error, feeling bad with, "Oh boy, am I stupid!" or "I always do things like that, what's the matter with me?", diminishing your self-esteem level. Or, you can *use* the error to do a better job in the future. Instead of wallowing in "how awful it was," or "how dumb I was," or "how clumsy I was," look at that particular situation and think, "Well, that didn't work out very well; next time here's how I'll handle it differently." **Pre-program the system** so that should that same kind of event come up again you are ready to handle it in a more productive, more effective manner.

When you are tempted to hang a negative label on yourself, there is another useful phrase which can help you to remind yourself of the fact that you are constantly changing.

UP UNTIL NOW.....

Instead of, "I just can't make speeches!" it will be more accurate and more helpful to change to, "Up until

now, it hasn't been easy for me to speak to groups."
You are constantly changing, and there is no reason at
all why the way that you have done things in the past
will be the way that you will do them in the future.

Allowing your thoughts and feelings about yourself
to move in a positive direction is particularly important
the last few minutes at night, just before you go to
sleep.

I think it is very likely—and very tragic—that hundreds of thousands, perhaps millions of people lie in bed
for thirty minutes or an hour each night thinking, dwelling on, re-experiencing all of the things they have done
wrong all day—thus virtually guaranteeing that they are
going to do them all over again.

Just before you fall asleep is a very special time to be
sure that you are directing your thoughts toward the
things that you feel good about having done, or the
activities that you are looking forward to in the future.

Here's another way in which it is possible for you to
reinforce, develop, enhance your personal level of self-
esteem. You can build your own feelings of worth,
value, and significance by reinforcing and strengthening
the self-esteem of the epi-organisms of which you are a
part. Think about your family, the department in which
you work or some other group to which you belong.
Each member of the group has some feelings about the
value or significance of that epi-organism, and when you
put all of those attitudes together, you have a group
attitude—"How we feel about us."

Your family has a self-esteem level. Mom has some
feelings about the family, Dad has some, Judy, Mary,
Johnny—each member of the family has some feelings
about "our family." If you are very fortunate, you are
part of a family with a high self-esteem level, where the
prevailing attitude is, "What a terrific place to be!" or
"I'm proud and happy that I'm a part of this family. I
feel sorry for people that are not a part of a family like
this one. We love each other, we do things together and
express ourselves to each other. What a great family!"

Whatever potential exists within *that* family is likely to be flowing easily and naturally.

Unfortunately, all too frequently, we find families in which the prevailing attitude is: "How do you get out of this outfit?" That certainly says something about the self-esteem level of that group personality, and whatever potential exists within that group is probably locked up tightly. The brakes are on!

Look at this as it applies to a company. You may be part of a company—or other organization—in which the prevailing attitude is: "What a great place this is to work—I really like being here! I'm working with terrific people. We're doing important things and we're doing them well."

Your group's self-esteem level is somewhere on the scale from low to high.

If it is in the lower range of the scale, maybe it would be to your advantage to get busy and do what you can to move it up. Consider that carefully. Can you see that it will be to your personal profit and benefit to help the group feel better about itself? There are at least two important ways in which it will be to your self-interest. First, you will find it much easier to achieve your own goals if the groups within which you are living and working are functioning effectively. Second, when you know that you are a part of a winning team, you feel better about yourself and that helps to release your own abilities.

How much value will it be to the tackle on the football team to go into the huddle between plays and say to his teammates, "Boy, we are a bunch of clods!"? If you have ever played on any kind of athletic team, you know how dramatically productive it is for someone on the squad to "talk it up." It is contagious; before you know it everyone is more energetic, better coordinated, and expecting to win the game. That surge of positive self-talk within the team and the resulting feelings *do* increase the chances of victory.

Because the athletic world in our culture is so visible, it is easy to see a process like this at work in a team of professional athletes. What happens when a player is traded to the top team in a league? Whether it is in baseball, hockey, basketball or soccer, when that player puts on the uniform of the championship team, his performance improves. Just knowing that he is good enough to have been traded to the top team causes him to walk taller, play better. The new uniform doesn't change his potential—it stimulates a thought and feeling sequence which releases his brakes!

You can see this same phenomenon with certain branches of the armed services, too. Some units "know" that they are the finest—and they *act* that way when they are in combat. In every industry there are companies which have that same atmosphere of high self-esteem, and it is no coincidence that they are leading the way and attracting the best people from their competitors.

Take a very close look at this idea—again from your own selfish viewpoint. See if you could profit by spending a little more time reinforcing the positive feelings about your group. Look at the application to your family, your bowling team, your company, your department, your service club, trade association, church, community, and your country. Anything that you can do, say, express in any way that will reinforce the good feeling within that group about the group will help the group to function better, achieve its goals more easily, and help *you* to get where you want to go a lot faster.

How long has it been since you sat at the dinner table and said to your family, "I'm really proud to be a part of this family. We are really terrific!" Don't say it unless you feel that way about the family, but if you do feel it, why not express it? It may feel a little uncomfortable the first time. That goes back to some childhood programming about not expressing your emotions, but go ahead and release that brake. When you have a positive feeling about your group, *say it!* You will enjoy the results.

When the group does something badly, use NEXT TIME to avoid wallowing in the error and reinforcing it. When others in the group slip into the trap of "That's like us, we're always goofing things up!", step in, gently, with a question: "What could we do to handle situations like this better in the future?" Help the group to find a way to change the procedures which led to the difficulty so that it is less likely to happen again.

Nations have self-esteem levels, too, and they are constantly changing, just like those of individuals. A look back through the pages of history will disclose some dramatic examples of the ebb and flow of self-esteem within various nations, and the relationship between how a country felt about itself and its ability to use whatever potential it possessed. Great Britain, Russia, Germany, Israel, Japan, Mexico—as you think of each country can you see how the national self-esteem level has changed, and how that has affected progress, productivity and the effectiveness of the citizens of the country?

How valuable is it to our country—and to you as a citizen of the country—to talk about and reinforce all of the things we have done wrong? Might it not be more useful to dwell on the incredible successes of our nation and feel good about them? In those areas where we have failed, what can we do to correct the system so that if we ever encounter a similar situation again we will be more likely to handle it well?

Now let's look at how you can help other people to reinforce *their* feelings of self-esteem. This may be the most exciting and productive way of building your own feelings of value and worth. One of the interesting peculiarities of this basic releasing mechanism is that the more you give away to other people, the more you get! The more you reinforce, enhance, undergird the self-esteem of the other people in your world, the better *you* like *you*. The reverse is also true, and perhaps even more obvious. Anything I do to cause you to dislike yourself creates an uneasy feeling within me about myself.

So, one of the ways that you can build your own personal self-esteem level is by helping others to build and reinforce theirs. And, there is an extra bonus benefit to this process. By providing other people the opportunity to enhance the positive feelings they have about themselves, you are enriching your environment.

Pause for a moment and think about the dozen most important people in your world—the people you live with, work with, have frequent contact with on a social level. Who are the twelve most important, significant other human beings in your world? They might include a mate, your children, people with whom you work closely in your professional or vocational activity, close friends or neighbors. Think about those people for a moment and ask yourself this question, "What would it mean to me if those individuals, in the next month, really, honestly, deeply liked themselves better?" What would that mean to you? Would it be useful, to your advantage—or would it be harmful, unpleasant? Would it be a plus or a minus if those people with whom you interact every day, people with whom you have daily contact, were to move up that self-esteem scale and really like themselves better?

I feel certain that as you think about this idea you will see that life is a lot easier when you are dealing with people who have a high level of self-esteem. Instead of working (or living) with people who are defensive, withdrawn, inclined to "shift the blame," you have a more open, honest, trusting relationship with mutually set goals and more direct communication. Much more exciting, positive things happen when people who have an abundance of self-esteem are working together. Try this. Set yourself a project in the next month. Pick out specific people with whom you have regular, frequent contact, and decide that you are going to do whatever you can to help those individuals to genuinely, honestly feel better about themselves.

How do you do that? By spending more time and effort putting those people up, and less time and effort putting them down.

An exercise that you may want to test came from one of our *PACE* Youth Conferences. One of the most important—and exciting—programs which my organization offers is a Conference for teen-agers in which we explore the entire *PACE* framework as it applies to young people. In the summer of 1968, one of the participants in a *PACE* Youth program created this exercise and called it "The No Put-down Game." The way to play it is simply to time yourself and see how long you can go without putting anyone down. Can you go for fifteen minutes? An hour? It may not be as easy as it seems.

The rules prohibit putting anyone down, out loud, including yourself, even in jest. The "joking" put-down is outlawed because it usually has a sharp barb attached to it. It is certainly possible to tease someone in a warm, loving way, but to rule out the possibility that the teasing, joking put-down is just a clever way of sneaking in a little dig, avoid it as you play this game. Moreover, this is an individual, personal, private project. Do not tell anyone else what you are doing; just time yourself and see how long you can go. You are only working on *yourself*! Calling another person's attention to the fact that he has just put someone down is a put-down, even if you were the one being attacked.

When you find out how long you can go without any put-downs, then see if you can break your record. See if you can go for a longer period next time.

At the same time, develop the habit of putting other people *up* instead of down. See what happens if instead of undermining other people you reinforce their good feelings about themselves. Be alert to the positive feelings that you have about another person. Be aware of what is going on inside of you and when you feel a sense of admiration or regard or warmth for another person, go ahead and express it. You will be delighted with the results. As you spend a little more time putting people up and less time putting them down, you will not only be enhancing your environment, but you will find yourself liking you better, too. You will be building *your* feelings of self-esteem as you develop the ability to reinforce the positive qualities of others.

In your dealings with other human beings, you always accomplish a great deal more by praising the qualities that you admire than you can ever accomplish by criticizing those that you condemn. I'm sure you have noticed that. It can be very tempting sometimes to criticize the behavior or attitudes of other people when they are doing something "wrong"—which means they are not doing it the way that you would do it. But it is much more productive to reinforce the behavior—or qualities—that you admire.

Imagine a husband and wife sitting in a restaurant. One of them says to the other, "You're not really going to eat that piece of banana cream pie, are you?" The question (and the tone of voice that goes with it) has a reinforcing effect, but probably not in the direction the person who asked it had in mind! Calling attention to behavior you do not admire and would like to see changed often has just the reverse effect. It might be better to wait until the other person passes up dessert to comment on that in a positive manner. "I know how much you like desserts, honey, and I really admire your decision to not have any."

If you are in a management role, or if you are a parent, you will occasionally encounter situations in which someone under your supervision has done something badly. Your child crawled up on the counter, reached for a cookie, and broke the cookie jar. Something needs to be said, but what the child does *not* need is to have someone tell him, "You broke the cookie jar!" He knows that. He's already aware of the fact that the cookie jar is broken, and he probably feels bad about it. Now there are a lot of little pieces of ceramic mixed in with the cookies and they don't taste as good. So, he's upset enough with himself and with the situation without having someone help him to feel worse about what he's done.

What he needs is some help in how to handle this kind of project differently—better—NEXT TIME. He needs some loving, coaching guidance about how to get cookies without breaking cookie jars. It might be more productive to say, "Next time, get a taller chair," or "Next time, call me and I'll get the cookie for you." Sometimes a question can be valuable. "That didn't work out so well, did it? How could you handle that differently the next time you want a cookie?"

A sales manager might say to one of the sales people,

"When the telephone rang in the middle of your pre-sentation, you lost your momentum and never quite got back on track. Next time a phone call breaks your stride, how can you handle it better? What can you do to get back on track and close the sale?" In many cases it will be desirable to give your opinion about something which might work well next time. Above all, be sure to discuss the *activity* or the *behavior,* not the *person.* The coaching kind of helpfulness on the part of a manager or parent is more likely to be in the category of a "next time" message and an expression of opinion, rather than advice.

Before we leave self-esteem, there is one other puzzle it will be valuable to examine. What about the person who has so much self-esteem that you can't stand him? I suspect that if you really think about that person, the one who is always bragging and boasting about past accomplishments, you will probably find that you are not dealing with someone who has an overabun-dance of self-esteem. Chances are that a person who blows his horn all the time is pretty near to the lower end of the self-esteem scale.

the person who seems to be off the top of the scale is, more likely, compensating for low self-esteem.

Here is someone whose "REALITY" structure is saying, "I know that I am worthless; and if anybody else ever really knew me, they wouldn't like me either. So, I can't let that happen." He presents a facade self, a false front. Talking con-stantly about something that he has done well, he tries desperately to con-vince others that he may have some value—and at the same time, he is trying to convince himself! Of course, the transparent facade evokes a flood of messages from other people that they don't admire the fraudulence, the falseness; and so he tries harder and harder to be a likable person and to pretend that he is more worthwhile than he really believes that he is.

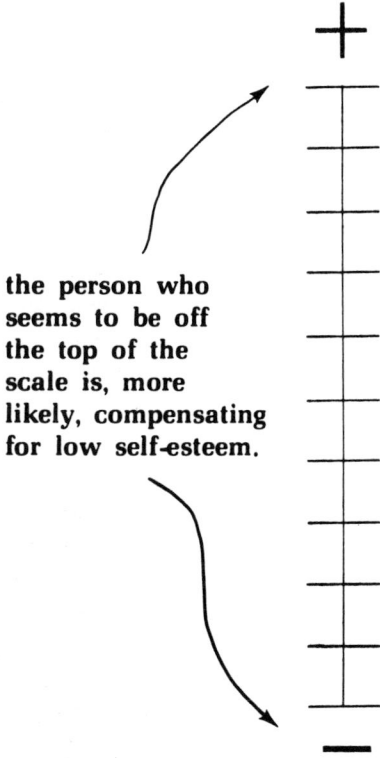

If you have someone in your world who is trying to compensate for low self-esteem with bragging and conceit, your natural inclination may be to get out your needle and see if you can pop his balloon. When someone is blowing his horn all the time there seems to be an almost automatic urge to whittle him down to size. But the reverse approach is much more productive. It may not be easy, but if you think it through you will find that it is much more profitable. If you will devote some time and effort to reinforcing that person's inner feeling of value and significance, you will find that the bragging diminishes.

That may be just the opposite of your initial impulse, but try it. When you run across someone who seems to be trying very hard to impress everyone, look for something that the person does that you feel good about. Find something that you can genuinely, honestly, sincerely compliment. Not flattery, but something about that person—his taste in shoes, the idea he presented at the staff meeting—that you admire, and express that positive feeling to the person. Express your admiration instead of reinforcing the low self-esteem by reacting negatively to his bragging. Remember that how you feel as you do this is what really counts. Set aside the external behavior of that person for a moment and acknowledge the true worth and value that is there if he will only let it out.

Another possible indication that a person may be at the lower end of the self-esteem scale is a negative reaction to compliments. That is not a universally dependable symptom, but it can often provide an interesting clue that a person's self-esteem is sagging. When you admire a person's clothing, saying, "That's certainly an attractive jacket you are wearing," the response of, "Oh, this old thing?" may tell you something about how he feels about himself—especially if the jacket is obviously brand-new. When a person is uncomfortable about a compliment, what is probably happening in his mental system is, "I know I have terrible taste, and here is someone telling me that my jacket is attractive." The conflict between what he is perceiving and his "REALITY" is uncomfortable.

Sometimes people don't wait for the compliment to run themselves down. "I'm sorry that I look so awful today," or, "I'm sorry the house is such a mess." You might not have noticed if they hadn't brought it up!

So, one possible signal which can tell you something about a person's self-esteem is his response to a compliment. If you say to a person with very *high* self-esteem, "You really did a fantastic job on that project, Shirley," what will her response be? Probably a simple, "Thank you." Or perhaps, "Thank you. I appreciate your saying that. I feel pretty good about it myself." Praise is more acceptable to the person with a solid sense of personal worth, because it is consistent with what he knows and feels about himself.

You are "they"

The next symptom of excellence we want to examine is probably the most basic, most essential, and most universal attribute of the high performer. In a very real sense, this entire book—the entire *PACE* philosophy and method—is based upon the concept that we are now approaching. I urge you to study this chapter with special care. Re-read it, discuss it, challenge and test the ideas you are about to encounter. They can provide you with the most exciting, productive and immediate releasing mechanism!

The label that I will use for this quality is **responsibility,** but what that label stands for can, as with all words, mean something quite different to one person than it means to another. My first objective will be to define or clarify just how this term is being used—the meaning it is intended to convey.

> RESPONSIBILITY IS THE DEGREE TO WHICH A PERSON FEELS COMFORTABLE WITH THE FACT THAT HE/SHE LIVES WITH—AND IN THAT SENSE IS ACCOUNTABLE FOR—THE CONSEQUENCES OF HIS/HER BEHAVIOR

Let's explore that definition in a little more detail just to be sure that we are on the same track.

We start with the basic principle that nearly all of your behavior is volitional—conscious choices, decisions, selections of the most desirable (or least undesirable) alternative available to you. Sometimes your behavior is more automatic—more toward the subconscious, pre-programmed *reaction* department of the mental system. Whether what you are doing is clearly of a conscious decision-making nature or more like a conditioned reflex, **you** have built the "REALITY" structure on which that behavior is based, and **you** live with the consequences of those actions and reactions.

This is a little like the law of gravity in the world of physics. It is simply the way things are—a dependable principle that always works. If you don't like the law of gravity—or don't believe in it—it goes right on working anyway. We did not get to the moon by violating the law of gravity, but by understanding it and putting it to use to help us achieve a goal.

The law of accountability is equally immutable in the field of human behavior. It goes on working, whether or not you know about it, accept it or like it. And the better you understand it, the more positively you **feel** about it, the easier it becomes for whatever potential you have to flow effectively and productively.

Look at the **Responsibility Continuum.** After you have examined it carefully, go back and reread the definition on page 171.

The person who is very high on this scale is not just *comfortable* about the fact that his behavior is taking him where he is going—he is *excited* about it! Wouldn't have it any other way! And, as a direct result of this very positive **feeling,** the responsible person is in a position to correct for errors and reinforce

Very enthusiastic about the fact that your decisions, actions and reactions have brought you to where you now are, and are taking you where you are going.

Able to recognize that you are making decisions (or neglecting to do so) and that your behavior influences your progress.

Convinced that external forces are in control — other people or the hidden, mystical forces of "luck" — and that what you say or do is completely impotent in its effect on your destiny.

RESPONSIBILITY CONTINUUM

successes. This is the essence of why this quality has such a profound effect on a person's ability to use his potential. When things go *well,* you are able to *feel good* about whatever part you played in the success, and thus *reinforce* the behavior that *worked!* When things go badly, you are able to acknowledge the error—"I blew it!"—and then think about how you might handle such situations differently, better, NEXT TIME. Reinforce successes—correct for errors.

Think about the first time you pitched a horseshoe, tossed a ring at a peg, or shot with bow and arrow. Chances are that the first time you tried you were quite a bit off target. If your first attempt fell short, you thought about how you could correct for that and then tried again, probably coming a little closer to the target. As you found out what worked, and what didn't, the pattern got tighter and tighter. Your performance improved, largely because you were accepting full personal responsibility for the consequences of your behavior.

If you had transferred the responsibility to someone else, or to "circumstances" or "luck," there would have been little or no improvement. When you think you have had a "lucky shot," you don't think about what **you** did well so that you will do it again. You just hope that you will have another lucky shot sometime.

A person at the lower end of this scale—the nonresponsible person—responds to his successes and failures as events which have happened because of some external force. When things go well, he thanks his lucky stars, sees the success as a lucky break, or is grateful that "they" let him have a win. When things go badly, he responds with, "Just my luck!", blames the failure on the fact that he walked under a ladder, or resents the fact that "they" did him in. This person is usually very superstitious and his motto in life is: "If at first you don't succeed. . . . fix the blame fast!"

But even worse, he fixes the blame for his successes, too! There is no reinforcement of effective behavior and no correction for errors. Only a great many superstitious rituals and taboos, and the all-consuming hobby of getting "them" shaped up—a very difficult, frustrating task which further limits his effectiveness.

There are signals which can tell you something about where you are on this *Responsibility Continuum.* They are language signals—verbal indicators you can watch for in your thinking or in your conversation with others.

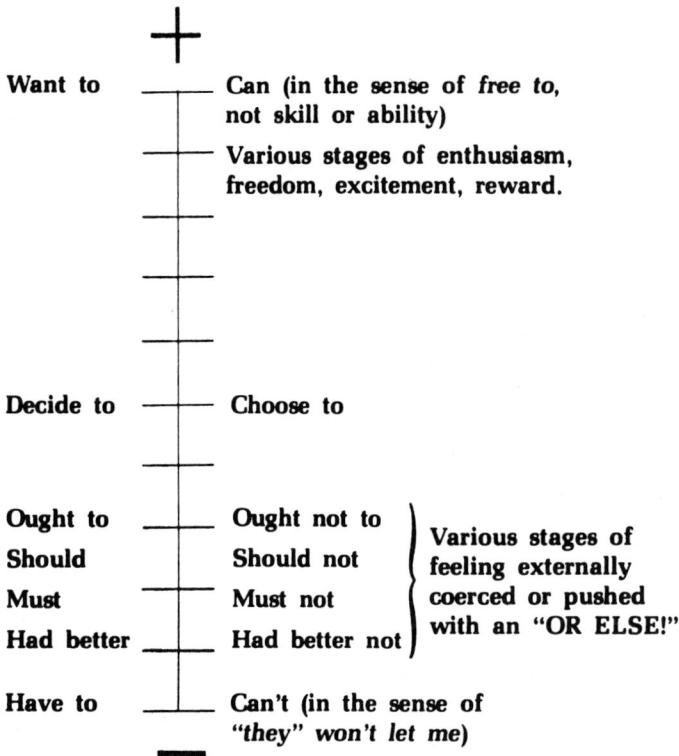

If you examine that scale carefully, you will find that everything below the mid-point (*decide to/choose to*) is false and non-responsible. However, to the degree that you have adopted this framework within your "REALITY" structure as valid, "the way things are," then, of course, you will behave in a manner which reflects that "REALITY." Just as people who "knew" that the earth was flat behaved as though they lived on a flat earth, people who know that the entire continuum is an accurate representation of the real world will behave that way. I believe that most people today accept the entire continuum in the diagram.

Want to	Can (in the sense of *free to*, not skill or ability)
	Various stages of enthusiasm, freedom, excitement, reward.
Decide to	Choose to
Ought to	Ought not to
Should	Should not
Must	Must not
Had better	Had better not
Have to	Can't (in the sense of "they" won't let me)

Various stages of feeling externally coerced or pushed with an "OR ELSE!"

Thus, non-responsible behavior is predictable—inevitable.

I do not expect you to pounce on this idea and immediately accept it. You have been so thoroughly immersed in a world which regards the lower end of that scale as valid that this may very well require a substantial revision of the way you see yourself and your behavior. But, stick with it! As you grasp this idea and become increasingly comfortable with it you will find it to be the most exciting releasing device you have ever encountered!

Let's look at some extreme examples of this principle. Most of our discussion throughout this book is focused on high-performance activity, but for a moment I want to deviate from that approach. A look at people with the brakes pulled back about as far as they will go may help to explain why this concept is so critically important.

Some years ago when I was in college I had the opportunity to observe a patient in the Missouri State Mental Hospital who had moved all the way to the bottom of the *Responsibility Continuum.* Charlie "knew" that there was a gang in Chicago who controlled his behavior with a very complicated "machine." He could tell you all about the machine, the dials, gauges, switches, and buttons, and he could listen in on the gang's deliberations and discussions. He was entirely under their control. Everything that Charlie did—from getting out of bed in the morning to falling asleep at night—he *had to* do. And everything that he did not do he knew that he *could not* do. The OR ELSE! in Charlie's case was a migraine headache. If he disobeyed instructions from the gang in Chicago, they would push a button on the machine and Charlie would immediately suffer the terribly painful symptoms of a very real migraine headache.

Of course, there was no gang, and there was no machine—except in Charlie's "REALITY" structure. He had so vividly experienced their existence in his imagination that they had become completely real to him. It made perfectly good, logical sense to Charlie that there were eight men in Chicago who had nothing else to do, twenty-four hours a day, but to decide what he had to do and what he could not do.

If someone said, "Come on, Charlie, it's lunch time. Let's go eat," he might reply, "I can't eat lunch yet. They are having a conference about that now." Then, a few minutes later Charlie would say, "I have to go eat lunch now." And off he would go to the cafeteria. He would put his tray on the rails and move from station to station, awaiting instructions from Chicago about what he had to eat today. He sometimes had some strange combinations of foods on his tray—but he had to eat every bite, OR ELSE!

After lunch one day someone suggested, "Let's go into the lounge and listen to the radio, Charlie." He reacted immediately, "No. I can't listen to the radio at all today. I have to go outside now and walk around the old willow tree fourteen times and await further instructions."

This was an extreme, pathological case. Charlie's "REALITY" had become severely distorted. But do you see that he had, progressively over the years, moved all the way to complete non-responsibility? He could not receive the credit for anything that he did well, nor the blame for anything that he did badly. If he didn't show up for breakfast, if he neglected to make his bed, if he threw his dinner on the floor or violated a rule of the institution, no one could blame Charlie—take it up with the gang in Chicago!

Now certainly you don't believe that there is a gang in Chicago controlling your behavior. But look very carefully and honestly at the possibility that you occasionally slip across that center line into various degrees of non-responsibility. As soon as you cross that line—in your *thinking*—you are pretending that someone else is in partial control of your system. Not only is that inaccurate and non-responsible, but the impact on your behavior—your effectiveness—can be disastrous. What are some of the behavioral consequences as you move into the lower range of that scale? Whatever it is that you are doing—going to work, getting married, eating lunch, cleaning the garage, studying for an examination, writing a letter, terminating an employee, or countless other activities—to the degree that your attitude is toward the lower end of the scale, these are some of the predictable results:

1. You will tend to procrastinate. When you feel *pushed* (even if you yourself are doing the pushing) you will *push back,* resist the pressure. You will find creative "reasons" for putting off that activity until later. You will discover other pursuits which are suddenly much more important.

2. When you do get around to doing it, you will find the task more distasteful than it really needs to be. You will feel such emotions as resentment, anger, frustration, and disgust, both toward the task and toward "they" who are forcing you into such an unpleasant activity. All of those negative, braking emotions will severely limit your effectiveness, and your relationship with whoever "they" are.

3. You will not perform as well as you are capable of performing. You will be inclined to "get it over with," settling for whatever minimum level of quality that you believe is absolutely required.

4. You will not use your experiences as learning processes. Instead of correcting for errors and reinforcing successes, you will see the event as an unpleasant "nuisance" imposed upon you by "them."

5. Your awareness of available alternatives will be limited. If you have "made up your mind" that you *have to* do something, you will see only two possible courses of action: do it, or else! Life is almost never that simple. In the real world there are many alternatives open to your consideration, and since you are making the selection, it helps to be able to examine as many of those which are available as possible.

Here's an example. In a *PACE* Seminar I asked one of the participants, "Do you have to pay income tax, Ted?" His answer was classic, "No, you can always go to jail!"

Sounds so simple, doesn't it? Either this or that. Either pay income tax or go to jail. When you "know" that something is a *have to,* you will see only those two possibilities.

I asked the Seminar group, "Can you think of any other alternatives?" It was not easy to break out of that either/or lock-up, but as each new suggestion was offered it became easier to see others. Here are some which the group listed:

A. You could decide not to earn any money and go on welfare.

B. You could cheat and take your chances of being

caught. (That, they agreed, was pretty close to the "go to jail" alternative.)

C. You could move to Montana, raise your own food, and live off the land without any taxable income.

D. You could find some tax-sheltered ways of earning income.

E. If you have enough capital you could invest in tax-free municipal bonds and live on the dividends from your investment.

F. You could have so many children that your deductions make your income not taxable.

G. You could simply earn less—lowering your income below the taxable level.

H. You could commit suicide. (The group agreed that this was an even less desirable alternative than going to jail.)

I. You could move to another country where there is no income tax. One of the members of the Seminar group had a list of places—some of the Carribean islands, Lichtenstein, Costa Rica, Monaco, or Tahiti among others.

So there *are* alternatives. Some are more appealing than others, but that also depends upon the individual's background, values, and goals. The point is that if you pay federal or state income taxes it is because you have decided that, of all the courses open to you, that is the most desirable (or least undesirable) action. It is your choice.

Look at some of the other "have to" and "can't" imperative in you life. Track them down and you will see that none of them will really stand up under careful scrutiny.

What about the "if—have to" sequence? "*If* I want good grades, I *have to* study." Or, "*If* I want to keep my job, I *have to* do what the boss tells me to do." You will find that even in these cases there are other alternatives and you are, in fact, making a choice. Try substituting "because—decide to" or "because—choose to" and see how it feels. "*Because* I want good grades *I have decided to* study for this test." "*Because* I enjoy my job, *I choose to* do what the boss wants me to do."

It may occur to you as you work with this idea that the one certain "have to" is dying. In this context, we have a different usage of the words. What we are really saying is, "Death, so far as we know, is inevitable." There is no OR ELSE! implicit in this use of "have to." It is rather like saying, "The law of gravity *has to* work." A more useful expression is, "So far as we know, the law of gravity always does work."

Think of some people whom you really admire and respect. People in your profession, neighbors, relatives, nationally prominent men or women for whom you have a very high regard. As you have the opportunity to observe those people you will notice that in every instance they live their lives almost totally in the upper range of the *Responsibility Continuum.* They do what they do because it is what they want to do—or at least, because they have decided to do it—and that is one of the key reasons why they do it so much better than other people—why the potential they possess is flowing so consistently.

Then consider the people who are accomplishing little. The criminal, the assassin, the chronic non-producer. You will see that these people live in a prison of *have to, can't, should* and *ought to.* It is a psychological prison to be sure, and one which they have constructed brick by brick, bar by bar with their own thought processes. Still, it is just as limiting as any steel and concrete prison could be.

Do you recall what Jack Ruby said just after he killed Lee Harvey Oswald? "I had to do it!" We may never know all of the reasons or motives which impelled Ruby to commit that murder, but that is the typical language—the typical mode of thinking of the criminal. "Something came over me," "I couldn't help myself," "I was only following orders," "They made me do it."

Have you ever noticed a newspaper story about someone about to be released from a prison who pleaded *not* to be released? Most people find that kind of behavior puzzling—contradictory. Why would anyone want to stay in a prison when he could be out, free of the steel bars, guards, and rigidly controlled activity? Because being *free* means being *responsible*! Inside the prison nearly all the choices and decisions are made by someone else. The prisoner is told when to sleep, when to wake up, when to eat, what to eat, when to work, when to play. On the outside, one makes choices, decisions, selects alternatives—and lives with the consequences. If a man has been in the prison for a while, the prospect of making decisions can be frightening.

But that is exactly what freedom—personal liberty—is all about. The only important kind of freedom is the freedom to choose, to decide, and to live with the consequences of our behavior.

True *freedom* is the right to be *responsible*! That includes the right to succeed and the right to fail—to make decisions that help you to achieve your goals, and also to make decisions that turn out to be counterproductive. Whenever someone tries to sell you on the idea that you should let him make your choices for you, look out. Whenever someone insists on protecting you from the consequences of your behavior, tells you that he knows what is best for you better than you do and he is going to help you whether you like it or not, listen for the clanging of the prison door—you are about to be locked up! You may, of course, *choose* to follow someone else's counsel. If you regard your physician as an expert regarding your health, you may decide to accept his suggestions regarding diet, exercise, medicine, or surgery. It is when someone else's opinion of what is best for you is *forced* upon you that you are in danger of losing your freedom.

Not *all* of life is a matter of choice, though. You did not decide which parents you were going to have. If the driver behind you in traffic has a brake failure and you suffer a rear-end collision, it certainly is not because you chose to do so. When there is an earthquake, when a hurricane blows, or when lightning strikes, the people whose property is destroyed or damaged can hardly be held accountable for the forces of nature.

Yet even in those areas where dramatic unexpected changes take place in your environment or in your physical system, you are accountable for your *reactions.*

You live with the consequences of your responses to change. The event may be very negative—illness, loss of a loved one, increased taxes, theft—but your response can range all the way from a determination to take creative, constructive action to anger, depression or even suicide.

In Chapter 18 we will look at how you can re-program your reaction mechanism so that your response to pressure is automatically more positive. At this point it is important to recognize that not only in the area of overt action and decision, but also in those aspects of your life where you are *reacting* to what is happening, you live with the consequences of your behavior. How you **feel** about that fact will have a lot to do with what kind of choices you make and how well you handle the unpredictable emergencies of life.

Now let's look at what you, personally, can do to move up this scale. It won't happen instantly, but the more that you can edge upward on the *Responsibility Continuum,* the more your potential will be released, available for your use in achieving your goals.

First, use Constructive Imagination. Practice in your imagination responding to various situations in a responsible manner. A useful affirmation might be, "I am excited about the fact that my choices, decisions and reactions are guiding the direction of my life. I reinforce successes and correct for errors, using my experiences to become increasingly effective." Practice responding to real life events with that kind of attitude, in your imagination, and let the *feeling* of freedom flow through your system!

Next, watch your language. Not only in your vocal conversations, but the language of your verbal thought processes as well. Be alert for "should" and "shouldn't," "have to" and "can't" and the other prison words. When you catch yourself with one of those OR ELSE!-oriented thought sequences, pause for a moment, go back and re-phrase the same idea with "I'm going to....," "I've decided to....," or even better, "I want to...." Especially look out for the expression, "You have to.... (or should or ought to, etc.)" when the word "you" is used to include everyone in the same prison. For example, the statement, "Well, you have to make money and support your family!" is just an attempt to make that particular "have to" sound like a universal rule which applies to all mankind. A more honest expression is, "The way I see things, I have no choice but to work, earn money and support my family." Changing "I" to "you" is a subtle way to further duck the responsibility. Even in the example which I have used, there are other alternatives which are open to consideration. The more responsible expression might be, "Of the alternatives open to my consideration, the one which makes the best sense to me in the long run is to earn the money that I want to have in order to make my family comfortable and happy." Or, "I love my family and I want the best for them."

Practice the idea of reinforcing successes and correcting for errors as you release this brake. When you find yourself in the upper end of the *Responsibility Continuum,* feel good about your progress, notice the positive impact it has on your performance. When you sense that you have slipped below that center line, correct for the error. Re-phrase the sentence. Consider how you can handle that kind of situation better NEXT TIME!

Watch the news media for stories which illustrate varying degrees of responsibility. Listen to politicians, business and labor leaders, educators and other public figures and notice where they seem to be on this scale. That will help to increase your awareness and alertness to this important concept.

Now let's turn to how this applies to the epi-organism. Your family, your department, your club or any other group has a feeling about the degree to which "we are responsible for our own destiny." To the degree that the group is convinced that "they" are in charge of our future, there won't be much creativity, not much inclination to set goals, and a minimum tendency to reinforce successes and correct for errors.

In a company, for example, if the consensus is that our competition is determining where the industry is going, or that the government is running our business, or that some other "they" are in charge, then why do any thinking? Certainly there is competition, and of course there are a multitude of government regulations, but do what you can to help the group realize that even within those very real constraints, we can make choices, set goals, develop new products or services, find better ways to increase our share of the market, improve our quality and our reputation in the market place. And we, as a group, live with the consequences of our behavior.

When you hear someone in your group saying, "We can't do that, they won't let us," or "We have to do it this way," step in and ask, "What are all the alternatives available to us?" and "Which course of action will really take us where we want to go?"

If you want to do so, you can have a powerful effect on the degree to which your group feels comfortable about the fact that "we are taking us where we are going." Everything you do to strengthen that attitude will help you to achieve your own personal goals that much faster.

How about other individuals whom you care about? What can you do to help someone else who looks to you for leadership and guidance to release this very fundamental brake? I have two suggestions—both very simple. Not always *easy,* but very simple to state. First, give that person the opportunity to make specific, clear-cut choices, in increasingly significant areas, and permit the person to live with the consequences of those choices.

Whether it is your child, mate, employee, or any other person, look for opportunities to test this idea. With a small child, for example, you might ask, "Would you like to have tomato juice or orange juice for breakfast?" Or, if you have several options to offer, present them all. Then, when the child has made the choice, stick with it.

"*I want orange juice.*"

"*Okay, here is your orange juice.*"

"*I changed my mind. I'd rather have tomato juice.*"

"Sorry, it's too late for that. You chose orange juice and that is what you have. Now you have another choice. You can drink the orange juice or not drink it—and you will also live with the consequences of that *choice."*

Simple? Indeed it is. But what difference does it make? Why not let the child have the tomato juice? This has nothing to do with causing the parent some inconvenience—it is entirely in the category of a step-by-step training process to help the child learn about choices and consequences. It is an application which can be employed at a very early age. You would not, of course, offer a choice which could lead to disaster, or which you might not be able to see through to its conclusion. Remember, the purpose is to help the person learn—and to feel comfortable with—the principle that we do select alternatives and live with consequences. For most parents, allowing a child to "suffer" the consequences of behavior can be very painful, but in the long run it may save a much worse pain.

When my son was about eight years old he had saved enough money to buy a model airplane. We had put together some models as a joint effort, but he had decided that he would assemble this one by himself. He had worked hard to earn and save the money, spent two or three hours at the hobby store deciding on which kit he wanted, and finally went to his room to work on his project. He knew that I was available to help if he needed me, but this was a special "first"—the first model that he would assemble all by himself.

A few minutes after he had started, I happened to walk by his bedroom. As I glanced in, there was Jim, carefully gluing the wing on to the fuselage—backwards! I still remember the wrenching feeling I had as I kept on walking and let him go ahead and make the mistake. My impulse was to go in and help him— whether he liked it or not! Somehow I was able to resist that impulse and I am certain that he learned more from the mistake than he could possibly have learned if I had obeyed my impulse to "protect" him from the consequences of his behavior.

He learned something about accountability. He learned that someone would not always be available to bail him out when he goofed. And he had another very important learning experience—if all else fails, read the directions. How much better to learn that very valuable principle with a model airplane than to learn it later in life with an automobile.

Here's another example that you can try if you are a parent. At some point in your child's life give him or her the complete responsibility for a bicycle. It may take some delicate judgment to decide when the child is ready for that, and it will somewhat depend upon what other experiences or training he has had with responsibility. But somewhere along the line, tell him that the bicycle he has been given is really *his* property and *his* responsibility.

"We're not going to give you any more bicycles; this is the last one. If you take care of it you may be able to put some money with it and trade it for another one some day. But it is **your** *bicycle. You can leave it out in the rain, take it apart and never put it together again, trade it for a frog, or keep it oiled and polished. It is really up to you. If something happens to your bicycle, you will walk a lot—not because we are punishing you, but because that will be the direct consequence of your behavior."*

You might want to "insure" the bicycle. If something happens which, in your judgment, is beyond the child's control—the bike is locked in the garage but someone breaks in and steals it—then you will replace it; but if it is left lying out in the front yard all night and is stolen, then the "insurance" doesn't apply.

You certainly would not give this kind of responsibility to a four-year-old. You might at age twelve or fourteen. I hope that you will get around to it before your child is thirty-five! The goal is: the sooner the better. The earlier in life a child understands and feels comfortable with the idea that his decisions and actions are taking him where he is going, the more likely he is to grow into an effective, high performance adult.

One of the most valuable favors you can do for your children is to help them grasp this concept. It will be to your self-interest to get this message across while the child is still young. It can be very painful to a parent to see his or her teenager stumbling into all kinds of difficulties because of a lack of understanding about the importance of long-range consequences.

The other suggestion that I have for helping another person to release this braking mechanism is, for most of us, a lot easier to understand than it is to practice. Make it safe to make a mistake.

That doesn't mean make it rewarding or desirable to make an error, but establish the atmosphere and the relationship within which that other person can easily and freely acknowledge that he or she has done something badly—and thus be in a position to correct for the error.

Several years ago I saw a "humorous" sign hanging in a business office. It was supposed to be funny, and I suppose the reason people laughed when they saw it was because it was so close to being true. The sign said:

> TO ERR IS HUMAN.
> TO FORGIVE IS NOT COMPANY POLICY.

This attitude, which is so common in organizations (and in families) can be traced back to the restrictive conditioning of childhood which we discussed in Chapter 8. You may have learned as a child that you *have to* do things "right"—you can't make mistakes! When you did something which "they" did not approve of, you received a disapproving frown, scolding, or perhaps physically painful punishment. If that was where it stopped, all you learned was that doing something which others didn't like usually led to emotionally or physically unpleasant consequences.

In its extreme form this can lead to a constant level of anxiety and a continuous inclination to watch for other people's reactions to be sure that "they" approve before speaking or acting. It can even result in an unwillingness to do *anything,* for fear that it might be "wrong."

If your childhood environment was one in which those in authority—parents, teachers, etc.—accepted your errors as a normal part of your growth and development, and helped you to learn from them, this will be much easier for you to do with your own children, your employees, mate, and others whom you care about.

To the degree that you programmed your "REAL-ITY" structure with "you have to do things right!" and/or "you can't make mistakes!"—complete with the OR ELSE! feelings that go with *have to* and *can't*—you will find yourself feeling some anxiety when you "make a mistake." You will feel a similar anxiety when anyone else does something "wrong." Because of that anxiety, you will be more inclined to *punish* (get that person shaped up) than to *help* the person to learn from the experience.

When it is dangerous to make a mistake—in your home or your vocational environment—errors *increase.* When people are trying hard not to make mistakes, they are much more likely to make them. And the tendency to "shift the blame" to others increases, with an understandable decrease in morale and productivity. Worst of all, in that kind of atmosphere people do not *correct* for their errors, so they go right on making the same mistakes again and again.

Use Constructive Imagination to develop your ability to allow other people to learn from their errors. Eliminate "should have," and "if only." Instead of conveying the feeling of disapproval, make it safe for that person to acknowledge the error and help him to think about how it could be handled better next time.

Usually when someone "goofs" he knows it—and doesn't like it. It feels a lot better to do something well. If he needs any help at all it is a *coaching* kind of help— some guidance about how he might change behavior in the future. That may take the form of a question: "If something like that were to happen again, how do you suppose you could handle it differently?" Or it may be appropriate for you to offer your opinion about how it could be done in a better way.

My dear (and wise) friend, Betty Peters, helped me to understand the important difference between *advice* and *opinion.* Look at this carefully; it can have a profound effect on your leadership and on your relationships with others. Advice has strings attached to it. If I give you some advice, you'd better follow it, or else! If you don't follow my advice I will feel resentment and anger—which, of course, is more damaging to *me* than anyone else! If you don't follow my advice and what you do doesn't work out very well, then I will probably tell you, "I told you so," every hour on the hour for the rest of your life. That won't do much for our relationship either!

An opinion, on the other hand, is a free gift. If I give you my opinion, you may do anything with it that you want to do. You may ignore it, laugh at it, use part of it, or accept and use it all. In effect, I am saying to you, "You are much closer to this situation and much more involved in it than I am. You have different experiences and values influencing your decision and your behavior. And you are the one who will live with the consequences of your actions. So, here is an opinion, based upon *my* unique package of experiences. Examine and consider it if you want to do so, and use whatever part of it that seems to make sense to you."

The fact that you *label* something as an opinion is not what counts, of course. The question really is: how do you **feel** about it? If there is a feeling of freedom—that the other person may choose his own course of action, do what *he* thinks is best for *him*—then what you are offering is an opinion. If you find yourself thinking/ feeling that the other person *should, ought to, must,* etc., what you are giving is advice. You are putting yourself in charge of that other person's behavior.

You will do that certainly with a small child. The parent *is* responsible for the survival and well being of a baby. But shift that responsibility to the other person just as quickly as you can do so. Not only will it help the other person to grow; it will accelerate your own growth and build a lasting relationship of mutual respect as well.

With another adult, try to stay on the *opinion* track. Provide that other person the freedom to function—the freedom to decide and to live with the consequences.

Building better bridges

As you read these words, you and I are engaged in one of the most fascinating, complex, and difficult of all human endeavors—we are communicating.

In this instance I am the one who is sending a message and you are the receiver. We are both working on the project of getting an idea across the space which exists between our systems. You devote a great deal of time and effort every day to the process of communication, both on the sending and receiving ends of the activity. Much of your success in every part of your life, particularly in your direct relationships with other people, depends on how well you practice this art or skill.

I would like to explore the communication process with you. What is it, what kind of media do we use, why do people often not understand each other, and what, exactly, can you do to build better bridges of understanding between you and the other people in your world?

Our difficulties with the communication process start with the fact that we have not yet discovered a way to transplant an idea. We can transplant a kidney, a cornea, or a heart, but so far we do not have any way of transplanting an idea! There is no closed circuit cable between your head and mine across which we can transfer what is happening in one brain to another. Thus if we are to communicate we need to find some vehicle or medium with which we can convey the idea.

Doubtless the first such medium to be used by human beings was the system which we now call nonverbal communication, or "body language." Gestures, postures, physical contact, and facial expressions must have been the way that the cave men and women conveyed their ideas to each other. Next came verbal or symbolic communication. Sounds or designs were agreed upon to "stand for" ideas at various levels of abstraction. Then followed the extraverbal system of exchange—the meaning which could be added to the verbal symbols with inflection, tone, loudness, and speed.

When we send a written message to someone else we are limited to the verbal and extraverbal channels. A letter or memo is made up of word symbols; if we want to do so we can add some meaning by underscoring or punctuating the sentences. Generally we are able to convey a richer meaning with a telephone conversation, because the extraverbal inflections are a lot clearer than they can be in a letter. Of course, the most complete mixture of messages is conveyed in a face-to-face interaction.

The sender starts off with an idea which he wants to get across to the receiver. There is some goal which he believes can be better achieved if the other person has some grasp of that idea. The sender "encodes" his idea into symbols which stand for what he has in his mental system, adds a tone of voice, facial expression, posture, or gesture, and sends the coded message to the receiver. The sender's code book is, of course, *his* "REALITY" structure. In trying to convey his idea to another person he can only use the symbols and signals which he has already experienced and assimilated into his own unique "REALITY."

When the message reaches the receiver, he tends to pay attention in direct ratio to the value it seems to have to him. Both sending and receiving are purposeful, goal-directed, selfish activities. To the degree that the

receiver becomes aware of the message, he then consults *his* code book—his equally unique "REALITY" structure—in an effort to find meaning in what he is perceiving. The image or idea in the mental system of the receiver is never identical to the sender's idea—because they have different code books! The receiver may have a very clear, vivid image in his thinking, and it may seem as though it is exactly what the sender intended, but that is impossible.

No matter how hard we try, how much time we invest, how much we care about each other, or how important a particular project may be to both of us, we will never achieve a perfect match between what *you* are thinking and what *I* am thinking. The words, gestures, postures, inflections, and tones will never trigger exactly the same images and experiences in your system that they stimulate in mine. We have had different encounters with those symbols and signals and different emotions will be connected to them in my system than in yours.

This morning as I was walking along the street in our neighborhood, I saw a dog in the driveway of the house next door.

Look at what happened in your thinking as you read that sentence. Did you get an image of what happened? What kind of dog did you picture in your thoughts? The chance that your picture is anything like the one I have is pretty slim. We could spend a lot of time discussing the breed, gender, size, configuration, color, and other characteristics of the dog I saw, but no matter how much time we spent and how much detail I gave you, we would never achieve an exact match. You have had different experiences with dogs than I have had, hundreds of different experiences. You have some very different feelings about dogs, and no matter how we work at it, we can never go back and re-program either your "REALITY" or mine.

If we use the word *understanding* to mean the degree to which what you have going on in your mental system matches what I have going on in mine, we can make some real progress in the direction of more meaningful communication. Understanding is a matter of degree, not an absolute that you either have or do not have. This puts an entirely new light on such expressions as, "Do you understand me?" "Have you got that?" "Have I made myself clear?" Those questions are not only useless; they are downright dangerous! If you ask one of those questions and get a "Yes" answer, it can give you a very false and perilous sense of security.

A better procedure is to invite a more expressive feedback. "What do you understand from what I just said?" Or, "I'm not sure that came out the way that I intended; would you mind telling me how you understood it?"

The important point is this: perfect understanding is an impossible and frustrating objective. The legitimate goal to strive for is a meaningful, profitable, adequate *level* of understanding which will make it possible for us to work together, live together, get the job done, close the sale, run a business, or whatever it is that we are working on together.

With that objective in mind, let's see what the emotional releasing mechanism is which will allow you to make productive use of your potential as a high performance communicator.

WHO BEARS THE RESPONSIBILITY?

SENDER

RECEIVER

When two people are communicating, who is responsible for seeing to it that an adequate level of understanding has been reached? What do you think? Much more important, how do you **feel** about that?

When you are the sender, how much of the responsibility are you willing to assume? How much do you assign to the receiver? When you are on the receiving end, to what degree do you see yourself as the one whose job it is to be sure that a reasonable level of understanding has been achieved? Do you see it as a fifty-fifty proposition? Each should carry half of the load; we should meet each other half way. "I'll do my part if you'll do yours." That sounds very reasonable and just, doesn't it? But we are not dealing with justice or fairness. We are concerned with achieving a profitable level of understanding.

I believe that the most useful attitude you can have with respect to the responsibility factor in communicating is the willingness (perhaps eagerness) to assume the full, complete, one hundred per cent responsibility for reaching an adequate level of understanding, whichever role you happen to be playing.

When you are sending a message to someone, there is some reason for your action. In some way it is going to be of value to you to get an idea across to that other person. Therefore, it will be to your own personal self-interest to do whatever you can do to be reasonably sure that you have been adequately understood.

Complete responsibility for being adequately understood

Complete responsibility for adequate understanding

SENDER

RECEIVER

When you are on the receiving end of the exchange it is also to your self-interest to adequately understand what the sender is trying to convey, and it will be worth the effort to do whatever you can possibly do to insure that a profitable level of understanding has been reached.

Recognize, too, that some delicate judgment may be required to gauge just what will be an adequate level of understanding. When I talk about the dog that I saw in the neighbor's driveway, we may both be quite willing to stop right there—unless you have lost your dog! Then you might want to take some action to upgrade the

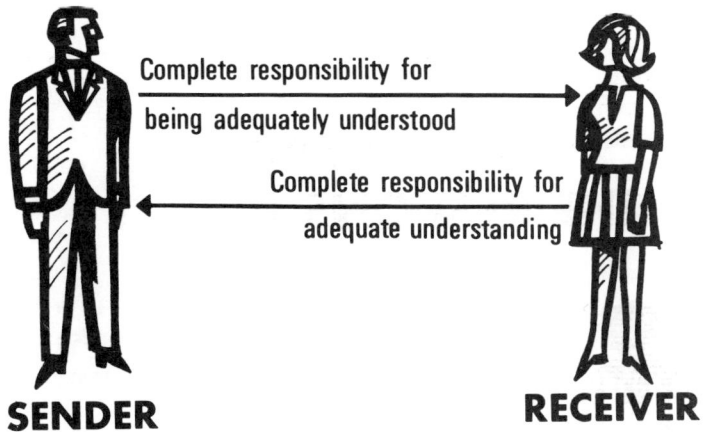

accuracy of your understanding. If you are making a sale, filling a customer's order, delivering a summation to a jury, or making an airplane reservation, it may be even more important to be reasonably sure that you have reached a level of understanding which will help you to accomplish your objectives. That's a lot more likely to happen if you do everything that you can do—reach for the complete responsibility.

I am not suggesting that it will be possible for you to achieve that one hundred per cent goal in every case—only that it is worth striving toward. Try it for the next few days and see what happens. Leave as little to chance as you possibly can. In all of the professional, family, and social relationships of your life, recognize the value to *you* which will result from doing everything that you can do to increase the probability that the people in your world will reach that level of understanding which will help to get the job done.

Excited about doing everything you can do to improve the level of understanding

Determined that if any useful communication takes place it is up to the other person.

The releasing mechanism is the degree to which you feel comfortable about being completely responsible for the degree of understanding which is achieved in your communications with others.

As you move up this scale, whatever talent, knowledge and skill that you have acquired in the field of communication is likely to flow easily and naturally in the way that you want it to flow. Some of the things you know about how to get your ideas across to others will begin to work for you better than they ever have, and your ability to listen—really listen—will flourish, too.

Practice this with Constructive Imagination. Project yourself into real communication situations in your imagination. Experience a selling situation, a discussion with your teenager, giving instruction to someone you work with, a difference of opinion with your mate. Let yourself reach across that gap and assume the responsibility for understanding—and *feel good* about being that kind of person and about the results you are achieving.

Several years ago a restaurant owner in the Bahamas told me about an experience he had had with the complexities of communication. I think that his experience provides a dramatic illustration of the ideas we are examining.

As we enjoyed our lunch I noticed that the sugar bowls were filled with the little paper envelopes—individual servings sealed against the humidity of the tropics. While those packets of sugar were fairly common at that time in the U.S., this was the first place I had seen them in the Carribean. When the man who owned the restaurant came over to have a cup of coffee with us as we finished our dessert, I complimented him on having gone to the extra trouble and expense of protecting the sugar from the bugs—and from people who stir their coffee and put the spoon back into the sugar bowl.

He thanked me for the comment, then said, "Let me tell you a story about the sugar packets. I was over in Miami about a month ago and I saw these for the first time in a restaurant there. The minute I saw them I knew that they were just what we needed here, so I went right to the phone in the restaurant and called the wholesale food broker who supplies us. I ordered a case of these packets, and they arrived about a week later. It was about four o'clock in the afternoon when the delivery came.

"I put the carton of sugar up on one of the tables here in the dining room, called all of the Bahamian waitresses together, and opened it up. I took one of the packets out of the carton, showed it to the girls and said, 'We've got something new! From now on we're going to use *this* sugar in the sugar bowls instead of that stuff we have been using.' Then I went on home.

"When I arrived here at the restaurant the next morning I was surprised to see that the sugar bowls still had the loose sugar in them—until I noticed the carton in which the new packets had been shipped. There it was, filled with empty paper packets! The waitresses had carefully, laboriously emptied every one of them into the bowls."

Fortunately, the restaurant owner had a good sense of humor. He could see that it was just as much his sending as their receiving that had caused the breakdown.

He had a perfectly clear image in his mental system about what he wanted the waitresses to do. He encoded his image in very simple language and sent the message to the waitresses. When they received his message they de-coded it and did exactly what they understood that he wanted. But their code books were different.

How much would it have helped if he had stopped on his way out and asked, "Do you understand what I want you to do?" Probably not much. Chances are he would have heard something like, "Sure, we understand."

Here's another example of how different "REAL-ITY" structures can foul things up. A man was driving along a rather remote road late one night when he had a flat tire. He pulled off to the side of the road and exchanged the flat tire for the spare that he had in the trunk. He had not had much experience changing tires, and it took him a long time to figure out how to use the jack. The lug-nuts were very tight and he spent considerable time getting them loosened. All the while, in order to see what he was doing and as a safety measure, he had left his headlights on.

When he had the tire changed and got back in the car to drive on, the battery had run down and he couldn't get the car started! He stood out on the roadway for some time, trying to flag down a passing car to give him some help. Finally, another man stopped and offered to take him into town. The stranded motorist explained that it would not be necessary to go into the next town; he only needed a push to get his car started. The good samaritan agreed.

"Oh, there is one important point," said the man whose car was stalled. "My car has an automatic transmission and it will be necessary to get up to about thirty-five miles an hour in order to get it started."

The other man nodded and went back to his own car. The driver who had suffered the flat tire waited patiently for a few minutes; then, wondering what was taking so long, he looked in his rear-view mirror. There came the other automobile—at thirty-five miles an hour!

Sometimes your willingness to assume the entire responsibility for reaching a profitable level of understanding can be almost a matter of life or death!

Based upon this very important releasing attitude pattern, let's look at four practical communication skills which you can practice right away to build better bridges. Remember, you can understand these skills thoroughly and still not use them very effectively, depending upon how you feel about your "share" of the responsibility for understanding.

The first communication skill that we will look at is a process called **empathy**. I am sure you are already familiar with that word, and with the kind of behavior for which it is a label. I want to describe how we will be using it, and then suggest a very simple but productive step-by-step process with which you can make the practice of empathy a habit.

> EMPATHY IS THE ART OF GRASPING
> OR UNDERSTANDING ANOTHER PERSON'S
> POINT OF VIEW, LOOKING AT
> A SITUATION OR AN IDEA
> THROUGH THE OTHER
> PERSON'S FILTER OR
> FRAME-OF-REFERENCE

Notice that *empathy* is not the same as *sympathy.* If you sympathize with another person, you feel the way he feels; to some degree at least you adopt that other person's viewpoint, belief, or attitude. With empathy you *understand* what the other person is thinking and feeling, but you need not adopt it, agree with it, or even approve of it.

Very often empathy and sympathy are found together, particularly in close, caring relationships. Yet they can be separated. Can you think of a situation in which you might have a great deal of sympathy and very little empathy? One possibility might be listening to a recording of someone laughing or crying. You may have little or no grasp of why the person is feeling that emotion and expressing it; yet you may find yourself feeling that way, too—sharing the feeling without understanding the reason for it. Sometimes people at a football or soccer game find themselves "caught up" in the excitement and enthusiasm of the crowd, yelling and jumping without much understanding of how the game is played or scored, or why everyone is behaving so wildly.

How about practicing empathy without much sympathy? An example of that combination might be seen with the physician, salesperson, psychotherapist, or criminologist. These professionals want to *understand* the other person's viewpoint as clearly as possible, without adopting it. Their lack of sympathy does not mean that they do not *care,* only that they realize that they can perform their function much more effectively by understanding than by feeling the same way that the other person feels.

To understand empathy better, and as an aid in developing the skill, let's break it down into three phases or steps. At first this may seem a little mechanical, but as you put these three stages together and practice them they will become as natural and automatic as tying your shoelaces or dialing a telephone.

The first stage in the practice of empathy is by far the easiest. It is simply the recognition or acknowledgment that the other person's "filter" is different from yours—that he is looking at the world through his own unique and different accumulation of experiences and attitudes. This is a very rational, logical, intellectual observation which most people find quite obvious and easy to accept. Some people like buttermilk; others can't stand it. Some enjoy opera; others prefer rock bands. Some get a kick out of sky diving; others prefer scuba diving. We can stand side by side looking at the same scene and have something very different going on inside our systems. Our filters are different.

The second step is more difficult—feeling comfortable about the differences in the way that we see ourselves and the world around us. Now we are getting into the emotional area of the system, how you feel about the fact that the other person has a different set of values, a different "REALITY" structure. This second step does not require that you feel the way the other person feels, only an easy, comfortable willingness to allow the other person his or her uniqueness. It might be expressed in this way, "I know that you are looking at this situation differently than I am, and it's all right with me for you to have a point of view different from mine. It's all right with me for you to be *you*."

Then, to the degree that you have been able to take the first two steps, you may be able to reach across the gap and understand that other person's different way of looking at what is happening. Not perfectly, remember, but the degree to which you are able to understand will depend a lot on your ability to go through these three phases in your own mental system:

> *"I recognize and acknowledge the fact that you have a "REALITY" filter through which you perceive yourself and your world that is very different from mine.*
>
> *"I feel very comfortable with the fact that your "REALITY" is different from mine, and that we can look at the same event or object and perceive it differently."*
>
> *"I really want to understand your different viewpoint—not judge it or attack it—just understand it as clearly as I possibly can."*

If you are a manager, try practicing empathy with your workforce. Recognize that they see you, themselves, your department, and everything else differently than you do. That's the easy step. Then see how you **feel** about that. Can you allow them to have a different point of view? Do you see that *different* doesn't mean *wrong* or *bad*, it just means *different*? Take a look at the world through the other person's point of view. If you were looking at things through that different "REAL-ITY" filter how would you see your job, your co-workers, your boss? What are that other person's hopes, dreams, fears? Let yourself go through that sequence every now and then and see what happens to your relationship with that other person.

If you are a salesperson, you already practice a lot of empathy. It is an occupational necessity for the successful professional salesperson! Still, it may be productive to spend some time practicing and further strengthening this skill. Your prospect or client has a way of looking at you, your company, your product, his company, his needs and your interview that is different from yours.

That's fine. If you and he had exactly the same "REALITY" filter, there would be no need for your services. His different viewpoint is not an obstacle to your success; it is the name of the game! Your whole task as a salesperson is to understand his way of looking at things, his needs and goals, and then to help him fulfill his needs with your product or service. One of the most important attitude structures the professional salesperson can cultivate and maintain is, "I really want to understand your point of view." That is only likely to happen as you recognize that each point of view is different and allow the other person to have his own ideas and "truths."

If you are married, or have a close loving relationship with another person, empathy is one of the most useful arts for strengthening and enhancing that relationship. Again, the easiest part is recognizing the fact that your mate does indeed have a different way of looking at life. Take a look at some of those differences and at the different experiences, relationships and thought processes which have created them.

Can you allow your mate to have different likes and dislikes, different values, different prejudices? When you are looking at a painting, listening to music, or watching a sunset, can you rejoice in the fact that something different is happening in each of your systems because of the multitude of different experiences you have had throughout the years?

As you recognize the fact of difference and feel comfortable about it, what do you want to do about it? Let yourself reach for greater understanding, listening with interest, asking but not challenging, discussing without judging.

I think this story illustrates the importance of empathy in a marriage. A mother was walking down the upstairs hallway one night. It was late and the children were all in bed. As she passed by the baby's bedroom she noticed that her husband was standing there by the crib in the dim light looking down, lost in thought. She tiptoed in and stood beside him for a moment; then she broke the silence and said, "A penny for your thoughts, darling." Startled as he discovered that she was there beside him, the husband said, "Oh, well as a matter of fact, honey, I was just standing here wondering how in the world they can sell a crib like that for $19.50!"

Just one more example of how two very intelligent, loving people can stand side by side looking at the same object or event and have something different going on inside their mental systems. Neither point of view is right or wrong. Each is quite reasonable for that individual.

Are you a parent? If so, that may well be the most productive area of your life in which to practice more empathy. If you have a small child it will be easy enough to see that the little person has a different "REALITY" filter. Not only *different* experiences, but so much *less* experience has been programmed into that mental system. Remember, too, the thought processes of the small child are still primarily on the emotional level. Not nearly as many abstract concepts or experiences have been assimilated, and the limited vocabulary allows less verbal thought activity.

Are you comfortable with the fact that your five-year-old thinks like a five-year-old? Can you find excitement in watching that filter system develop, allowing your youngster to see the world (and you) in a childish way? Do what you can to understand the child's viewpoint. What is it like to live with people who are much bigger than you are? How does it feel to always be told what to do, where to go, what to eat, how to do things? How much of what is going on in the world does the child miss because his vision is obstructed by objects which are larger than he is? How much empathy in the parent who says, "Shut up and go to sleep; there's nothing in the closet!" From the child's viewpoint there just *might* be something there. Try crawling into that little filter and see how the world looks from in there. Instead of "Don't be ridiculous!" try "I understand how you feel."

Several years ago in a *PACE* Seminar one of the women in the group told a personal story about empathy which I think provides a poignant illustration of the importance of this skill to a parent. She had been shopping in downtown Los Angeles about a week before Christmas, and had taken her five-year-old son with her. They had been in the department stores since they opened in the morning and at two o'clock in the afternoon she was tired, piled high with packages and still clutching her little boy's hand, pulling him through the crowd of shoppers. His shoe came untied. She stopped, put the packages down on a counter and impatiently stooped down to tie his shoes. "When I got down on one knee and was working on Timmy's shoelace I suddenly realized that I was seeing things the way he did— from his level," she said. "I could see what he had been seeing all day—the counters, people's legs, and rear ends. I thought about how it must feel to be dragged and pulled through crowds of people, wondering if I will be separated from my mother and maybe even lost, banging into people, told to keep quiet, not to touch things. I burst into tears, gave my son a big hug and headed for our car. We went home and I determined that I would never put him through anything like that again!"

Just the simple fact of different physical stature makes a big difference in how we see things, but there are a lot of other ways in which your child's filter is unlike yours. That doesn't mean that either of you is "wrong"—it just means that you have a very different set of experiences through which you are perceiving what is happening.

If you have a teen-ager you have an especially challenging opportunity to practice empathy, and you will find the process especially rewarding. Since you have been through the teen years it will be considerably easier for you to empathize with an adolescent than it is for the younger person to understand a parental viewpoint. Again, the responsibility is *yours.* What can *you* do to build better levels of understanding—better bridges across the generation gap?

The first step in empathizing with a teen-ager is by far the easiest; recognizing that the other person does indeed have a different filter. Not only different from your present point of view, it is a lot different from the filter you had when *you were a teen-ager*! The world is a lot different now and countless different thought/feeling experiences have been assimilated into that other person's "REALITY" structure. Most parents have little or no difficulty acknowledging the fact that "we are looking at life through a different set of values, goals, ideals and experiences."

But then you may feel that powerful impulse to get the other person's viewpoint shaped up! If you know that your way of looking at life is *right,* then of course a different viewpoint is *wrong,* and it is your duty—particularly in your role of parent—to get that other person's thinking straightened out!

Try a different approach and see how much better it works. Instead of searching for what is "right" or "wrong," reach for better *understanding.* See if you can feel more at ease with the fact that your offspring's viewpoint will *always* be at least a little bit different from yours—maybe a *lot* different in some areas. Since it is not going to be possible for you to force that person to think and feel exactly the way you do, might it not be profitable to develop an open, honest flow of ideas in both directions, a rapport, a climate in which it is possible to exchange ideas and share values? In that kind of atmosphere there is at least a chance that you might be able to *sell* your way of looking at life.

Remember that empathy does not require that you adopt the other person's viewpoint—or even that you approve of it—only a willingness to *understand* it.

When someone gives you the impression that he or she really is interested in your opinion—really wants to understand your thoughts and feelings—how do you feel about that person? How do you feel about someone who conveys a complete lack of interest in your ridiculous viewpoint, but a great determination to help you to see life *correctly*?

Now turn that around. If you were your teen-ager which kind of parent would you prefer to have?

In the *PACE* Youth Conferences which our company conducts one of the most common expressions we hear from young people is, "Adults don't listen very well!" The teen-ager discovers at an early age that when Mom or Dad (or teacher, aunt, uncle, etc.) asks, "What do you think about college?" or "How do you feel about marriage?" or drugs, religion, politics, business, sex, war or any other dimension of life, they are probably not really asking a question. It *sounds* like a question, but the chances are it is just a ticket to a lecture. If the teen-ager responds as he would to a real question, he will probably receive a long dissertation about the "truth"— the *correct* way for a person to think about that subject. So, instead of answering questions, the teen-ager develops defensive strategies and responds with, "Oh, I don't know," or perhaps with the answer he thinks the parent wants to hear.

You need to decide what kind of relationship you want to build with that person—your teen-ager. It may be that you really do not *want* to know what he is thinking and feeling about himself, about you, the future, about life. If that is the case, then you can easily maintain that situation by always being right and talking *at* instead of *with* your youngster.

If you decide that you want a more open, honest *exchange* of ideas, then develop the key emotional pattern which allows empathy to develop—"I really want to *understand* your point of view." Deliberately, mechanically *practice* the one, two, three sequence of empathy until it becomes an automatic part of your system. You will find that as *your* attitude changes there will be an automatic increase in the other person's willingness to reciprocate—to listen to your ideas and opinions. To the degree that the other person is *listening,* there will be a chance that he might find your ideas of value and perhaps even worth adopting.

The same method works in the other direction, too, of course. If you are a teen-ager, don't cop out with the excuse that you have not been a parent and therefore it is not possible for you to understand a parental viewpoint. Just go through the same three-step sequence with your Mother or Father. You will have no difficulty at all recognizing that they have different ways of looking at life than you do. Can you develop a comfortable feeling about that fact? Instead of requiring that they look at everything just the way you do, give them the same kind of freedom to have their own values and ideals that you would like to have them give you!

Then let yourself look at the situation through their filters. If you were your parents, had been born when and where they were, raised during those years, how would you be looking at life? Project yourself ahead a few years through the process of getting married, concern about family finances, the birth of your first child, and some of the other experiences which are now a part of your own parents' filters. If you had been through what they have been through how would *you* feel about some of the important aspects of our world? If you were your parents, how would you feel about having a teen-ager like you?

Be willing to assume the responsibility for building some bridges of understanding with your parents. It may not be easy, but at least you know why the barriers are there, and you know that it will be to your best interests to do whatever you can do to open up the channels.

When you find yourself thinking, "I just can't understand people like that," or "I can't understand how you can possibly think that way," remember that you *can,* if you just *will.*

There is a second technique that you can use to enhance your understanding in any kind of interpersonal encounter. It, too, may seem "mechanical" at first, but as you practice it and see it working it will become an automatic, flowing part of your interaction with others. This skill has been given different labels by various experts in the field of communication. I prefer the descriptive term used by Dr. Stephen Covey, the well-known author and professor at Brigham Young University. Dr. Covey calls it *the understanding response.*

Using this technique is simply a matter of re-stating what you have heard the other person say, in your own words, and offering that person the opportunity to check it—to see whether what you understand is a reasonably accurate representation of what he wanted to convey.

The following is a simple example of how the understanding response might save time and frustration.

"Excuse me, can you tell me how to get to the post office?"

"Sure. Just go straight ahead three traffic lights, then turn left, and it's about two blocks down the street on the right."

"Thanks a lot. Let me see if I got that right. I go on the same way I'm headed and turn left at the third signal. . . . ."

"No, don't turn *at* the signal. Turn left at the first street *after* the signal."

"Okay, one block after the third traffic light I turn left and then go about two blocks and it's on the right side of the street."

"That's it."

"Thank you!"

It may be very tempting to think that the person giving the directions was "wrong." Yet, knowing the area so well it made perfectly good sense to him to put it the way that he did. The important point is that delegating the responsibility for understanding can lead to trouble. Going that one extra step to check out your understanding can often save a lot of grief.

Here's another example. It's Friday evening. John and Mary are having dinner and she says, "I think we should work on the garage this weekend, John."

Which of these responses is most likely to be useful?

"I already have my whole week-end planned. We will have to do it some other time."

"Yeah, okay. I'll think about it."

"You think it really needs to be straightened out, eh?"

"Okay, we'll start on it first thing in the morning."

The third response is the understanding response and will probably be the most productive in most instances. It gives Mary the opportunity to further clarify what she has in mind. Even when it seems as though there could only be one possible meaning, it is often worth checking out. It might be that she is simply concerned about the oil spot on the garage floor, or the leak in the roof. The phrase "work on the garage" could have a lot of different meanings.

The understanding response flows easily from the *thought* process, "I really want to understand what you are saying; let's see if I do." It is not a challenging, judging, argumentative exchange—just a way of checking out the degree of accuracy with which you have received the other person's message.

There is a third technique for building better levels of understanding, particularly in situations which seem very tense or in which emotions seem to be blocking the flow of ideas.

In its most complete form this method has six stages, although in many cases not all six will be needed. The six steps are:

1. Here's how I am **feeling** about what is happening.
2. Here's what I **want** to have happen.
3. Here's what I am **willing** to do to make it happen.
4. How do you **feel** about it?

5. What do you **want**?
6. What are you **willing** to do?

Here is an example of how the **feel, want, willing** system might be applied to a management situation:

"Jerry, I feel very frustrated. We have had several talks about how important it is for you to get to work on time. I've tried to explain why it is important—to me and to the general morale in our office. Yet you still show up late about forty per cent of the time. We haven't been able to find an answer, and I feel frustrated about it. I do want to find a reasonable solution—some way to resolve this puzzle that we can both feel good about. I'm willing to set aside whatever time is necessary to work with you to find an answer.

"How do you feel about this, Jerry?"

"Well, I feel kind of guilty that I haven't been observing the company rules, and at the same time, I feel angry at the morning freeway traffic jams which keep me from getting in on time. I guess I want to find a solution just as badly as you do, Ed."

They are well on the way to finding an answer. Notice, though, that it is very important to express **feelings** in that first phase, not opinions. It would have been very easy for Jerry to say, "Well, I feel that the company policy about getting into the office at exactly 8:30 is too rigid." As soon as someone says "I feel *that. . . .*" you know that you are going to hear an opinion, not an emotion. Part of the magic of this method is your willingness to give the other person an honest expression of the emotions you have going on in your system—not what you think, but what you **feel**.

Then, express you goal. What do you want to have happen? And then, what are you willing to do to bring about that situation?

Often it will not be necessary to go into the second half of the pattern. Expressing your feelings, your goals and what you will do frequently stimulates an open response from the other person without your having specifically asked for it. To the degree that you have established an atmosphere in which it is *safe* for the other person to give you an accurate expression of his inner feelings, and you have done so to him, he will be inclined to reciprocate.

This system is not restricted to exchanges in which your emotions are negative. You may find it equally valuable in very positive situations:

"Joe, I want you to know that I feel very good about the job you are doing. I regard you as a very important person in our organization and I hope you will be a part of our team for a long time. And, I want to be sure that you know that I am eager to help in any way that I can to make our association a good one for you."

Practice using this sequence with Constructive Imagination. Prepare in advance when you have an important communications situation coming up. Project yourself, in your imagination, into that encounter and go through the sequence a few times so that you will be comfortable with it when the time comes. When you have had a communication breakdown, get off by yourself for a few minutes and think about how you could handle a situation like that differently if it were ever to happen again. Go through it in your imagination using this feel/want/willing process to establish an open flow of understanding.

In the first part of this chapter I referred briefly to the three media we use to convey our thoughts and feelings to each other. Let's take a little deeper look at those three channels now. I believe that a better grasp of their importance can help a lot in your effort to build better levels of understanding.

Verbal communication—using words to send a message—may seem like the most obvious system. Some people seem to think that the word *communicate* means *verbal exchange.* We have become so accustomed to the use of verbal symbols that it may be easy to forget that some very important messages are sent on the other two channels. Certainly words are important, as you well know if you have travelled in a foreign country without having studied the language spoken there. In the scientific community, where words and other symbols have more limited and precise meanings, progress would be nearly impossible without a commonly accepted vocabulary.

Most of our interactions, however, involve the use of extraverbal and nonverbal messages as well. Punctuation, emphasis, inflection, the rate of speed, the "tone of voice" with which something is said, all fall into the extraverbal department. These are ways in which we add extra meaning to what is being said (or written). You can use exactly the same words, but by adding just the slightest note of sarcasm the entire message is changed. Or, the tone may be one of irritation, anger, frustration, fear or condescension—or warmth, enthusiasm, excitement or joy.

Notice that the extraverbal messages are of an emotional nature. What one is *feeling* tends to come through on this channel—and usually the extraverbal, emotional message is more dependable, more authentic. When the words and the tone of voice are in conflict, you usually find yourself "believing" the extraverbal impression.

Nonverbal signals also convey what a person is feeling more accurately than the words being spoken. Gestures, body postures, facial expression do not "just happen." All behavior is communicative. While it is not possible to label a particular gesture or posture as one hundred per cent dependable—always indicating the same meaning—as you increase your awareness or sensitivity to this important signal system you will find yourself grasping the other person's viewpoint much more accurately.

Of particular importance are the messages of the eyes and the area immediately around them. Look for the emotions which come to you from that very expressive part of the person's face. Notice how difficult it is to communicate with a person who is wearing sunglasses. If the eyes are not available, the message is not as clear—and not as complete.

Here, then, is our fourth communication skill to develop: listen to the whole person—the words, tone of voice, and the postures and gestures. And be aware of the fact that what *you* are feeling—anger, joy fear, enthusiasm, frustration, affection—is being conveyed to the other person. It is almost impossible to block that flow. Instead of trying hard to come across like a particular kind of person, develop the kind of emotional patterns you want to convey to others; then relax and be the real you! Use Constructive Imagination to build the patterns you want to have, the positive emotions you want to have others see in you. Then, instead of tense, guarded communication you can allow a natural, spontaneous message to flow to others.

Here is one more suggestion—an emotional releasing mechanism which will help you to allow an easy, smooth flow of the potential you have to communicate well. Look upon every opportunity that you have to communicate with another person as a *"let's win"* situation. Recognize that a high level of understanding between you and that other individual will be rewarding to both of you, and that if your understanding breaks down you will both lose. Here is how a continuum might look in this area:

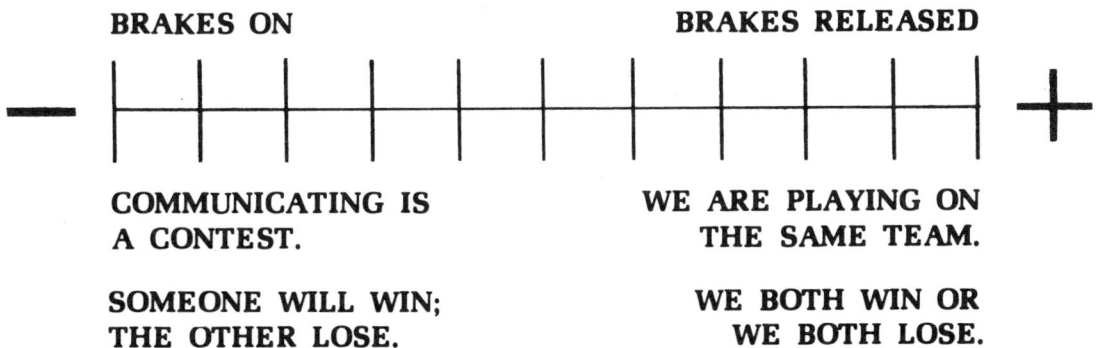

BRAKES ON   **BRAKES RELEASED**

$$-\ \vdash\!\!+\!\!+\!\!+\!\!+\!\!+\!\!+\!\!+\!\!+\!\!+\!\!+\!\!+\!\dashv\ +$$

COMMUNICATING IS   **WE ARE PLAYING ON**
A CONTEST.   **THE SAME TEAM.**

SOMEONE WILL WIN;   **WE BOTH WIN OR**
THE OTHER LOSE.   **WE BOTH LOSE.**

Professional selling provides us with a very useful example of this principle in action. There was a time when a salesperson was trained in a skill very much like fencing. His goal was to maneuver the prospect into signing the order. Any means were justified by that end result. Such expressions as "killer instinct" were widely used in sales recruiting and training manuals. If the salesperson made the sale the feeling was one of unilateral victory—"I won; the prospect lost." If the sale was *not* closed, the prospect won the contest. The entire selling situation was seen as a game or a hunting expedition in which the salesperson did whatever he could to "trap" the prospect into signing an order.

Today, the professional salesperson has moved to the positive end of our scale. The goal is to understand the prospect's needs and to help him to satisfy those needs with the salesperson's product or services. If we can work together to reach an adequate level of understanding and solve the prospect's needs, everyone wins. If understanding breaks down, or the product or service is not properly suited to the prospect's situation, everyone loses.

The professional sees the prospect and the salesperson as a working team striving for the same goal. The salesperson is a playing coach on the team—the expert who can best guide the process which will lead us to victory.

See if you can feel the difference in this very fundamental attitude structure. If you are a salesperson, it can multiply your effectiveness quickly and dramatically.

If you do not make your living as a professional salesperson, see if you can recognize that much of your life is devoted to selling—your self, your ideas, your values. If you are a manager you must surely know that the best way to get things done is to *sell* your subordinates on following the policies and procedures which will accomplish the results that you want.

Of course you can get things done with fear—"The reason you will do it this way is because if you don't, you'll be fired!"—but it requires a lot more energy on your part, and the other people in your group are going to be functioning with the brakes set. They will get a lot more done—and so will you—with much higher quality and a greater sense of personal satisfaction if they have *bought* your way of doing things. See if you can move your management style a little more in the direction of "let's win." That doesn't need to mean that your department is a democracy. It does mean that when people feel that they are important, that someone listens to their opinions, and that they are working as a team, they will feel a greater sense of personal commitment to the organization and to the team's leader.

How will this work around the house? How many sales do you suppose are made with, "Because I said so, that's why!"? In your relationship with your mate and in your interaction with your children search for areas in which you can communicate on the basis of this simple rule:

> **WE WILL KEEP THE COMMUNICATION LINES OPEN UNTIL WE FIND A SOLUTION THAT EVERYONE FEELS GOOD ABOUT.**

That may not always be possible, but give it a try and I predict that you will find that it works far more often than you might expect. If you can get just ten per cent more of the differences of opinion settled on a "let's win" basis it will make a wonderfully positive change in the atmosphere of your home.

We have looked at two emotional releasing mechanisms and four skills or techniques which you can use to upgrade the level of understanding you are able to achieve with the other people in your world. Let's review them briefly.

The releasing devices are:

1. **Develop an increasingly comfortable feeling** about assuming the complete, 100% responsibility for achieving a workable, profitable level of understanding. Delegate or shift as little as possible of the responsibility to the other person.
2. **Discover the excitement and reward** of building and maintaining a "let's win" atmosphere in as many of your communication situations as you possibly can. When you feel a contest developing remind yourself that the results will be far more satisfactory if everybody wins.

The four communication skills which we have examined together are:

1. **Empathy**—the art of grasping or understanding the other person's different point of view.

2. **The understanding response**—the habit of feeding back what you understand the other person to have said and giving that person the opportunity to check it out and see how accurately you have received his message.

3. **Feel, want, willing**—expressing to the other person what emotions you are experiencing, your goal in that situation and what you are willing to do to achieve that goal, and offering the other person the opportunity to reciprocate.

4. **Listen to the whole person**—be alert to the tone of voice and the gestures and postures which are conveying messages along with the words you are receiving. Develop the emotional patterns you want to convey to others, because whatever you are feeling about yourself, the other person and the situation in which you find yourself is going to be telegraphed to others.

Begin right now to practice these ideas. You will see an almost immediate change in the quality of your relationships.

There is a better way

One of the most exciting ingredients in the complex structure of your potential is your capacity for creativity—your talent for finding new ways of doing things.

Creativity is part of the original equipment dimension of your system, a built-in talent which we all have, probably in much greater abundance than we reflect in our behavior. Let's look at a working definition of creativity and then I would like to suggest three simple releasing mechanisms which have proven very useful to allow the natural creativity of a human system to flow more freely and consistently.

> CREATIVITY IS THE MENTAL MANIPULATION OF PAST EXPERIENCES INTO A *NEW* OR *DIFFERENT* WAY OF DOING SOMETHING.

In Chapter 6 I suggested that there is a tendency in your mental processes to "close the loop"—an inclination to arrange things as they are "supposed to be." Of course, each person has a different image of how the world is "supposed to be," and different feelings about how important it is that various parts of that world be "properly" arranged. Some will feel a strong urge to straighten the crooked picture on the wall, some will know that it is crooked but not be concerned about it, and others will not even notice that the picture is tipped.

When you notice that something (about yourself or the world around you) is not "right," there is a feeling

CHAPTER

17

of conflict or dissonance between what you are perceiving and what your "REALITY" structure "knows" to be the way things like that are supposed to be. Immediately your subconscious Conflict Resolution processes are stimulated to "search the experience files" and develop a solution to the puzzle—a way of setting things "right."

Simultaneously, there is usually a *conscious* attempt to find a solution, and that conscious activity may involve various degrees of creative thinking.

For example, when you notice that you are thirsty, you have become aware of a conflict or "shortage" in your system. Something is not as it should be. As you perceive that disturbance and associate the sensation with your past experiences—your "REALITY" structure—you recall how you (or others) have handled similar situations in the past. Then there is an evaluation. Which of those past actions seems most appropriate in this instance? On the basis of that evaluation, you make a decision.

That very common sequence of thought and action is simple and practical, but it involves no creativity. When you simply do what you have done before, your behavior may be very productive and sensible, but it is not *creative*.

Now, if none of the past experiences seem to provide an appropriate solution to this situation, or if you encounter an obstacle which doesn't allow you to implement any of those previous actions, you may shift into a conscious type of creative thought. That process will involve re-scanning whatever information you have accumulated from your own experiences and observation of other people and fitting those ideas together in new ways. It may be very logical, mechanical manipulation of related information or it can be a playful juggling of bits and pieces to see if something useful will evolve. Sometimes a combination of logical approach and playfulness creates something that works.

Puzzles can provide a demonstration of these two conscious approaches. Here is one which is probably best solved by a very logical, step-by-step sequence of thought.

Three women, Mary, Betty, and Dorothy, each have two of the following hobbies: golf, painting, ceramics, collecting antiques, tennis, and photography. No two of them have the same hobby.
1. The golfer went to visit the ceramicist.
2. Dorothy bought Christmas presents for Betty and for the antique collector.
3. The ceramicist and the tennis player went shopping with Mary.
4. The antique collector is the painter's cousin.
5. Betty asked the tennis player to have lunch with her.
6. The golfer sold a family heirloom to the antique collector.

Which two hobbies does each of the women have?

Find the solution to the exercise, and notice as you are working on it that your efforts follow a straight-forward logical sequence. You will find the solution on page 276, but please at least try to work it out on your own before you look.

Here is another puzzle which requires more than simple logic. To find the answer to this one you will need to take a more playful, imaginative approach.

A friend of mine had a very small window in his garage. He wanted to enlarge the original window which was only a foot high and a foot wide. One Saturday afternoon he went out to his garage, took a saw from his workbench, and, starting from the midpoint of the top of the window, he cut six inches to the left, twelve inches down, twelve inches to the right, twelve inches up and six inches to the left. That brought him back exactly to the point where he had started and he had exactly doubled the size of his window.

How is that possible?

Once again, I invite you to give that puzzle a good effort before you look at the solution on page 277. You may find yourself tempted to think, "That's impossible!" Or you may decide that there is something wrong with the description of what my friend did. Not so! It *is* possible, and the description is accurate without any tricky play on words.

One more exercise—one of my favorite puzzles—will further illustrate the idea that you have a lot more potential in the area of creativity than you may think you have.

There are three cookie jars on a shelf, high enough that you cannot see into them, but you can reach into them. There are labels hanging on the jars—one says "Chocolate Chip", one says "Oatmeal" and the third says "Chocolate Chip and Oatmeal." Each of the labels is incorrect, and your job is to rearrange the labels so that they are accurately placed. You may take only one cookie out of only one jar. Take the first one that you touch—no fair feeling around in the jar.

The answer is on page 278, but try to find the solution on your own before you look. The effort will help you to understand the rest of our discussion on creativity a lot better.

Thus far we have been looking at what happens at a primarily conscious level in your mental processes. Meanwhile, some very creative processes are going on subconsciously. In fact, very often the logical thought processes which are working on the conflict at a conscious level may obstruct the flow of a much more exciting solution which has been created without any awareness on your part of the mental activity which developed it. Let's see how that might happen.

Earlier in this chapter, and also in Chapter 6, I suggested that when there is a conflict between what you are now perceiving and what your "REALITY" structure has been programmed to regard as acceptable in such situations, the Conflict Resolution Processes are stimulated to find a solution—the best available solution from the point of view of your own self-interest—based on the information available. Moreover, that computation or creative development of the optimum solution happens almost instantaneously.

Let me say that another way. When your conscious perception of what *is* happening does not match your "REALITY" about the way things are *supposed* to happen, a subconscious activity is initiated or stimulated to search the experience files and compute an acceptable resolution to the conflict.

However, it seems that once the solution has been developed it must make its way through the existing "truth" patterns, preconceptions, and pre-judgments in order to get to a conscious level where it can be implemented.

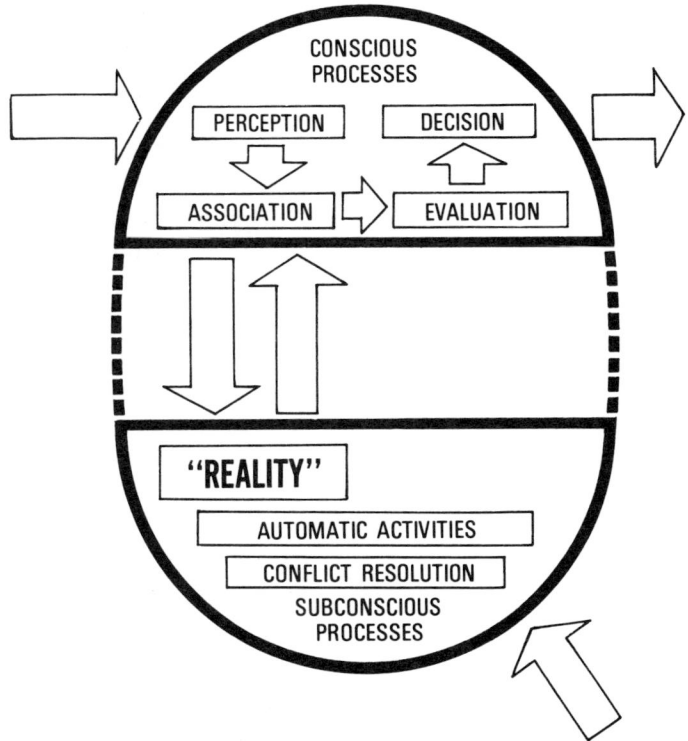

You have probably had the experience of working consciously to solve a difficult puzzle relating to your business, or perhaps having to do with a personal relationship. You wrestled with all of the various elements, listed all the alternatives you could think of, looked at the pros and cons of each possible course of action, but still were not satisfied with the results of your efforts. So, you walked away from the puzzle for a while—went on to something else with the intent to return and solve this one later.

Then, when you least expected it, the ideal solution popped to the surface. It may have happened when you first awakened in the morning, or even in the middle of the night! Or, perhaps, while you were sailing your boat or working in your workshop—a time when you were totally engrossed, consciously, in an unrelated activity. The "problem" had not been set aside after all. The creative part of your mental system developed a solution and then went to work on the project of finding a way to get it through the blocks, barriers and preconceptions. When you were relaxed—distracted—the answer popped up like a cork that had been released.

That solution may have been created almost as soon as you recognized and defined the difficult situation—the conflict. Or, if not enough information was available, there may have been a waiting period while you assembled more data. The rest of the time was spent opening up the mental blockages—releasing the brakes—so that the idea could get to the surface.

Based upon this model of how your creative thinking processes function, let's look at five braking mechanisms which limit the flow of your creative potential. As you might expect, they are attitude patterns, each with a negative emotional component. If you choose to do so, you can easily revise these restrictive attitudes and allow your creativity to flourish and work for you spontaneously and consistently.

1. Fear of change.
2. Knowing/feeling that you are not a creative person.
3. Labeling the conflict with a word which connotes "difficult" or "impossible."
4. Knowing/feeling that you *have to* do something in just one way.
5. Knowing/feeling that you *can't* do something in a particular way.

Fear of change is usually a combination of fear of failure, fear of the unknown, and the strong human tendency to cling to the familiar ways of doing things. You know that you can handle things the way that they are—perhaps not perfectly, but you are at least functioning reasonably well. If there is a change, will you still be able to function as well? Will you have the skills, the knowledge you will need to relate to that new way of doing things? If something changes will it take you out of your Comfort Zone?

Those fears can not only jam your own circuits and diminish the creative flow in your own mental system, but also cause you to react negatively to the new ideas and new ways of doing things which others may propose to you.

Here is an example.

All of the knowledge which has been accumulated by the human race since the beginning of time—everything in all the libraries, computers, and mental systems throughout the world—will be doubled in the next six years!

See if you can sense what your emotional reaction is to that idea. Not what do you think of it, but how do you **feel** about it?

Do you find yourself feeling a positive or negative reaction to that idea? Where are you on this scale?

If you find the idea of change threatening, then the rapidly accelerating rate of change that is going on in our world today will maintain a constant anxiety in your system. That negative emotion is a braking mechanism which you can work on if you want to allow your potential in this area to flow more easily.

Get acquainted with how you really do feel about change. I am not suggesting, of course, that all change is necessarily good, or that we should initiate change just for the sake of doing things differently. However, only those who have the positive feelings of enthusiasm and excitement

Change is exciting, stimulating, invigorating.

Change is frightening, threatening.
Let's do things the way we have been doing them.

about the *fact* of change will be able to get involved in what is happening and help to guide the course of the future in positive, constructive directions.

See if you can move your attitude in the direction of "What an exciting time to be alive!" Since the future—your future—*is* going to be different, start thinking about the way that you would like to have things go. As you are able to project your imagination into the future and anticipate the sort of changes which are likely to happen you will not only find new directions more familiar and hence more comfortable, but you will find yourself creating new ways of doing things which will help to bring about the changes that you want to have happen.

I am a very creative person.

Next, let's look at the self-image block to the flow of your creative talents. It is just possible that somewhere along the line you may have made up your mind that you are not a creative person. If, as a child (or during any period of your life) your self-talk has embraced such ideas as, "Some people are creative and some people aren't—and I am one of those who simply do not have any of that talent," then, SURE ENOUGH! that's the kind of behavior we will be able to expect. To the degree that you approach the puzzles of life with that "truth" you will be inclined to give up before you even start.

I have no ability at all in the area of creativity.

Where would you put yourself on this attitude scale? Can you acknowledge that even though you may not have been using much of it you probably do have a great deal of creative potential? Or do you regard that as an area in which you have been shorted, deprived? If you can accept the possibility that you may have more potential in this area than you are using, and that it would be to your advantage to use more of it, then put *Constructive Imagination* to work. Perhaps an affirmation like this would be productive: "I am excited about the fact that I am, by nature, a creative person and I

enjoy letting my creative ideas flow easily and spontaneously." Experience, in your imagination, how it
feels when you have a new idea. The next time that
your creative processes are working for you, notice that
it is happening and use that experience to remind yourself that such mental activity is a normal and exciting
part of your system.

Do you ever find yourself blocking your approach to
a situation you have encountered by giving it a label
which implies that this is going to be difficult—or impossible? Perhaps the most common example of this
braking mechanism is the very frequent use of the word
"problem." To the degree that you have programmed
your system with the idea that "problems are sticky,
difficult, require a lot of effort and may involve failure," then when you label a situation as a problem you
have instantly made it more of an obstacle to your
progress than it needed to be.

Remember that words are not just empty vehicles.
Every word that you have in your voluntary files is associated with the experience and the emotions which you
have attached to the word in your past thoughts and
feelings. See what happens if you use different labels for
the same puzzles. Instead of the word "problem" try
the word "situation" or if it is appropriate, "conflict."
In many instances, what you have been labeling as
problems are in fact *opportunities.* Chances are that
your family doesn't have nearly as many communication *problems* as you have thought. If you look more
carefully you will find that there are many exciting
opportunities for building better understanding and a
"let's win" atmosphere. When you start thinking about
the positive results of finding a meaningful, rewarding
solution to the situation then the creativity, the ideas
about how to accomplish that objective, will begin to
flow.

This is not to say that every situation that you encounter can properly be labeled an opportunity. Of
course not! There will be times when it would be a real
stretch to use that label. I recall an example of this
which came up in a *PACE* Seminar that I was conduct-

ing in Mexico several years ago. One of the participants was a top marketing executive from a major international airline. He came to me just before dinner one evening and said, "Jim, I've thought a lot about today's session on creativity and now I realize that we don't have any *problems* in our company. All we have are *insurmountable opportunities*!"

Try this idea. Next time you feel as though your thinking has clogged up and you are not making much headway in finding the solution you are seeking, look at how you have labeled the situation. If you have given it a negative label, one which carries the connotation of "difficult" or which implies that it will take a miracle to find a way out, try shifting your mental gears and think about how it will feel when you have solved it. Search for the opportunity that is probably hidden within the puzzle that you are facing. You will find that the positive emotions will help to release the creative ideas that you need.

Restrictive conditioning will also inhibit the flow of a creative idea. To the degree that you have made up your mind that certain kinds of activity *have to* be done in a particular manner, then even if your conflict resolution processes should develop a very useful, innovative way of approaching a situation, it will be unlikely to surface. The pre-judgment will block its flow. The compulsive pattern obstructs your awareness of alternatives because it implies that to do anything other than what you *have to* do will result in pain or unpleasantness. Even if an imaginative new thought should cross your mind it is very likely that the evaluation process will reject it as "unthinkable."

A similar blockage occurs with the inhibitive pattern. If you know that you *can't* do something in a certain way, then any thought which comes close to that direction will have difficulty reaching a conscious level, and if it does it may be rejected quickly. "You can't do things that way—OR ELSE!"

So, when it seems that you are making no progress in finding a solution to a puzzle, stop for a moment and ask yourself if you have any restrictive patterns working in this area to block your thinking. Carefully search for the *have to's* and the *can't's* and then play with this question; "How would I approach this situation if I *didn't* have to do things that way?" Or, "What would happen if I were really free to handle this in absolutely any way that I wanted to handle it, without any restrictions of any kind?"

There is a classic puzzle which demonstrates the limiting effect of *have to* and *can't* in approaching some of the real situations of our day to day lives. Again, I urge you to work on this and solve it without looking back at the solution on page 278. The thought processes that you will go through in attempting to solve the puzzle will help to reinforce the principle that is involved.

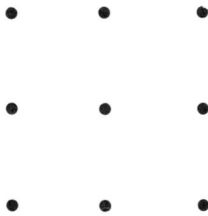

• • •

• • •

• • •

Draw four straight, connected lines (no more than four) without lifting the pencil from the paper, so that the four lines connect all nine dots. Lines may intersect, but not retrace.

When you have solved that puzzle—and the others presented earlier in this chapter—go back and look at how your thought processes worked as you approached each of them. See whether any of the five braking mechanisms we have reviewed may have limited your ability to find the solutions easily. Be sure that you understand the principles involved in each of those simple exercises, and especially be sure that you know how to *release* your creative ability the next time you encounter a similar situation in the real world.

Perhaps something should be said here about assumptions. I believe that a lot of unwarranted attacks have been leveled at the process of assuming or making assumptions in various management training programs, books etc. How do you feel about assumptions?

If you look at this subject carefully I feel confident that you will agree that it is impossible to live without making assumptions. You are assuming that the ceiling in the room where you are now sitting is going to stay where it belongs. That is not an absolutely predictable *fact,* but you are basing your behavior upon that assumption. And so it is with countless acts and decisions that we make all day long. The process of evaluation is a process of gauging probabilities on the basis of which we can make assumptions and then take appropriate or reasonable risks.

The hazard is not in *making* assumptions—it is in *not recognizing* that we are making them! When you *assume* something and treat it as though it were a *fact,* then you are very likely to get into serious trouble. It is impossible to avoid *making* assumptions, and extremely valuable to continually examine them.

There is one other aspect of the creative potential of your system which I believe is both challenging and exciting. It may well be the primary frontier in the next decade or two in the field of human behavior. That department is the **Eighth Arrow.**

It seems that at least some people—probably all of us—have the capacity to tap into some outside force or source of information or inspiration in our creative efforts to solve the puzzles of our lives. Many highly creative, innovative people have felt as though ideas or new thought processes were flowing *through* them instead of *from* them. Ralph Waldo Emerson said that sometimes it seemed as though an alien force guided his hand as he was writing an essay. He always read those writings with great interest and fascination because he said, ''They always contained concepts which were foreign to my thinking.'' He was perfectly willing to take credit for most of his writing, but he felt certain that in some instances what he was putting on paper was coming from another source than his own thoughts.

Mozart, who wrote some remarkable music at a very early age, commented that much of his music came into his head fully composed. He simply listened and wrote down what he heard. Tchaikovsky, Beethoven, and other great composers related similar experiences.

Thomas Edison, Charles Steinmetz, Albert Einstein— all felt that many of their great scientific breakthroughs came through them from some outside source.

Then, in somewhat recent times, we have had the research of Dr. J.B. Rhine and the extensive studies of the remarkable activities of Edgar Cayce, the clairvoyant who was apparently able to examine, diagnose and prescribe for a person several thousand miles distant while he was in a hypnotic trance state.

Much research is now being conducted in the area of parapsychology or extrasensory perception both in this country and in the Soviet Union. I expect that we will soon have a better understanding of such phenomena as telepathy and clairvoyance, and that practical methods will be developed so that anyone who wants to do so can further develop the ability to allow that talent to flow.

Meanwhile, one of the ways to release your creative potential is to be open to ideas which seem to come from "left field." When a thought pops into your mind which does not seem to be grounded in any of your past experiences, there may be a tendency to toss it out, regard it as nonsense. Instead, take a closer look at it. At least examine it carefully and see if it might be a practical solution to your puzzle even though nothing like that has ever occurred to you before.

One final thought in the area of creative ideas. When you have one, capture it! Sometimes when a great idea pops through, and you recognize it immediately as the simple, ideal solution that you have been looking for, you will find yourself trying, thirty minutes later, to recall what the idea was all about. It's almost as though the old habit patterns and preconceptions in the "REALITY" structure were so thoroughly ingrained that they obliterated the new idea or at least the memory of it. I have found it valuable to carry an "Idea Trap" in my pocket. It is a simple little notebook that fits easily into my shirt pocket. When an idea occurs to me—a new way of handling something, a project I want to start, a call I want to make—I simply note it in my Idea Trap. It may still be a while before I take action, but at least the idea is not going to get lost.

Remember, you are a very creative person. Accept that aspect of yourself and allow it to flourish, to flow, to work for you.

Pressure—turn-on or tie-up?

It's a very delicate operation. The Senator's mental functioning—indeed his life—will depend upon the next few movements of the surgeon's hand. The tumor must come out, but if the surgery is not precise some of the most important parts of the brain will be damaged.

PRESSURE!

The golf ball is four feet from the cup. It's the final hole in the last round of the tournament. As the professional golfer stands over his ball he knows that if he sinks this one he will lock up the first prize money of $25,000. If not, he will be in a sudden-death playoff with three other top pros.

PRESSURE!

It's opening night on Broadway and the star is in her dressing room putting the finishing touches on her make-up. The house is packed and all of the critics are out there. How they like what they see will have a lot to do with how long the play will run.

PRESSURE!

The small private aircraft is circling the field erratically. The pilot has suffered an apparent heart attack

CHAPTER 18

231

and is unconscious. The female passenger has never flown an airplane. Now the controller in the tower will try to help the distraught woman get the airplane safely on the ground.

PRESSURE!

What's next? What do you suppose will happen in each of those pressure situations? How would you expect each of those people to perform?

We need to know more about the *person,* don't we? The key factor is not how much pressure there is, but what is going on within that individual. How much potential the person has is very important, of course. But even more important is the degree to which he or she is able to apply the potential that is there. Some will crumple under the pressure, others will perform even *better* when it is critically important to do so.

One of the most fascinating attributes of the high-performer—the pro in any field who is using a lot of his or her available potential—is the way that person uses pressure as a positive, productive force. This positive response to the real pressures of life not only allows the potential to flow more easily and more consistently, it also allows the high-performer to move on up to the top of his profession—where the pressure is usually the greatest.

Consider that idea very carefully. When you reach the point at which pressure is frightening, overwhelming, too much to handle, your progress stops. You will tend to retreat to a safer, more comfortable level. So long as you see pressure as a stimulating, challenging, exciting adventure, you will continue to reach out and test your abilities at higher levels.

When a person first joins the Toastmasters, for example, the pressure of standing in front of a few friendly, encouraging people can be pretty heavy. Some will find very creative reasons for not being able to come back for additional meetings and others will return and further develop their skills. Those who return probably have no more *potential,* but they are responding to the pressure in a very different way. Later, when there is an opportunity to speak to a large group, the same screening process will be repeated. Some will find it an exciting adventure and others will falter. When you see an outstanding speaker performing with great enthusiasm and confidence, you can be sure that he has been subjected to the same pressures that have been felt by every other public speaker. He has not gritted his teeth and forced himself to continue—or if he has, he has *really* gotten there the hard way. Instead, he has formed the habit of responding to the successively higher levels of pressure in a positive way, using them as turn-ons instead of tie-ups.

Has it ever occurred to you that in nearly every field of endeavor the person who is recognized as the very best is under the greatest pressure? The *top* surgeon, athlete, executive, salesperson, musician or any other professional is under greater pressure, consistently, than the beginner or the person who has been in that field for many years and has stayed at a mediocre level. The corporate president feels the pressure from shareholders, directors and competitors to a much greater extent than others in his firm. The Olympic athlete competes with the world's best, and on world-wide television! Of course, the skills are there, the physical equipment, conditioning and the motivation. But the most important ingredient is the emotional element—how that person *feels* about the pressure.

How do *you* feel about pressure? Do you find yourself flinching when you just think about that *word*—and what it stands for in your "REALITY" structure? Or do you think of pressure as a stimulating, exciting part of your life? Chances are that your response to pressure will be different in various areas of your life. You may love the excitement of an important sales presentation, but not function very effectively when explaining sexual intercourse to your pre-teen daughter; or you might find it stimulating to go sky diving but fall apart under the pressure of making a speech to the local Rotary Club.

It's not so much the amount of pressure as what you do with it that really counts. That's very fortunate, because while it is not possible to get the rest of the world shaped up, there *are* some things that you can do about your own system. Pressure can be converted into positive, achieving, productive tensions or limiting, destructive, negative tensions—and it's up to you. You are in charge of that conversion process—or you *can* be if you want to be.

The first, and by far the most important, step in dealing with pressure more effectively is to strengthen your recognition and acceptance of the fact that *you* create your own tensions—positive or negative—with your reactions or responses to what is happening in your world. Or, with your reactions to what *seems* to be happening or what you think *may* happen. Tension in your system is a do-it-to-yourself project! Circumstances don't make you tense. Other people don't make you tense. *You* make you tense!

Are you comfortable with that idea? Listen to your self-talk when you are feeling negative tensions. Do you slip into such thoughts as, "Sales quotas make me tense," or, "People who drive like that really irritate me!"? It would be a lot more accurate—and more responsible—to acknowledge the fact that you are *reacting* to what is happening. "I react with tension when I am given a sales quota," or "When I see people driving like that I react with anger!"

Make a list of the pressures you encounter in your job, your family, social activities, on the tennis court—in all of the various areas of your life. List as many as you can think of, whether you now respond to them positively or negatively. Then look at each one and evaluate as honestly as you can whether you have been regarding it as an event or activity which has "made you tense" or as something to which you have been "reacting with tension." Spend some time with each one that falls in the first category and trace what is really happening. See if you can develop a comfortable feeling about the fact that it is not the event, but your response that is creating the tension in your physical system.

Before we look at what you can do to change those

responses, let's take a closer look at their nature. How do they get started in the first place? What is the essential difference between a positive tension response and a negative one?

Here's how it works. To the degree that you are thinking about the successful results of an outstanding performance—the rewards—the brakes are released and the potential which you have will flow easily and spontaneously. To the degree that your thoughts—and feelings—are focused on the terrible consequences you will suffer if you perform badly, muscles will work against muscles and the talents, knowledge and skills which you do possess will be blocked.

COERCIVE PRESSURE   **MAGNETIC PRESSURE**

HAVE TO   **WANT TO**

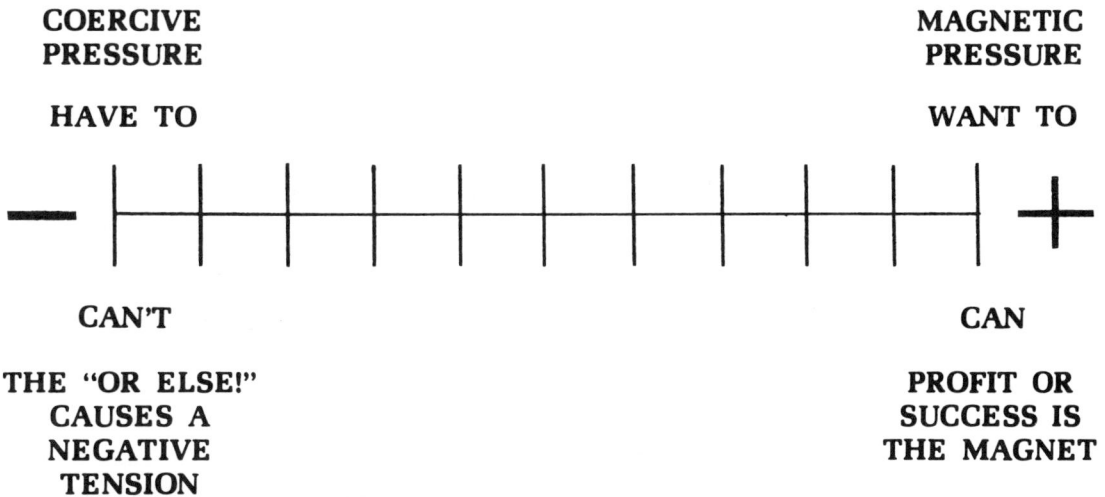

CAN'T   **CAN**

THE "OR ELSE!" CAUSES A NEGATIVE TENSION   **PROFIT OR SUCCESS IS THE MAGNET**

As in all of the other mechanisms of release that we have been exploring, this is a matter of degree. Rarely will anyone be all the way over at the positive or negative end of this continuum. Whatever potential you do have in any area of activity will tend to flow naturally and consistently as your perception of pressure leans toward the positive, reward end of the scale. The outstanding American swimming champion, Shirley Babashoff, said it all in two short sentences during the 1976 Olympics in Montreal: "The difference between winners and losers is that winners think about what they want to do. Losers think about what they are afraid might happen."

Have you ever walked over to the coffee pot, filled your cup with coffee and started back to where you were sitting? The cup was pretty full, but everything was going along quite nicely until some friendly, helpful person said, "Be careful, don't spill that!" Oops! As long as your attention was directed toward the goal of getting back to your chair, all was well. As soon as you thought about how messy it would be if you spilled the coffee, you were a lot more likely to spill it. If you type, you know what usually happens when you try hard not to make any mistakes. The golfer knows about the strange magnetic attraction of the sand trap or the water hazard—the more that you worry about it the more likely that your ball will find it.

Repetition can build a habitual, automated reaction pattern. As we saw in our discussion of the Restrictive Conditioning Process in Chapter 8, the repeated association of a particular kind of behavior or activity with a negative emotion will form a reflexive, automatic reaction. And to the degree that such a pattern is formed, any encounter with that stimulus will trigger the same kind of negative emotion and the same limitation on the flow of available potential.

It is almost as though you had installed a push-button in your system, wired into your mental processes so that when the button gets pushed a circuit is automatically closed to stimulate a negative tension response in the physical system. And each time the button gets pressed, the circuit is reinforced so that it is even more likely to trigger the tension reaction the next time it is pushed.

Here are two kinds of action you can take to release the very restrictive effect of these negative tension responses.

First, form the habit of directing your attention toward the rewarding results of successful performance whenever you approach any activity or project. When you find yourself thinking about (worrying about) the terrible things that may happen, do not grit your teeth and try hard not to think negatively. Simply acknowledge the presence of those negative images, recognize them as *possibilities,* and then let your thoughts and feelings move back to the positive end of the scale. Imagine how it will feel when you have successfully concluded the project, how rewarding it will be to have established a meaningful relationship or how exciting it is to close a sale like this one.

Trying hard not to think negatively is like trying hard not to think about alligators. The harder you try *not* to, the more you will find yourself thinking about them. The best way not to think about alligators is to become absolutely fascinated with giraffes. And the way to avoid the destructive effort of dwelling on the negative things which might happen to you is to become absorbed in the image—and the emotions—of the positive consequences of effective performance.

I hope that it is clear that I am not suggesting that you ignore all hazards, dangers or possible difficulties. The pros and cons should be carefully considered. Sometimes it is valuable to ask the question, "What is the worst thing that can possibly happen?" It is always useful to be aware of the dangers which may be involved and just what their consequences might be. But then, having acknowledged and evaluated those negative possibilities, focus your attention on images of successful behavior and on the positive emotions which go with that success.

Next, if you want to do so it is possible to re-wire your buttons. In those areas where you have developed automatic reaction mechanisms and the negative tensions are instantaneous reflexes, you have the ability to "re-program" the system so that when that same button is pushed the automatic response will be different.

First, list some of your buttons. Use the form on page 279 to identify some of the situations to which you now automatically react with a negative emotion and the resulting destructive tensions. Do you have a door-slamming button? A four-letter word button? How about a tail-gating button? Look at buttons relating to your job, your family, social areas, sports—every aspect of your life. Then, when you have made a list, go back and look at each one of the buttons you have identified and ask yourself, "Is this a button which is to my advantage to have in my system? Do I choose to nurture and cultivate this reaction pattern or would I be better able to achieve my goals if I were to change it?"

Then, on page 280, describe the kind of reaction you would really *like* to have to that kind of stimulus. If you were to develop the kind of response that you would admire, respect, feel good about, what would it be? Sometimes it helps to think about this as it might apply to another person. If you knew someone who handled that kind of situation in a very mature, effective, profitable manner, how would you describe that person's behavior?

Next, on page 281, write out an affirmation, following the guidelines which start on page 270. A positive, present-tense statement which describes the kind of automatic response pattern you would like to have in that area.

Here is an example. Suppose that one of the buttons on your list is a tail-gating button. When someone follows very closely behind you in fast-moving traffic you react with anger. As you review that response mechanism you can see that it is not really to your advantage to keep it and reinforce it. Anger in fast-moving traffic could lead to a lot of trouble. So, you decide that this is one button that you would really like to re-wire.

What kind of reaction would you like to have become the genuine, free-flowing reflex in your system when someone is tail-gating you in fast traffic? Perhaps a calm, relaxed inclination to move over to the next lane and let the other driver pass you. Then translate that into a personal, positive, present-tense affirmation. It could be as simple as, "When someone is following very closely behind me in traffic I calmly move over to the next lane and let him go by."

Add that affirmation to your list. Program it into your "REALITY" structure by experiencing, in your imagination, exactly that kind of event. Imagine yourself pulling over and watching the other driver pass you. Let yourself feel the positive emotion, the calmness and the pride that you are able to respond to a potentially dangerous situation in a mature, safe manner.

As you work with that affirmation repeatedly, vividly experiencing the kind of behavior that you want to have become your normal, natural reaction and the emotion that goes with it, the reflex will be revised. The next time you are in traffic and someone is following behind you only a few feet from your rear bumper, you will be more inclined to react with calmness and just move over to the next lane. You may want to add four or five affirmations to your list which relate to the buttons you want to re-wire. As you notice that the reactions have changed, you can substitute new affirmations to modify some other negative reflexes.

These affirmations can be used along with your others at night, in the morning and any other time during the day. However, I do not recommend that you attempt to re-wire a button when it has just been pressed. As long as that negative tension response is still a part of your system, when the button is pushed you are in no condition to work on the project of revising the circuit. Wait until later, when you have cooled down and you are able to think more rationally. Then, look back, acknowledge that you didn't handle that situation very well and practice the kind of response you'd like to have the next time something like that happens.

Is there a danger that you will become some kind of placid, unresponsive vegetable by re-wiring all of those buttons? Not likely. There will probably be some irritations which are just not worth taking the time to revise, and a person whose primary emotional response to life is positive—enthusiastic and optimistic—will scarcely be regarded as a vegetable.

Still another area of concern in the general department of pressure and tension is the very hazardous process called "stress." So long as you have any buttons left
which trigger negative tensions, and you live in a social
structure, there is the danger of stress developing in
your physical system. I am using the word *stress* to
mean the build-up of unresolved tensions in your
system.

If you feel angry and you go ahead and hit something—or someone—then the tension is cancelled. The
chemicals which were released into your bloodstream to
prepare you for the expression of your anger were used
and the physical system returns to normal. But if you
do *not* express your anger, if you bottle it up inside of
you, then the chemical changes are not immediately
dissipated. They will be, of course, over a period of
time, unless another situation comes along to which you
again react with anger. If you chronically bottle up such
emotions as anger, fear (or anxiety), frustration or grief,
the resulting chronic change in the body's chemistry can
result in physical disaster.

Because we live in a social world, there will be times
when it is appropriate to "swallow" our emotions. If
you were swimming from one end of the pool to the
other, under water, it would be wise to hold your
breath. And there are social situations in which it is not
profitable to "blow your top." So, you don't show the
emotions that you actually are feeling. You bottle them
up inside you. If that happens frequently, you are probably asking for trouble in the form of serious physical
illness.

Research teams in the medical profession have found
statistical indications that people who suppress the emotion of grief—people who find it difficult to cry when
they have suffered a deep personal loss—are about four
and one half times as likely to contract lung cancer as
those who express their grief easily. The chronic suppression of anxiety—over deadlines, finances, relationships or just "the future"—may lead to ulcers, sexual
disfunction, ulcerative colitis, and blood sugar im-
balance. A chronic feeling of frustration in children—

confrontation with what physicians have come to call "smother love"—seems to be one of the primary causative factors in the development of asthma. A recent study has indicated that females who chronically suppress their anger are more than twice as likely to contract breast cancer as those who are able to express the anger which they feel. The probability of coronary heart disease, skin disorders and even arthritis are all linked to stress. Your resistance to infectious or contagious illnesses also seems to be largely a function of your stress level. You are more likely to catch a cold, the flu or the measles when you are under stress than when you are not. If you are interested in more detailed information about the relationship between stress and your physical health, you will find several excellent books dealing with that subject listed in the bibliography at the end of this book.

But let's see what you can do about *releasing* the stress which may impair your good health. Many years ago Dr. Hans Selye suggested a simple method which we have been teaching in our *PACE* Seminars with excellent results since 1961. We call the system Gross Physical Impact Activity, and it simply amounts to having a good, violent workout with a punching bag or a reasonably exact facsimile.

If you have access to a gymnasium or a health club, make use of the training bag for stress release. The training bag is the large cylindrical one—about sixteen inches in diameter, four feet tall, hanging from a chain. If you do not have access to a place where there is a bag like this, you might want to get one of your own and hang it in the garage or the family room. I can promise you that if it is there, people will use it—and the cost will be returned in reduced medical bills. Look in your telephone directory under gymnasium equipment. Many of the companies with which we work have installed punching bags in the manufacturing area and have found that relationships improved and time off the job because of illness diminished.

If there is no punching bag available, try pounding on a piece of wood or a log with a hammer. Or beat the dust out of some throw rugs. Every time you change the sheets, hit the mattress fifteen or twenty times—and do that with each bed, because the more beds you have the more stress you are likely to be experiencing.

Any kind of gross physical impact activity will serve to release the stress—restore the normal chemical balance in your system. Skillful activity does not seem to be as effective. Playing golf does involve impact, but there is the danger that the golf game may create more stress than it is releasing! Handball or racquetball are excellent, particularly if you can go on the court by yourself and practice.

Of course, many forms of exercise—running, swimming, calisthenics—are beneficial to your system in building your heart and keeping your body in condition. For releasing stress, however, the exercise should involve impact and should not require skill. Gross, Physical Impact Activity.

There are two applications of this stress-reducing method. As a preventive device, have some Gross Physical Impact Activity at regular intervals. Once each week, or even more frequently than that, depending upon how much stress you are likely to build up in your system.

The second application is when you feel the stress building up. When you have felt a lot of pressure from your job, when things aren't going as smoothly as you would like around the house or when there has been a major change in your life will probably be appropriate times. If you will be alert for them, your body will give you signals that the stress is developing in your system. I cannot tell you exactly what they will be, because each person has a different pattern. When you notice something different happening like a skin rash, headache, a muscular twitch, at least look at the possibility that it may be an indication that your stress level is reaching the danger point. Try some gross physical impact activity and see what happens. Of course, it may be that you just need a good night's sleep or that your nutritional intake has been inadequate, but if it is due to a stress buildup, then having a good workout with the punching bag will help to release it.

There is one other area that is related to this whole department of tensions and stress which I would like to explore with you—headaches. Since the American population spends hundreds of millions of dollars each year on various headache remedies, most of which are the result of tensions which stem from a particular kind of emotional conflict, you may find value in a very simple technique which will eliminate most headaches—and other functional tension pain—quickly and easily. I call this process "Manipulating The Conflict" and it is very easily applied, completely portable, healthier for your system than chemical pain relievers and usually works faster than they do. If it doesn't work, then take an aspirin or consult your physician.

We have been teaching this method in our *PACE* Seminars for many years and have not only found it to be extremely effective, but we have also noticed that as people who have had frequent headaches use this a few times they often stop having the headaches altogether. I believe that this stems from an understanding of the basic principle which underlies the process. As you become better acquainted with the type of conflict which causes such tensions to develop, it is possible to free yourself of the conflicts and thus eliminate the tensions.

There are three simple steps to this technique.

First, get acquainted with the tension.

Second, test three images to see which will cause an increase and which will cause a diminishing of the tension.

Finally, use those images to increase and diminish the tension until it is eliminated.

To get acquainted with the tension means just sit quietly in a fairly comfortable position, close your eyes and carefully examine the tension. Describe it to yourself in as much detail as you can. Where is it located? Is it well defined or fuzzy around the edges? Is it steady or does it pulsate? Is there any temperature difference—is that particular area warmer or colder? Does it feel like an ache (dull) or a pain (sharp)? Does it feel like something pressing—and if so from the inside or the outside? Or does it feel like a violin string that is being pulled tight? As you look at it is it moving around at all or changing in any way, or is it steady? If the tension is painful in more than one area, which is the most intense, moved to another area, changed shape or changed in any other way? Just note the change, if any, and then go on to the next image.

Now put yourself into three different kinds of situations in your imagination and notice whether the tension changes in any way with each of them. There is no way to predict what change will happen, or even if there will be any change, so do not try to anticipate—just observe. The first image is one of being in a situation where you are doing something unpleasant, distasteful, that you really do not enjoy, but you have put it off as long as you can and now you are doing it. It can be something like cleaning out the garage, firing an employee, working on your income tax—anything that you regard as unpleasant. Crawl into that situation and experience the *emotion* that goes with it, the irritation, resentment or frustration that goes with, "I don't want to do this, but I have to!"

When you have let that build up in your mental system for about half a minute, take another look at the tension. Has it changed in any way? More or less intense, moved to another area, changed shape or changed in any other way? Just note the change, if any, and then go on to the next image.

Now imagine that you are in a situation where you have been planning on and looking forward to doing something that you really enjoy, but now at the last minute something has come up and you can't do it. You really want to, and you have made all the necessary preparations, but something has happened which makes it impossible for you to go ahead. It could be a golf game, a fishing trip, a date with someone you like a lot or any other activity that you really enjoy. Let yourself *feel* the let-down, frustrating, disappointed emotion that goes with, "I really want to do that, but I can't!" Stay with that for about half a minute and then once again look at the tension to see whether anything has happened to it. Just observe the change, if any, and then go on to the last image.

Imagine that you are off by yourself in a situation where you can do anything that you want to do and you don't have to do anything that you don't want to do. You are able to call the shots just the way you want to, completely free to do whatever you want. You can walk in the woods, lie in the shade of a big tree by a stream on a warm summer day, stroll along the beach, listen to your favorite music—whatever you want to do. Let yourself get into that situation in your imagination and feel the emotion that goes with, "I am completely free to be myself, to do what I want to do. There's no one to tell me what to do or what not to do. Free!"

Now, again check the tension to see whether there is any change.

Nearly always one of the images will cause a noticeable increase in the tension and one will cause it to diminish. If that is the case, then simply alternate between those two images, going back and forth with the emotions that go with them. Each time that you go from one to the other, the tension will increase a little less, diminish a little more and after a few of those alternations you will find that it has completely dissipated and that neither of the images will bring it back.

You may find that only one of the images will cause a change in the tension, and the other two do not affect it at all. In that event, alternate between the one which caused a change and either of the other two. Again, go back and forth until the tension is eliminated.

If none of the three images causes any change in the tension you may want to try some gross physical impact activity, and if that doesn't release it then try an aspirin or other analgesic. If you frequently have headaches which will not yield to this process, I suggest that you discuss them with your doctor.

Try to use this technique just as quickly as you possibly can when you first have an inkling that a headache may be developing. You may find, if you catch it soon enough, that just the process of describing the tension, acknowledging it, will release it.

The reason that this method works so easily and quickly is directly related to the ideas we explored in

Chapter 15. As you are able to accept and feel comfortable about the fact that there are no "have to's" or "can'ts," as you break out of that psychological prison and recognize that all of your behavior starts with decisions, selections of alternatives, choices, you will find the headaches come less often and finally not at all! When you find yourself in a situation in which you feel as though "they" (or circumstances) are keeping you from doing something that you want to do, or in which you feel as though you are being forced to do something that you don't want to do, that conflict between the pressure of the perceived external coercion and the internal motivation to "do it your way" may lead to a headache or other painful tension. It may cause you to tighten up some muscles and hold them in a state of suspended tension for a period of time. As the muscles fatigue, the waste acids which are produced by the fatigue cannot be carried off by the blood stream fast enough. The nerve cells which are imbedded in the muscle fiber react to that build-up and send pain signals to the brain. Then there may be a "vicious cycle" or spasm reaction. The more the headache hurts, the more tense you get and the more tense you get the more it hurts.

If you lie in bed in the morning thinking, "I don't want to get up, but I have to," you may be asking for some painful tension in your system. Or, it could just as easily be, "I want to stay in bed, but I can't." The long-range solution is to really accept the fact that it is your choice. If you do get out of bed it will be because you have decided that in the long run that will be more advantageous to you than spending the day in bed. You are, in fact, *free* to make that judgment and that choice.

Sometimes an intense pain can stem from the "double bind" feeling that you *have to* do something, but you *can't* do it. I remember an attorney who attended one of our *PACE* Seminars who was suffering from a recurring headache nearly every day that he went in to his office. As we discussed what was happening at the office the cause of his tension and the resulting pain became evident right away. His secretary had been with him for many years, helped him build his practice and was a loyal, dedicated employee. Over the past year, though, she had begun to show signs of senility. She misfiled important documents, cancelled appointments with important clients, transcribed dictation erroneously and forgot where she had stored supplies. Without realizing it, the attorney had slipped into a dilemma. "I *have to* let her go because she could have a disastrous effect on my practice, but I *can't* fire someone who has put in so many years of loyal service!" Each day on his way to the office that pressure would build up in his system and by the time he got to the office the pain was unbearable.

As soon as he identified the conflict he took appropriate action—retired his secretary with a nice pension and replaced her with an efficient, younger person. Presto, no more headaches.

It is not necessary for you to know what the specific conflict is which is causing the headache in order for the manipulation of the conflict to be effective. When you feel the tension beginning to develop simply use this process to release it. It may be that after you have sent it on its way you will want to ask yourself, "What is the conflict I am experiencing which could have caused that tension to get started?" When you have identified it then take it apart and confront the fact that you are in charge, you are going to make a choice selecting the most desirable or least undesirable course of action. Remember that responsibility—as defined in Chapter 15—and freedom are two sides of the same coin!

Now, let's review the five key concepts we have been examining in this chapter.
1. Tension in your system—positive or negative—is a do-it-to-yourself project. "They" do not make you tense, *you* do. Work on the project of becoming comfortable with that idea.
2. When you are under pressure, in your job, family, social activities or sports, focus your attention on the rewards of outstanding, successful perform-

ance. Think about what you want to have happen and how good it will feel when it does.

3. Some of your response patterns have become pretty automatic—instantaneous emotional reactions when the "buttons" are pushed. If you want to, you can identify those buttons, decide what kind of reaction you would like to have and re-wire the buttons with Constructive Imagination.

4. If you hold in your emotions, bottle them up inside, they may build into stress, disrupt the chemical balance of your physical system and cause serious illnesses. Release stress with Gross Physical Impact Activity.

5. When conflicts in your mental system result in such painful physical tensions as headaches, Manipulate The Conflict to release the tensions.

Try these simple methods in your own life. You will find that they will increase your energy level, improve your health and release vast new amounts of your potential!

Learn how to relax

When you were a child, one of the things you did very well, easily, and quickly was to relax. Not only when your fatigue level turned off the tensions, but at any time that you wanted to do so you could sit down or lie down and simply let the tensions go. For many reasons you may have partially lost that ability. Many adults find it quite difficult to relax, not only at night when they want to go to sleep, but at other times as well. When you want to do some creative thinking, when you are involved in athletic activities, when you are getting ready to give a speech or an important sales presentation, it might be helpful to be able to let your physical system relax for a moment.

There is a very simple technique which you can use to practice and develop the ability to relax. I call it **Deep Relaxation.** There are seven steps to the practicing sequence, but as you go through them repeatedly you will lose track of the steps and the entire process will become automatic and easy to use.

1. The first step is to put yourself into a position in which it will be easy for you to relax. I do not recommend that you lie down on a bed for this purpose unless you want to go to sleep. The bed is so thoroughly associated with sleep that if you relax deeply while lying there you will almost surely go to sleep. As you develop the use of this skill, it will not be so important, but, at least in the early stages of practice, other locations are preferable. Lying on a couch (unless you associate that couch with taking

naps), sitting in a comfortable chair with a high back, or lying on the floor, perhaps with a pillow under your head, are all acceptable positions. Select one which seems to you to be a good place to relax. Whether you are sitting up or stretched out, you should be in an "open" position. Your feet should be apart and one hand or arm should not be touching the other.

If you are sitting in a chair without a high back to lean your head against, sit so that your head is balanced on your shoulders, with a minimum of muscular effort required to keep it erect. If you are sitting up very straight, there is the possibility that your head will drop forward as you relax; if you are slumped down in the chair your head may fall backward. Sit with your head nicely balanced so that you don't need to exert much effort to keep it there.

Your eyes should be closed.

2. Take a deep breath and hold it for just a few seconds. As you hold your breath, notice the tensions in various parts of your body. Exhale. As you let the air out of your lungs feel the tensions draining out of your system in much the same way that the tension drains out of a balloon when the air is let out. Then simply breathe normally, deeply.

3. Next, dwell on some images of relaxation. Think of yourself as a cloud floating softly in the air—or as a heavy weight sinking into a pile of soft, foamy cushions. Some people find it more comfortable to work with a feeling of lightness; others find that they relax more easily as they think of themselves becoming very heavy. Try both if you wish and see which one seems easiest for you to use. Tell yourself that you are relaxing now, letting the tensions drain out of your system. As you think about how good it feels to relax, experience the feeling in your imagination as vividly and realistically as you can. Go over your body, letting each part relax easily and smoothly. Your feet and legs, hands and arms—feel the relaxation spreading into your body, notice that the

muscles in your face are relaxing, easily letting the tensions drift away. Tell yourself that with each breath you take you are relaxing more and more deeply.

After a minute or so of imagery, start a countdown from one to ten. With each count notice that you are relaxing more easily and more deeply. Count slowly and let yourself revel in the good feeling of allowing your tensions to slip away. Do not "try hard" to ignore distractions or noises that may be going on outside your room. Simply acknowledge them and let yourself become increasingly fascinated with the feeling of relaxation that is spreading through your system.

4. When you reach the count of ten, think to yourself, "I am now in Deep Relaxation and ready for Constructive Conditioning." At this point you can dwell on one of your affirmations, experiencing it vividly in your imagination several times with the positive emotion that you want to associate with that behavioral pattern or attitude. In this state of Deep Relaxation your Conscious Mental Processes are "turned down"—especially the process of evaluation. Thus, your affirmation will have a dramatically powerful impact on your "REALITY" structure. You have reached a state in which your central nervous system is operating in a slower, more regular cycle. Your subconscious "REALITY" storage process is more open and receptive at this time and you can use the relaxed state very productively to accelerate the changes you want to make in your attitude patterns.

Or, if you want to do so, you can use this period of relaxation for some creative thinking. If you have been struggling with a "problem," take it with you into this Deep Relaxation state. Quietly define the situation as you see it and let the solution flow. You may feel a little startled the first time that you use Deep Relaxation for this purpose because you will find some exciting and brilliant solutions flowing very quickly. While you are relaxed, the preconceptions which have been blocking your progress can more easily be bypassed and your creative abilities will become much more apparent.

Of course, if you want to use this technique to help you fall asleep, just get into bed and go through the first three steps, focusing your attention on how good it feels to be so relaxed. Next thing you know, it will be morning.

5. When you have worked with your affirmation for a minute or two—or you have done the creative thinking you set out to accomplish—then think to yourself, "Each time that I practice Deep Relaxation it becomes easier and easier for me. I relax easily and deeply whenever I want to do so." This is, of course, a reinforcing affirmation to help you to develop this technique more quickly.

6. Now, count backwards from ten to one. With each count, tell yourself that you are becoming more alert, awake, and energetic. Notice that you can feel the energy returning to your physical system as you count back to a wide-awake state of mind.

7. When you reach the count of "one" stand up, stretch, walk around a little. Notice that you are more alert and energetic than when you started. One of the real benefits of this method is the extra energy it can give you when you are feeling logy or sluggish.

Practice Deep Relaxation at least once each day until you are able to relax easily and quickly under almost any kind of circumstances. At first it will help to practice alone with a minimum of distractions, but you will soon reach the point that noises and activity which once were distracting no longer are disturbing. Learning this method is much like learning the scale on the piano or developing your forehand stroke on the tennis court. With practice it will become automatic, and when you have learned it you will find that it is an invaluable skill.

Not only will it help you to effect changes in your attitudes and behavior much more quickly than by the use of Constructive Imagination at night and in the morning, it will help you to create new approaches to puzzling job and family situations; it will give you a simple method with which to counteract any tendency you may have to slow down in the middle of the day; and you will know that any time, anywhere you are, if you want to do so you can sit down for a moment and relax the tensions you are feeling in your physical system. If you feel tense when you fly, use Deep Relaxation as soon as you have fastened your seat belt.

You will find many practical applications for this process in your day-to-day life, not the least of which may be the ability to go to sleep much more easily and quickly than has been possible for you in the past.

Practice Deep Relaxation and let it work for you. One more way to **release your brakes!**

You are changing the world

In the first chapter of this book I urged you to adopt a very *selfish* attitude toward its contents—to search for ideas which might help you to lead a more fulfilling, happier life and achieve your goals more easily and quickly. I hope that you have done just that and that you are already aware of the changes which have come about in your thinking and in your behavior. Now I would like to pursue that idea of self interest to one more level.

Rational self interest requires a larger perspective of how you fit into the overall scheme of things. A time perspective, a grasp of the importance of relationships and the various epi-organisms of which you are a part, and an understanding and acceptance of the degree to which you can influence or control events in your universe.

Let's look at the time element first.

Behavior which seems to be to your self interest in the short range can often prove to be disastrous in the long run. The small child who sees a bowl full of jelly beans on the coffee table may try one, like it, and devour the whole supply. Next day the child has a stomachache. What will happen the next time that youngster sees a bowl full of jelly beans on the table? Chances are that they will all disappear again. The child may realize that there is a probability of a stomachache, but that won't happen until tomorrow—and it just *might* not happen at all. The same sequence can, of course, be translated to "adult" levels, substituting alcohol, drugs, or various foods for the jelly beans.

Mature behavior is based on an evaluation of the long-range consequences—selecting the alternative course of action which will probably be most advantageous (or least disadvantageous) in the long run. With an incomplete and distorted "REALITY" structure the basis for making those evaluations, it will not always be possible to predict long-range consequences accurately. But this evaluation is certainly worth striving for, and it is an area in which we all have a great deal more potential than we are now using!

When you are confronted with a difficult decision, try jumping ahead in time and asking yourself, "When I look back on this moment several years from now, what will I be proud to remember that I did?"

Another aspect of this larger perspective of self interest is the impact of your decisions and behavior on the people part of your environmental system. There are other individuals who, perhaps without your knowing it, are looking to you for leadership. There are people who admire you—want to be like you. Your children, of course, are in that category. The example you are setting for them will have an effect on their lives and on future generations as well. If it is to your advantage to enhance your environment (part of your Whole Person System), then it will be to your self interest to *be* the kind of person you want your children (or others) to become. They will surely follow what you *are* much more consistently than what you *say*.

Look at the epi-organisms to which you belong. We have seen several examples illustrating that groups have personalities which are very much like those of individual people. The attitudes and behavior of each person within the group have an effect upon the personality and the effectiveness of the group. Every thought that each person has influences that person's behavior; the behavior is communicated to the group and contributes to the group's self-image and to its ability to function effectively.

It may be easiest to see this process in action within a family group or a small athletic team. The attitudes of each member have a contagious impact on the entire group. Some will have a more powerful effect upon the activity, progress and achievement of the team or family than others, but each member makes a contribution—positive or negative.

The same pattern can be traced in a company, in a club, a community, a church group, an association, trade union, political party, neighborhood, project team, sales organization or branch of the armed services. We can see the phenomenon in a gang, a lynch mob, or a group of terrorists. Each person in the group makes his or her input. Individual personalities meld with others to become a group personality, but that group personality would not be the same with any one of its members absent.

You are a part of many such groups, and whether you try to do so or not, you are making a contribution to the personalities of those groups, to their effectiveness (the degree to which they use their potential) and their impact on the larger group, society. Will it be to your self interest to make an increasingly positive contribution to those epi-organisms?

There is an interesting possibility that you may want to spend a little time thinking about. I believe that the primary purpose of a living creature is to become what it is capable of being—to fulfill its potential. We can see this principle in action with animals at all levels of the evolutionary scale. Particularly, we can see it with human beings—with you and me. People who address themselves to that project, people who focus their attention and thoughts on that primary purpose, seem to be the ones who enjoy the highest level of joy, happiness, and contentment. If that is true, and I believe that all of our experiences tend to support or corroborate that premise, then the same should apply to the group personality which is so similar to that of an individual.

The primary purpose of an athletic team should be to fulfill its potential, to become the best athletic team that it is capable of becoming. Not necessarily the best team in the world, but the best that it is capable of being (which just *might* also be the best in the world). That objective will be reached most easily if there is an internal consistency—if each player is working to fulfill his or her own personal potential, helping to facilitate the growth of other members of the team, *and* helping the team to release its brakes, too!

The purpose of your family is to explore and actualize the unique potential which it possesses. The family can accomplish things which no individual could achieve alone; it can be exciting to get acquainted with the talents and skills which *we* have as a group and then work together to develop and use those abilities.

The primary purpose of a nation is to become the very best country that it can become—to fulfill or make maximum use of whatever potential it possesses. Not at the expense of other countries, not necessarily becoming the "best" country in the world, but the best that it can possibly be. Once again, that goal will be achieved far more easily if the individual citizens and groups within that nation are applying themselves to the project of fulfilling their own potentials in a manner consistent with the larger purpose of actualizing the national potential.

The same concept can be followed to its larger context—that of the human race as an epi-organism. The primary purpose of humanity is to fulfill *its* potential, to explore and to utilize the vast store of talent and knowledge which mankind possesses and our built-in desire or motivation to use that ability productively. Do we, as a species, have potential that we are not tapping?

What a question! Talk about driving with the brakes on! If our primary purpose is to become the kind of society that we are capable of being, to release the vast potential of the world's population, then we have a long way to go. But that purpose will be achieved much more quickly as each member of the group, each person on our planet, addresses himself or herself to the project of fulfilling that person's individual potential in a manner that is consistent with the larger purpose of releasing the potential of the human race!

If we, as individuals and as groups, will set our goals, make our decisions, take actions, select alternatives in a manner that will not only help us to accomplish our immediate needs and desires, but also contribute to the longer range purpose of fulfilling the potential of humanity, then each person, each group of people, will find the path smoother, easier, and far happier.

There is no goal in life that you cannot achieve as easily (probably far *more* easily) within the framework of this concept as you could by working against the stream. When you harm another person, destroy or confiscate someone's property, or accomplish your goal in a dishonest manner, the effect on the groups of which you are a part is destructive. In a very direct and often immediate sense, that is not to your own self interest!

In today's world it is very easy for a person to feel insignificant. Just trying to conceive of one billion of anything is difficult. Realizing that you are one of four billion people on this planet could easily cause you to adopt the attitude that what you think or what you do has little meaning in the course of history. Nothing could be further from the truth!

Who you are, what you are, what you do and how you do it are all having a profound effect upon this world. You are neither the *most* important nor the *least* important human being who has ever lived, but your existence—and what you do with what you are—is *very* important. How do you feel about that?

The human race is a system, and we know that any change in a system affects the entire system. If we dump some chemicals into a river, the whole ecology of the area reacts to the new input. If there is an increase in sun-spot activity, changes can be observed throughout the entire solar system. The fact that you are alive has already had an impact on the system of humanity. If you had not happened, or if you had not lived to your present age, the world would not have been the same. And your existence will have an unpredictable, reverberating effect for many years to come.

If you were to go back through history, you could find countless examples of people who felt quite insignificant during their lifetimes, whose lives and examples helped to mold the character of inventors, composers, authors, or statesmen. People who had an idea which all by itself did not amount to much, but which sparked the thinking and enthusiasm of others and led to major changes in the history of mankind.

No matter what you do in this life, or what you neglect to do, it is having an effect on your own future, on the future of the other individuals with whom you come in contact, and on the various epi-organisms of which you are a part—including the very destiny of the human race.

I am not suggesting that you *can* change the world if you want to do so. I am asserting that you *are* changing the world! Now the question is, what kind of change are you making? What sort of impact is your life, your activity, your achievement having on our planet?

The only system over which you have any direct ability to exercise some control is your *own* system. And the only part of that system that you can change is what is going on right now in your conscious mental processes. You cannot change what has happened there in the past, but you can *use* your past thoughts and feelings in the present, either positively or negatively. You cannot control tomorrow, either, except by guiding and directing what is going on in your mental system right now. You can decide what you want to accomplish—what goals you want to achieve in the future—and you can use your present thoughts to point yourself in that direction and release whatever potential you have to get there, but still the only control you have is over your present thoughts.

At first it doesn't seem like much. The only event in the entire world that you can control is what you are thinking and feeling at the present instant—but that is enough! That's all you *need* to be able to control.

As you take charge of that process and use it to release your brakes, to allow the vast untapped potential which you have to flow naturally and spontaneously, not only you, but your world will be happier, healthier, and a lot more fun to be around!

Constructive Imagination Project

Here is a list of the kinds of characteristics and skills which you may want to strengthen with **Constructive Imagination**. Other areas will probably occur to you which will be of particular interest to you; this list is only intended to be a "thought starter."

VOCATIONAL/PROFESSIONAL

Organization—use of time.
Long-range planning.
Helping associates to grow.
Communication of ideas.
Listening for understanding.
Getting things done promptly.
Willingness to delegate.
Willingness to assume responsibility.
Attitude toward "routine" activity.

Attitude toward mate's vocational activity.
Decisiveness.
Persuasiveness.
Attitude about organization and its product or service.
Response to change.
Awareness of opportunities.
Perseverance or follow-through.

FAMILY AND SOCIAL

Spending time with family.
Sincere expression of warmth.
Enjoyment of leisure activities.
Skill in bridge or other games.
Conversational communications.
Empathy.
Enjoyment of social activities.
Accepting and encouraging mate's individuality and interests.
Reinforcing family self image.

Dancing skill.
Earning respect of family members.
Sex.
Interest in children's activities.
Patience.
Attitude toward parents.
Attitude toward in-laws.
Development of self-reliance and responsibility in children.
Helping children build self esteem.

PERSONAL

Feeling and showing enthusiasm.
Honesty with self and others.
Public speaking.
Golf, tennis or other sports skills.
Self esteem.
Ability to relax easily.
Cheerfulness.
Calmness.
Flexibility.
Health.

Artistic or creative skills.
Reading rapidly with comprehension.
Legible handwriting.
Freedom from smoking habit.
Grooming and appearance.
Eating and nutritional habits.
Mature view of life.
Concentration.
Memory.
Emotional spontaneity.

The forms on the following pages are intended as guides. You will probably want to use additional sheets of plain paper for your projects, following the pattern set forth here. Take your time and feel free to make changes as you think of more important areas or ways of expressing your ideas more clearly.

Step 1	**Step 2**
Areas in which more positive emotional patterns will help to release my potential:	Probable significance to my future achievement and happiness:

VOCATIONAL/PROFESSIONAL

1 _____

2 _____

3 _____

4 _____

5 _____

FAMILY AND SOCIAL

1 _____

2 _____

3 _____

4 _____

5 _____

PERSONAL

1 _____

2 _____

3 _____

4 _____

5 _____

Step 3

(Use a separate sheet of paper for
each area you have decided upon.)

Characteristic, attitude or skill selected: _____

Probable significance to my future: 1   2   3   4   5

What does that mean to me? Exactly what do I want to strengthen?

What are the emotions I want to cultivate about this area of myself? How would I like to
feel about it?

When I have made the change I want to make, how will I be able to describe myself?

Step 3 (Example)

Characteristic, attitude or skill selected: _____*Concentration*_____

Probable significance to my future: 1   2   ③   4   5

What does that mean to me? Exactly what do I want to strengthen?

The ability to become thoroughly engrossed in a project or activity, to find what I am doing so fascinating that I don't notice what else is going on.

What are the emotions I want to cultivate about this area of myself? How would I like to feel about it?

Enthusiasm, excitement, eager anticipation.

When I have made the change I want to make, how will I be able to describe myself?

A person who easily and quickly allows his/her attention to become fascinated or engrossed in an activity or in another person.

Step 3 (Example)

Characteristic, attitude or skill selected: *Public Speaking*

Probable significance to my future: 1   2   3   ④   5

What does that mean to me? Exactly what do I want to strengthen?

The ability to think on my feet in front of a group of people. Speaking easily, confidently, with enthusiasm and conviction.

What are the emotions I want to cultivate about this area of myself? How would I like to feel about it?

Confidence, enjoyment, at ease - the same feelings I have about talking to one or two people about something I am familiar with.

When I have made the change I want to make, how will I be able to describe myself?

A person who enjoys addressing groups of people and who expresses himself / herself easily, enthusiastically, conversationally.

Step 4 (Example)

Appropriate affirmations for the examples on pages 266 and 267:

Concentration: It is easy for me to focus my attention and become fascinated with a project or activity.

Public Speaking: I have an enthusiastic, conversational style of public speaking and I enjoy the excitement of sharing ideas with large groups of people.

Remember, your affirmations are neither true nor false—they are tools with which to build a more accurate self-image. They will not describe your *present* behavior, but they *will* reflect a more valid image of your real potential!

Review the design rules on pages 270 and 271 before proceeding with *Step 4.*

Step 4

Design a positive verbal affirmation for each area selected.

1 _____

2 _____

3 _____

4 _____

5 _____

6 _____

7 _____

8 _____

9 _____

10 _____

11 _____

12 _____

13 _____

14 _____

15 _____

Now check your affirmations carefully against each of the ten design rules on pages 270 and 271 to be sure that they are properly worded.

DESIGN RULES FOR
WORDING YOUR VERBAL AFFIRMATIONS

1. PERSONAL. Be sure that **you** are in the affirmation. Use a first person pronoun such as "I," "me," "my" in each one. It may be tempting to use a platitude like "Patience is a virtue," or "Enthusiasm makes sales," but such sentences will have no effect whatever on your behavior. If you find yourself feeling some tension about your frequent use of "I" in your affirmations, simply recognize that tension as one more illustration of the effect of childhood programming on your behavior. The purpose of this entire exercise is to bring about some lasting changes in the self image, and the only way that will happen is with first person experience in your imagination, stimulated by a first person affirmation.

2. POSITIVE. In each case, the affirmation must describe the attitude that you want to cultivate or move **toward,** not what you want to diminish or move **away** from. Instead of, "I don't lose my temper," the better affirmation would be, "I am calm and even-tempered."

3. PRESENT TENSE. Reference to the past or the future in an affirmation will diminish or destroy the effect of the triggering sentence. "I am getting things done more promptly than I used to" will stimulate the experiences and emotions related to past behavior—and that is not what you want to be dwelling on. An affirmation phrased in the future tense always remains in the "some day" category and reinforces the fact that you are not behaving that way here and now. Instead of "I am going to be more patient," or, "One of these days I am going to get organized," the better affirmations are, "I am a very patient, understanding person," and, "I organize my time very carefully and follow the plans that I have made."

4. ACHIEVEMENT. The affirmation should indicate that the desired change has been achieved, not that you are growing or progressing in that area. Thus, "I have a sincere, outgoing, warm regard for others" will have a much greater effect than "I am steadily improving my warmth toward others." Your objective is to develop an affirmation which will easily evoke an imagined experience, and it is much easier to imagine the accomplished change than a changing process.

5. CATEGORICAL. Do not compare yourself with others in your affirmations. Instead of, "I am the most productive sales person in our company," a better wording is, "I am an excellent sales person and my production is very high." Comparing yourself with others opens the door to unconscious acts which might impair the effectiveness of other people rather than strengthen your own.

6. ACTION. The affirmation should represent an action, not an ability. Wording such as "I have the ability to remember names," or "I can relax," simply makes the affirmation more difficult to experience in the imagination. Better wording is, "I remember people's names easily," and "I relax easily and quickly whenever I want to do so."

7. EXCITEMENT. Whenever possible put the positive emotion you want to cultivate right into the wording of the affirmation. For example, "I am very proud to be free of the smoking habit, and I feel terrific!" or "I am a very enthusiastic person and I enjoy expressing my enthusiasm and excitement to others," are affirmations which are enhanced by the positive feelings included in them.

8. ACCURACY AND BALANCE. In those areas where a specific, measurable objective is part of your definition, do not overshoot in the hope that results may be achieved more rapidly. If you are affirming a particular weight level, golf or bowling score, or some other change which can be measured, then pinpoint the affirmation to the exact level you wish to achieve. Be careful what you affirm—it will happen!

9. REALISTIC. Do not affirm perfection. Such affirmations only lead to frustration, and in some cases are not truly representative of what you actually want to accomplish. For example, the affirmation, "I am always enthusiastic," may lead to frustration—and there are some occasions when it is not desirable to be enthusiastic. Look out for words like "always," "perfectly," and "completely."

10. YOURSELF ONLY. Sometimes it may be very tempting to write out an affirmation about someone else's behavior, such as "People like me," or "My children admire and respect me." Unfortunately, your affirmations will only have an effect upon *your* behavior. In fact, there can even be a "backlash" effect if your affirmation develops an expectancy which conflicts with the perceived behavior of the other person. Better affirmations are, "I enjoy building friendships with others," and "I am the kind of parent who earns and deserves the respect and admiration of my children."

APPENDIX
2

Goal-Setting Project

The following is a list of some of the categories you may want to consider as you set your goals. These are only intended to be "thought starters." *Your* goals should be the changes that *you* want to make in *your* world.

VOCATIONAL/PROFESSIONAL

Earnings.
Net worth.
Position within your organization.
Expanded (or reduced) staff.
Gross sales volume.
Profit percentage.
Professional certification.
Investment account.

More (or less) diversified product line.
Opening (or closing) branch offices.
Public offering of stock.
New buildings or facilities.
New equipment.
Modernizing plant or offices.
Geographical expansion.
Degree or other educational goal.

PERSONAL/FAMILY

Home.
Vacation and travel.
Automobile.
Marriage.
Mountain cabin.
Camping equipment.
Boat.
Beach or lake cottage.

Airplane.
Musical instrument.
Photographic equipment.
Art lessons.
Retirement fund.
Educational fund for children.
Sports or hobby equipment.
Art collection.

COMMUNITY

Volunteer work in a hospital.
Church building fund.
Junior Achievement.
Big Brothers, YMCA, etc.
Community fund.
Political activity.
Service club committees.
Boy Scouts, Girl Scouts, etc.

Teach a Sunday School class.
Run for political office.
Chamber of Commerce.
Working with retarded children.
Red Cross, Salvation Army, etc.
Local musical or dramatic groups.
Parent Teacher Association.
Foundations.

STEP 1

List your goals in each of these three categories:

VOCATIONAL/PROFESSIONAL

1 _____

2 _____

3 _____

4 _____

5 _____

PERSONAL/FAMILY

1 _____

2 _____

3 _____

4 _____

5 _____

COMMUNITY

1 _____

2 _____

3 _____

4 _____

5 _____

STEP 2

Define each of the goals that you have listed. Be very specific. Give as many details as you can about each goal, and reasons why it will be meaningful to you. You may want to use several sheets of paper for this step.

_____

_____

_____

_____

_____

_____

_____

_____

_____

_____

_____

_____

_____

_____

_____

_____

_____

STEP 3

Translate each goal that you have selected and defined into a simple, positive, present tense affirmation. Refer to the rules on pages 270-271 to be sure that your affirmations are well designed.

1 _____

2 _____

3 _____

4 _____

5 _____

6 _____

7 _____

8 _____

9 _____

10 _____

11 _____

12 _____

13 _____

14 _____

15 _____

APPENDIX
3

Solutions To Puzzles

Solution to the Puzzle on page 219:

The information in number *2* tells us that Mary is the antique collector.

Statements *3* and *5* show that neither Mary nor Betty is the tennis player, so Dorothy must have that hobby; and *3* then fixes Betty as the ceramicist.

Number *6* informs us that Mary is not a golfer and *1* rules Betty out as a golfer, also. That leaves Dorothy with that hobby.

The painter, then, must be either Mary or Betty, but number *4* tells us that it cannot be Mary—so Betty is the painter.

That gives Betty and Dorothy each two hobbies and Mary only one, so she must be the photographer.

Notice that a simple, logical process of elimination provides a means of solving this exercise. It is creative—a new sequence of thought for the person solving it. Next time you encounter a similar puzzle, the effort will be less creative because you now have an understanding of the concept—the kind of sequence that will work. Even though the actual situation is different, the principle will apply.

Solution to the Puzzle on page 219:

Here is what the original window looked like:

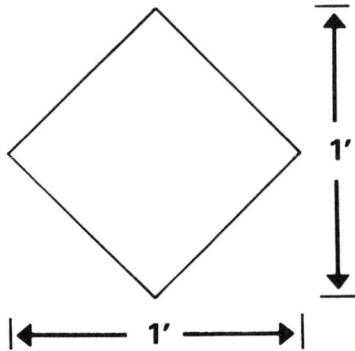

It really *was* a foot high and a foot wide. And when my friend was finished, the new window was still a foot high and a foot wide, but it was exactly twice the size of the original opening.

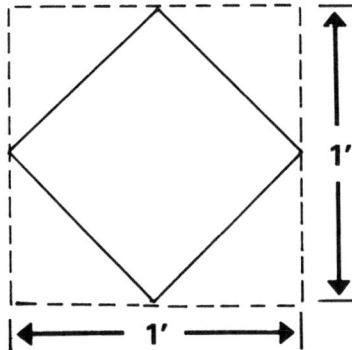

Notice the trap you fell into with this puzzle. When you read the word "window" you immediately popped up a mental image of a window. And it probably was an image of a regular, normal, straight up-and-down window. Without realizing it you locked *on* to that first image and thus locked *out* the possibility that not all windows look like that. From that point on, nothing made any sense. If you solved this one it was probably by playing with images and re-examining your assumptions—a different sort of creativity than you used to solve the preceding puzzle.

Solution to the Puzzle on page 220:

The fact that all three labels are incorrect provides the means to solve this one.

Take one cookie from the jar marked "Chocolate Chip and Oatmeal." Since we know that the jar is incorrectly labeled, we know that there is only one kind of cookie in that jar, the kind that you took out.

If you found an Oatmeal Cookie there, then we know that the jar marked "Oatmeal Cookies" is not only wrongly marked, but that it must have Chocolate Chip cookies in it. If it had both, then the third jar marked "Chocolate Chip" would have a correct label and we know that it does not.

Or, if the jar marked "Chocolate Chip and Oatmeal" has Chocolate Chip cookies in it, then the Chocolate Chip label should be changed to "Oatmeal" and the "Oatmeal" labeled jar should be changed to "Chocolate Chip and Oatmeal."

Once again, it helps to use your imagination, to play with alternatives until a workable approach is created.

Solution to the Puzzle on page 227:

When you first started on this puzzle you probably drew a line through three of the dots, stopped and thought about which direction to go for the second line. Most people do.

Without realizing it you had allowed a *have to* or a *can't* to block your success. The rules do not refer to a rectangular shape, nor do they say that you *have to* stay within the rectangle formed by the dots or that you *can't* go outside of them.

However, you probably introduced those restrictions without even knowing that you had done it. When you broke through that barrier it became possible to find a solution.

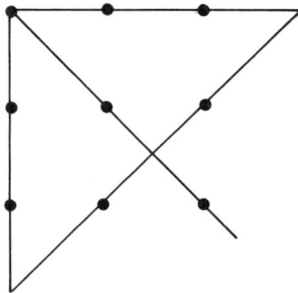

It may still have taken a little time and effort, but now at least there was a chance. How much of your life is limited in this way? Getting "outside of the dots" can open up a great many more approaches to every aspect of your vocational and personal life.

Re-wire Your "Buttons" Project

List on this page as many negative "buttons" as you can identify in your own system.

Is this a button that you choose to keep in your system?

1. _____   _____
2. _____   _____
3. _____   _____
4. _____   _____
5. _____   _____
6. _____   _____
7. _____   _____
8. _____   _____
9. _____   _____
10. _____   _____
11. _____   _____
12. _____   _____
13. _____   _____
14. _____   _____
15. _____   _____
16. _____   _____
17. _____   _____
18. _____   _____
19. _____   _____
20. _____   _____

Now list the buttons that you would like to change, and identify the kind of reaction that you would like to have to that situation or stimulus.

BUTTON	DESIRED REACTION
1. _____	_____
	_____
2. _____	_____
	_____
3. _____	_____
	_____
4. _____	_____
	_____
5. _____	_____
	_____
6. _____	_____
	_____
7. _____	_____
	_____
8. _____	_____
	_____
9. _____	_____
	_____
10. _____	_____
	_____

Next, translate each of the desired reactions you have listed on the preceding page into a simple, positive, present tense affirmation. You may want to review the design rules on pages 270-271.

1. _____

_____

2. _____

_____

3. _____

_____

4. _____

_____

5. _____

_____

6. _____

_____

7. _____

_____

8. _____

_____

9. _____

_____

10. _____

_____

Glossary of **PACE** terms

AHA!   A sudden feeling of discovery. Particularly the feeling one has upon first awareness of something which has been right there for some time but has not been perceived.

ASSOCIATION   The conscious process of relating what is being perceived with the existing "REALITY" structure.

ATTITUDINAL BALANCE SCALE   A symbolic representation of the idea that attitude patterns are inclinations or leanings either in a positive or negative direction. Every conscious thought/ feeling process makes some contribution either to the positive or negative side of one or more scales (See *ROCKS*).

BRAKING MECHANISM   An attitude pattern with a negative emotional component which restricts the flow of one's potential.

BUTTON   The *PACE* symbolic representation of a reaction or response which has been reinforced and re-affirmed to the degree that it has become automatic.

COMFORT ZONE   The *PACE* term for the kinds of behavior and the environments to which one responds with relatively little uncomfortable tension. One's image of "the way things are supposed to be."

CONCEPTUAL THOUGHT   The capacity to think with those experiences or abstract concepts which have occurred before in one's conscious thoughts, and which are now a part of one's "REALITY" structure.

CONSCIOUS   Mental activity of which one is aware. That awareness is a matter of degree.

CONSTRUCTIVE IMAGINATION	The deliberate, conscious direction of imagined experience for the purpose of modifying one's "REALITY" structure in order to release potential and facilitate the achievement of goals.
CONSTRUCTIVE PATTERN	A habit, skill, or attitude which has been formed with primarily positive self talk. Tends to be flexible, easily modified.
CREATIVITY	The mental manipulation of past experiences into a new or different way of doing something.
DECISION	The conscious process of selecting a particular alternative or course of action (or inaction).
EFFECTIVENESS	The degree to which a person uses his/her potential in a natural, free-flowing, spontaneous and consistent manner.
EFFECTIVENESS REGULATOR	The *PACE* symbolic representation of the regulating mechanism in the human system which tends to stimulate the kind of behavior that will keep a person within the Comfort Zone.
EIGHTH ARROW	An input channel to the mental processes at a subconscious level which is not yet thoroughly understood, but which seems to be a part of all human systems.
EMOTIONAL THOUGHT	The capacity to think with the feelings which one has associated with various symbols and/or concepts.
EMPATHY	The art or skill of understanding or grasping another person's way of looking at something. The ability to put one's self into another person's point of view.
EPI-ORGANISM	An organism made up of organisms—a group of individuals with a personality and behavioral characteristics similar to those of an individual.

EVALUATION — The conscious process of estimating the probable validity, usefulness, value of what is being perceived on the basis of the person's current "REALITY" structure.

IMAGINATION — The mental process of combining familiar objects, ideas or events into unfamiliar forms or relationships.

MENTAL PROCESSES — The activity or flow of information (electro-chemical impulses) within that part of the physical mechanism called the nervous system.

MOTIVATION — An inclination to behave in a certain way. "Outer" motivation is the tendency to behave in a particular way because of an externally offered reward or penalty. "Inner" motivation is the built-in drive to grow and to use whatever talent and information one has available.

PACE — An acronym made up of the first letters of the words: Personal And Company Effectiveness. The word "Company" is used here to mean any group of people. (See EPI-ORGANISM) Also a label for a comprehensive philosophy and methodology of personal growth and development.

PERCEPTION — The fraction of what is happening in the various parts of the Whole Person System of which one becomes consciously aware.

POTENTIAL — The present combination in one's system of talent, information and inner motivation.

"REALITY" — The present, cumulative total of what one knows and feels about one's self and his/her world. Always incomplete and inaccurate.

"REALITY" FILTER — The accumulation of experiences and attitudes through which a person perceives events in the environment and within the physical system.

RESPONSIBILITY	The degree to which one feels comfortable with the idea that he is accountable for the consequences of his actions, decisions and reactions to unexpected events.
RESTRICTIVE PATTERN	A habit or attitude which has been formed with primarily negative self-talk. Tends to be rigid, limits awareness of alternatives, restricts use of one's potential.
ROCKS (Positive and Negative)	The *PACE* symbolic representation of the effect of a thought sequence on an attitude pattern in one's "REALITY" structure. The "weight" of a rock is a function of the amount of emotion. Whether the emotional component is positive or negative determines the effect upon existing patterns. (See *ATTITUDINAL BALANCE SCALE*)
SELF-ESTEEM	The degree to which one has a feeling of worth, value and significance as a person.
SELF-IMAGE	The portion of one's "REALITY" structure which relates to one's own physical/mental system. What you know and how you feel about you.
SELF-REINFORCING CYCLE	The sequence of thought and behavior which tends to cause positively inclined attitudes to become more positive and negatively inclined attitudes to become more negative.
SELF-TALK	The internal Verbal/Conceptual/Emotional thought processes which continually modify one's existing attitude patterns.
SUBCONSCIOUS	Mental activity which happens largely or entirely without conscious awareness or direction.
SURE ENOUGH!	The *PACE* label for the phenomenon of the self-fulfilling prophecy. When one expects something to happen in a certain way, the expectancy tends to influence behavior and, SURE ENOUGH! it tends to happen that way.

SYMPATHY   Feeling the way another person feels.

TALENT   The original blueprint of a human system, the genetic, inherited characteristics and capacities.

"THEY"   The *PACE* label for groups, individuals, circumstances or mystical forces or beings which seem to control one's destiny or behavior.

UNDERSTANDING   The degree to which two people have the same idea/image/emotion in their mental systems.

VERBAL   The capacity to think with words (and other
THOUGHT   symbols).

WHOLE PERSON   The complex interaction of the physical mechanism,
SYSTEM   the environment and the various processes within the physical body, especially the mental processes.

The **PACE**™ Organization

P.O. Box 2949
Del Mar, California 92014

Telephone (858) 755-8604
Facsimile (858) 755-8468

Web Site   http://www.paceorg.com

Lindsey L. Davidson
President and CEO

Afterword

Where we are today ...

PACE™ *Seminars and Workshops*

The **PACE**™ *Organization* curriculum is extensive–filling the needs of individuals, couples, small groups, and organizations. The following five courses form the core of this curriculum.

COURSES FOR INDIVIDUALS, COUPLES, AND SMALL GROUPS

The **PACE**™ *Organization's*
Communications Workshop

This four-hour workshop focuses on the process of communicating. You will engage in participative discussion and exercises that will help you understand why the communication process breaks down so easily and how you can avoid or quickly recover from these breakdowns.

The **PACE**™ *Organization's*
Release Your Brakes! Seminar

This one-day seminar explores the core principles and applies the essential tools of the **PACE**™ technology. This seminar is far more than a typical motivational or "battery-charging" session: The insights and tools that you learn will become an integral part of your thinking and self-expression.

The **PACE**™ *Organization's*
High-Performance Workshop

In this two-day workshop, *The* **PACE**™ *Organization* provides a unique opportunity for a small group of business and professional people and their spouses or partners to actively explore and apply a "tool kit" of techniques that enhance and reinforce personal excellence.

TEAM-BUILDING PROGRAMS

The *PACE*™*Organization's*
Team-Building Seminar/Workshop

In this intensive two-day seminar/workshop, team members actively explore and apply proven techniques for enhancing personal and organizational excellence.

The *PACE*™*Organization's*
Team-Building and High-Performance Seminar/Workshop

In this three-day *PACE*™ seminar/workshop, a small group of business and professional people–and their spouses or partners–actively apply a "tool kit" of techniques which enhance personal and team excellence. We focus on the company's mission statement and incorporate it into the workshop to increase team effectiveness.

We also offer a ten-week version of this seminar/workshop. Team members attend three hours per day, once a week. The seminar/workshop includes a pre-course needs assessment, and course materials are specially designed according to that assessment. This is an excellent option for companies wanting more focused, on-site training that accommodates busy executive schedules.

Follow-Up Meetings

Follow-up meetings are available and encouraged for all our team-building programs.

PACE™ *Products and Services*

In support of the above curriculum, *The PACE*™*Organization* provides consulting services and publishes books, pamphlets, and other training media. These products and services are available through the various courses, or they can be purchased separately.

Here is a partial list of additional products:

- The *PACE*™ Palette
- *PACE*™ Palette Leader's Guide
- *PACE*™ Palette Participant's Guide
- *PACE*™ Palette Empathy Card
- *PACE*™ Palette Training Tape (Brian Tracy on single-cassette audio tape)
- High-Performance Behavior (six-cassette audio tape series)
- Deep Relaxation–Manipulate the conflict (single-cassette audio tape)
- Five Keys to Excellence (single-cassette audio tape)
- You've Got to Have a Dream! (single-cassette audio tape)
- Release Your Brakes! (single-cassette audio tape)

Please contact *The PACE*™*Organization* by phone at (858) 755-8604 or through our web site at http://www.paceorg.com to enroll in any of our programs, make a purchase, or obtain further information.

New programs and training materials are constantly under development.

Consulting is also available.

PACE™ Principles

All our programs are based on the groundbreaking principles in Jim Newman's book, *Release Your Brakes!* These principles have supported the development of powerful tools, processes, and techniques for releasing human potential. *The **PACE**™ Organization* has been delivering these breakthroughs for the past 40 years. Described below are some of the ideas you will explore in a **PACE**™ seminar.

What Has Changed...and What Has Not

In the 40 years since the creation of **PACE**™ there have been dramatic transformations in the nature of human enterprise and the economic environment in which it occurs. Computers move us at virtual light-speed through transactions that required considerable deliberation in more contemplative times. We have witnessed dot-com empires rise from thin air into millions of dollars in revenue in a matter of weeks–and then in as short a time plunge completely out of sight. A major stock exchange, the NASDAQ, has lost as much as 39 percent of its value at various points in recent time, and yet it chugs along. Change, as always, is the constant.

So changed is enterprise and the climate of enterprise that we might be fooled into thinking that the fundamental governing principles have changed. They have not. People like you and me are still the players in this game, and we are, after changes upon changes, more or less the same. This does not mean, however, that the tools and methods we use cannot be improved; they can, and they have.

The **PACE**™ principles are expressions of major discoveries about the untapped potential of human interaction. In the present climate of staggering re-direction and re-creation, The **PACE**™ Organization's commitment to converting these discoveries into useful tools is more vital than ever. Today these tools are necessary to keep up, let alone excel.

Every seminar, every workshop, every action or discussion about **PACE**™ principles leads to a deeper understanding of them. Our programs today reflect that deeper understanding.

As Jim Newman said in the final chapter of *Release Your Brakes!*, you and I, whether we know it or not, are constantly making changes in our environment. This becomes clear when you complete the Constructive Imagination and Goal Setting projects found in the appendix of the book. We can enhance the power and scope of these environmental changes by thoughtfully enlisting the help of those with whom we work.

Realm of High Performance

At some point in every **PACE**™ seminar that I lead, I receive questions from participants about how to bring the information they have learned into their workplace. The subjects we cover pertain to all human systems, and the workplace is, above all, a human system. Knowing this is step one in the process of leading your company into the realm of high performance. Only in this realm can your company hope to function as a team. Only in this realm can your company hope to achieve the highest goals of the enterprise for which it was created. Only in this realm can full potential be reached.

Initiating the Inquiry

"Potential" is the combination of talent, information, and motivation. (See "Potential and Performance," Chapter 3, of *Release Your Brakes!,* for an excellent discussion of this.) In our **PACE**™ seminars we write this combination as a simple equation:

Potential = Talent + Information + Motivation

Or...

P = T + I + M

This equation applies equally to individuals, teams or entire companies. To create a high-performance job environment, you must strengthen specific elements on the right side of the equation. To do this requires an inquiry focused on those elements. For example, what *talent* can we add to our team? What *information* can we learn? How can we increase our internal and external *motivation* to achieve this goal?

Asking these types of questions, even in an informal setting, will lead to a very rich list of suggestions which can be fleshed out as the process continues. For example, plans can be devised to hire more talent, training can be provided to increase information, relationships and working conditions can be developed to encourage new internal and external motivation.

In the process of conducting this inquiry, you will see enthusiasm in some, resistance in others. You may even discover pockets of enthusiasm and resistance in yourself. All of this is useful in advancing toward the ideal of high performance. However, it is important, especially in the beginning, to involve co-workers who feel positively about the company. The valve that allows potential to flow at a rapid rate is *positive emotion.* Therefore, it is far more productive to plan with co-workers who feel positively about the company—no matter where they may work. You will obtain marvelous suggestions from surprising sources in this way, and that is a big part of the fun of these discussions.

Continuing the Inquiry

Once you have created a team to lay the groundwork for positive change, others—some who may have resisted initially—will want to become involved. Human beings are a gregarious species. I truly believe that at some level we all want to grow and develop and become what we are capable of becoming. As this spirit is teased into the light, most employees will want to contribute to the company and to each other. They will be willing to discuss candidly what is and is not working. A high-performance team will begin to emerge.

When Strong is Weak

Another common question in my seminars is, "How can I get my different departments and divisions to go beyond protecting their turf and come together as a team?" I cover this extensively in the **PACE**™ Team-Building Seminar/Workshop. This is a special concern of upper management because it can affect the bottom line significantly.

When a department or division does not operate according to high-performance principles, the employees and managers in it seek to be held responsible only for their own results. At first glance, this seems to make perfect sense. Looking a little deeper, however, we see that a strong department reaching its isolated goals is not enough. In fact it may be detrimental to the company as a whole if the stronger department manifests an *attitude* that does not support other, perhaps weaker departments, in reaching their goals. Paradoxically, the destructiveness of this attitude is in proportion to the isolated strength of the department. In this case, strong is weak, and the company as a whole suffers. A strong department with the wrong attitude can be the worst enemy of efforts to develop a high-performance workplace. (See discussion of general system theory in Chapter 4 of *Release Your Brakes!*)

According to the well-established principles of the general systems theory, whenever anything changes within a system, the whole system changes. In other words, a positive event in one part of the company will have a positive effect on the whole company. It also follows that a negative event in one part of the company affects the entire company negatively. By definition, then, all the members of a company are personally and collectively responsible for the well-being of the whole company. Winning widespread acceptance of this responsibility is the first step in producing positive change in any organization.

The Myth of Null Effect

A person's thoughts and behavior take them toward a goal or away from it. It is surprising how many people hold to the notion that there is a third effect, a null effect, a do-nothing, play-it-safe position. This notion is false. A neutral position cannot be "held" at all, for it does not exist in time. It is a "no-place" that we pass through on the way toward or away from a goal. We cannot occupy it, even for an instant. This reality is explored in **PACE**™ workshops.

For example, you may be sitting at your desk, eyes closed as you reflect on your goal to be promoted to a higher position in the company. This moment of reflection may generate a fabulous idea that will take you toward your goal, or, viewed by your boss from across the room, it may earn you a rebuke and take you away from your goal. Focusing carefully on making choices that clearly take you toward or away from your goal is a simple, easy and conscious way to checking and correcting the effectiveness of the steps you are taking. Using this same method, you can help others evaluate their effectiveness: Are the steps you see them taking moving them toward their goal? If yes, ask them to observe carefully what worked in order to reinforce the success achieved. If not, invite them to correct for errors. (See "Next Time," Chapter 14, *Release Your Brakes!*)

The Communications Gap

I have consulted with many companies over the years, and I have yet to find one that is not seeking to improve the effectiveness of internal and external communication. In fact, *all* of the surveys I conducted over the years uncovered a weakness in this area. This is why communication effectiveness is a significant ingredient in all **PACE**™ training. (See "Building Better Bridges," Chapter 16, *Release Your Brakes!*)

Personal Responsibility–More Than a Slogan

Personal responsibility in the **PACE**™ program is defined as the degree to which a person feels comfortable with the fact that he or she lives with and is therefore accountable for the consequences of his or her behavior. Where you find high levels of performance, you will find high levels of personal responsibility. For this reason, the principles of personal responsibility are addressed in all **PACE**™ programs.

The language of personal responsibility is a key part of responsibility training in **PACE**™ seminars and workshops. Freedom is one of the highest ideals most of us hold. Personal responsibility takes us toward this ideal; personal irresponsibility takes us away from it.

In **PACE**™ workshops, I introduce The Responsibility Continuum as a tool for gauging whether your speech is advancing you one way or the other.

For example, if I hear myself using the words, "I can't," I realize that at some unconscious level I am feeling coerced. I am moving away from personal responsibility and thus away from freedom. Changing my words to "I won't" advances me toward personal responsibility and freedom. In the next step, I ask myself, "Why won't I?" This usually brings up the emotion I am feeling, which in turn reveals the attitude I hold. Now I am in a position to act, to become personally responsible, to be free–and to be effective.

Reality Structure–Not So Real After All

Our *reality structure* is full of incomplete and erroneous information. We have stored this information, this data, over a lifetime, and we base our judgments and decisions on it. This data is usually invisible to us. Just as a fish does not see the water and a bird does not see the air, we do not see our reality structure. We can monitor its functioning, however. In **PACE**™ courses, we discuss "prison words" (ought, should, must, had better, have to, can't) and learn how to adjust them to effect changes in attitude and thus in effectiveness. (See "You Are They," Chapter 15, *Release Your Brakes!*)

The same holds true when we are listening to others, and certain **PACE**™ processes are designed to develop these listening skills. For example, if we hear, "I have to do this," or, "I can't do this," we understand that the reality structure of the speaker has a stored experience attached to a negative emotion, causing the person tension or even anxiety. That negative emotion is acting like a valve which is inhibiting the speaker's flow of potential. Therefore, the person is likely to stay nestled in a comfort zone.

In **PACE**™ team-building workshops, participants are guided to seeing an issue in a different way. Often it helps to say things like this:

- "I understand you feel that way. For fun, though, what would happen if you could do what you say you're not able to do?" or
- "What do you feel is standing in the way of your doing that?" or
- "What do you think you need to have in order to do that?"

The answer will fall somewhere in our **P = T + I + M** equation. Often the invitation to look at an issue in a different way is all that is necessary to initiate conflict resolution. (See "Subconscious Mental Processes," Chapter 6, *Release Your Brakes!*)

The **PACE**™ Palette

People are interesting. Each of us has our unique way of viewing the world. In my work with corporate teams, one of the first issues addressed lies in the question, "What's in it for me?" I am aware that without the promise of a measurable personal gain (positive emotion), the training process will not flow smoothly. Each person will want something different from the training and that "something" is largely dependent upon each person's temperament pattern.

The **PACE**™ Palette is a simple and effective tool for determining temperament pattern. It is one of the keys to the effectiveness of **PACE**™ training. It is an invaluable aid in increasing the quality of the communications within a team.

The **PACE**™ Palette uses colors (Red, Yellow, Blue and Green) to represent four basic personality temperaments. We each have all four temperaments; however, one is generally dominant from birth. Using the Palette, participants choose what they think is their dominant temperament and therefore their color. The differences and similarities of the different temperaments are covered extensively. By the end of the session, team members clearly understand that they and their co-workers have different values and are subject to different sources of both joy and irritation.

For example, Reds will love adventure and new territory and be irritated with details, while Yellows value tradition and organization and may be annoyed with those who like to break the rules. Blues value harmony and abhor cruelty. Greens embrace logic and become very irritated with anyone or anything which does not seem logical.

The **PACE**™ courses, especially those which focus on team building and conflict resolution, make extensive use of the **PACE**™ Palette. The **PACE**™ Palette helps participants explore the different temperaments and avoid the breakdowns in communication which are so common between people with these different temperaments. Emphasis is placed on why and how to speak in the other person's language in order to reach an adequate level of understanding. Using the association of traits with colors and various other techniques assist tremendously in resolving conflict and enhancing motivation.

Bottom Line

PACE™ courses and publications emphasize techniques that empower participants to make a difference in their workplaces and their lives. **PACE**™ graduates know how to make it safe to be personally responsible. They are not "blamers" and "finger-pointers." They know the power of assessing *behavior* rather than condemning the *person* to resolve conflict and achieve bottom-line results. They know how to create an environment where it is safe to make the kind of courageous efforts that inevitably lead to some mistakes. They know that where it is safe to make mistakes, creativity flows. They know the negative influence of fear–fear of reprisal, fear of attack, fear of fellow team members' negative judgments. They know that fear leads away from the goal, not toward it. People who apply **PACE**™ principles reduce fear around them and increase personal responsibility–in themselves and their teammates. This leads to success in life and in work.

PACE™ *Alumni*

Over the past 40 years, we have found that people who are already successful benefit the most from a **PACE**™ *Organization* experience. Here is a list of some of our better-known alumni. Nearly all participated with their spouses.

In the world of business...

Richard Archer, Chairman of Jardine Emmett & Chandler
Tom Cleary, Chairman & CEO of G & H Technologies
Jim Collins, Chairman of Collins Foods International
Dr. Stephen Covey, Founder and Chairman of the Covey Leadership Center
Dr. Malcolm Currie, Retired Chairman of Hughes Aircraft Company
Jim Heavner, President of The Village Companies
Hugh Jacks, President of Bell South Services
Sanford McDonnell, Retired Chairman of McDonnell Douglas Corporation
Dan Pefia, President, Great Western Development Corporation
Hyrum Smith, Chairman, Franklin Quest Company

In the world of professional and business associations...

Wayne Comils, Radio Advertising Bureau
P. D. Herman, Associated Equipment Distributors
Roderick L. Geer, The Million Dollar Roundtable
William D. Nelligan, American College of Cardiology
Walter L. Cook, Building Services Contractors Association
Mike Welch, Credit Union Executives Society

In the world of government...

Former Secretary of the Army, Howard Calloway
Former Secretary of Housing and Urban Development, Jack Kemp
Former Los Angeles County Supervisor, Pete Schabarum
California Senator, Newton Russell

In the world of athletics...

Dennis Connor, America Cup Champion Skipper
Tom Gorman, Davis Cup Tennis Captain
Payton Jordan, Stanford and Olympic Coach
Pro Golfers Gene Littler, Ken Venturi and Billy Casper
Football Quarterbacks Jim Plunkett and John Brodie

In the world of arts and entertainment...

Television and radio star, Art Linkletter
Motion picture star and founder of the WAIF program, Jane Russell
Actress, director and producer, Joan Hotchkiss

Our Invitation to You

Jim Newman's legacy is in the work being done today by *The **PACE**™ Organization*. Jim founded *The **PACE**™ Organization* in 1961. Millions have benefitted from the work done by and through this organization. We hope that reading this book will inspire you to join with us in striving to do more than we thought we could do and to be more than we thought we could be. We invite you to follow that inspiration.

Lindsey L. Davidson
President and CEO
*The **PACE**™ Organization*
Del Mar, California

January 30, 2001